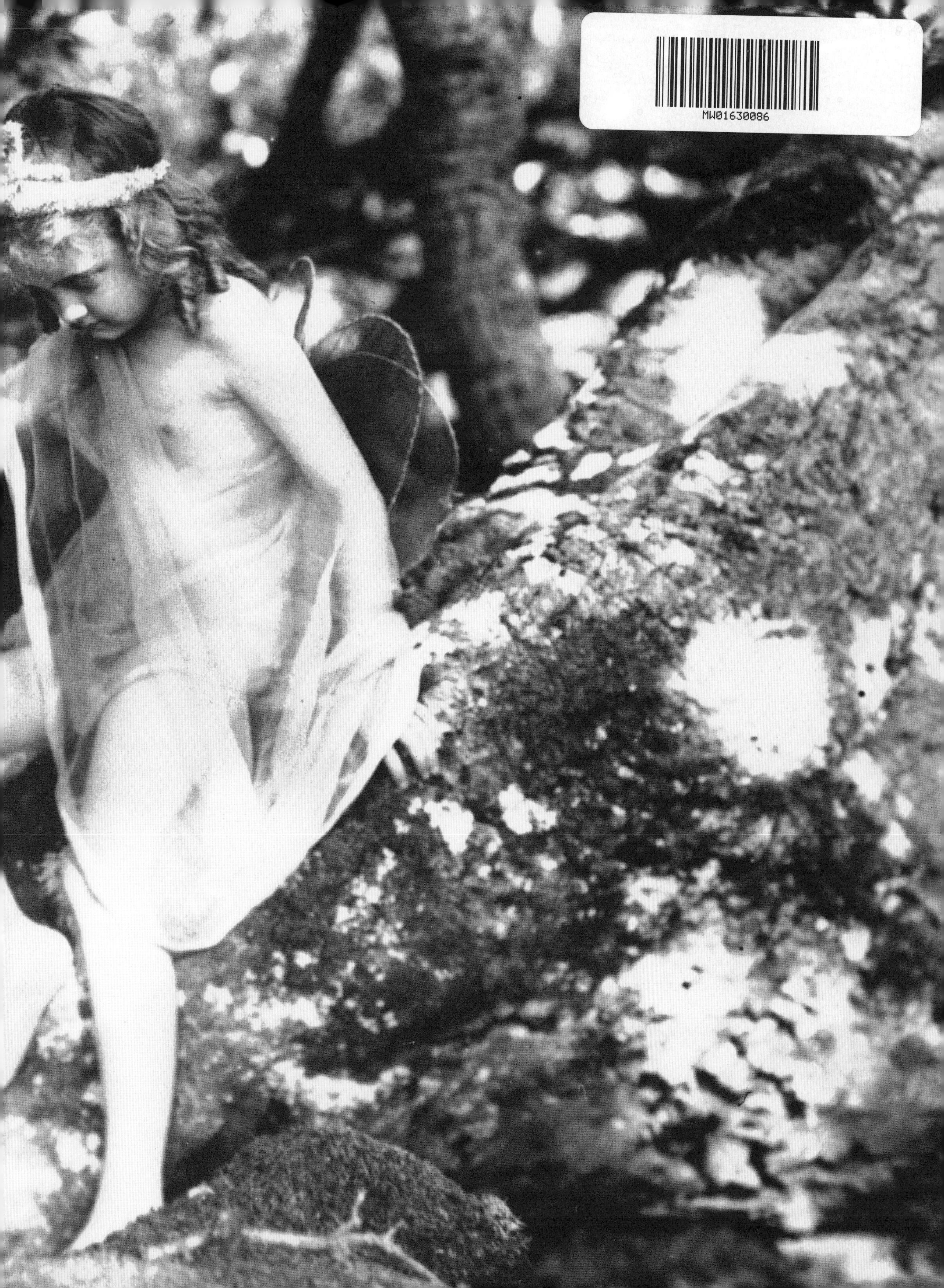

The Life and Art of
Elizabeth "Grandma" Layton

Tim,

A gift from your aunt Pauline, this book's story has been an inspiration to many, including your mother whom Elizabeth considered a friend.

D— Lambert

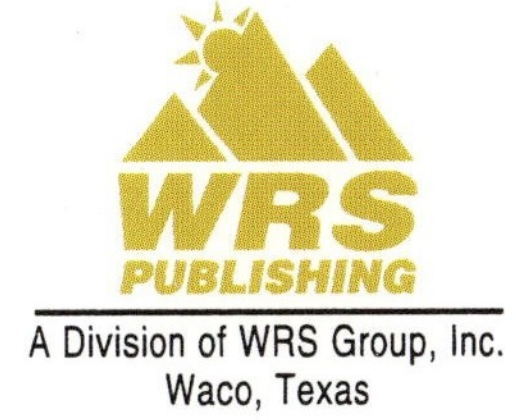

WRS PUBLISHING

A Division of WRS Group, Inc.
Waco, Texas

To Tim
with love
Auntie D
December 1996

First published in the United States of America in 1995
by WRS Publishing, A Division of WRS Group, Inc.
701 N. New Road, Waco, Texas 76710
Book design by Kenneth Turbeville
Jacket design by Joe James and Kenneth Turbeville
Jacket electronic imaging by Joe James
Vintage photogtaphy by Maude Frink Crawford, Elizabeth's aunt

Printed in Hong Kong

10 9 8 7 6 5 4 3 2 1

Library of Congress Cataloging-in-Publication Date

Lambert, Don.
      The life and art of Elizabeth "grandma" Layton / by Don Lambert.
         p.   cm.
      ISBN 1-56796-116-9
      1. Layton, Elizabeth, 1909-1993. 2. Artist--United States--
Biography. I. Layton, Elizabeth, 1909-1993. II. Title.
NC139.L37L36   1995
759. 13--dc20
   [B]   95-13661
                                                CIP

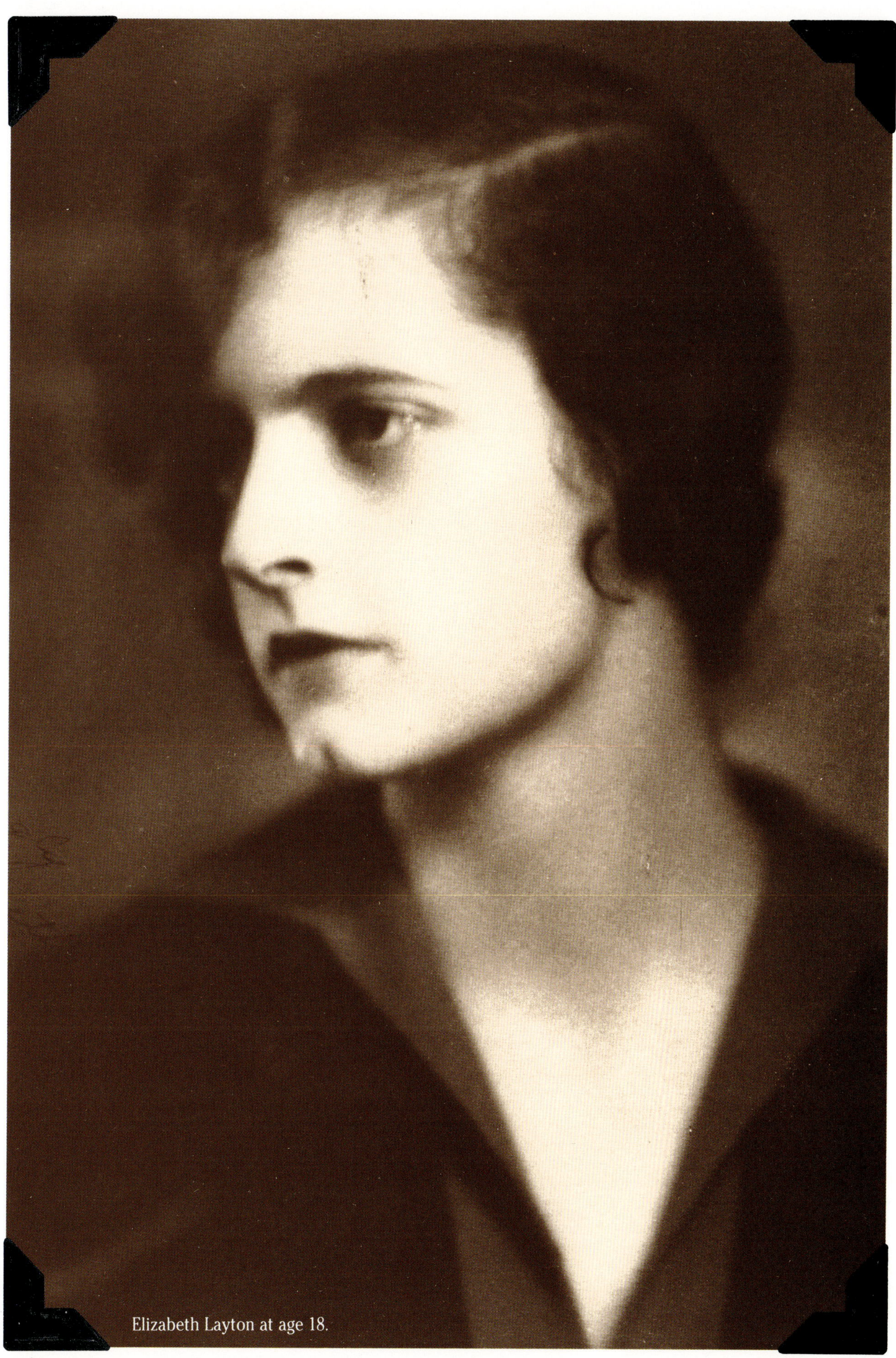

Elizabeth Layton at age 18.

TABLE of CONTENTS

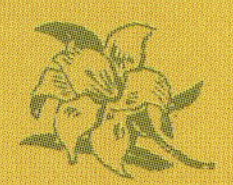

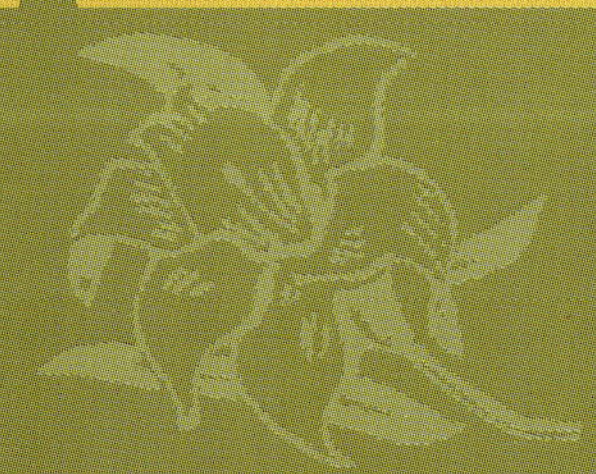

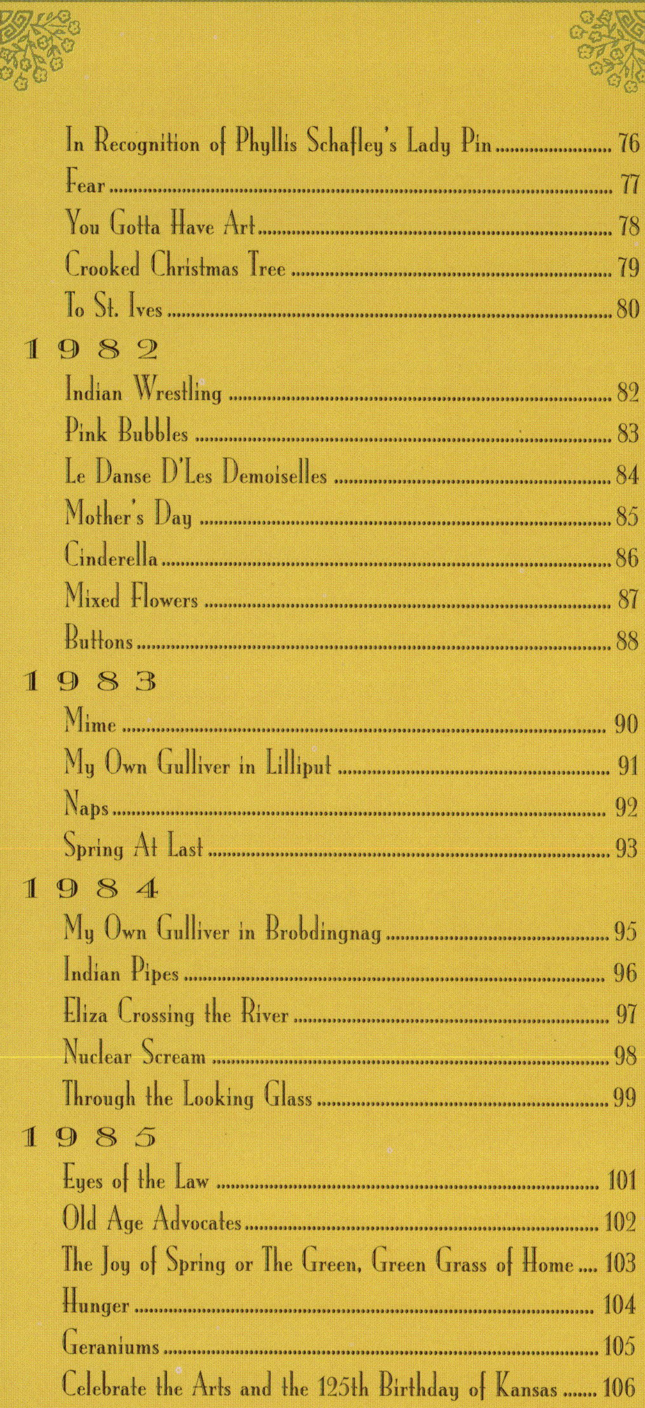

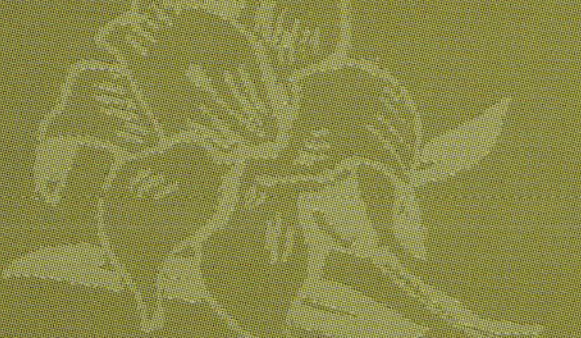

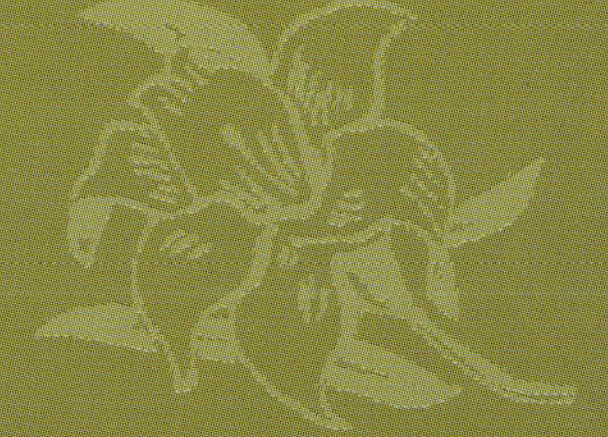
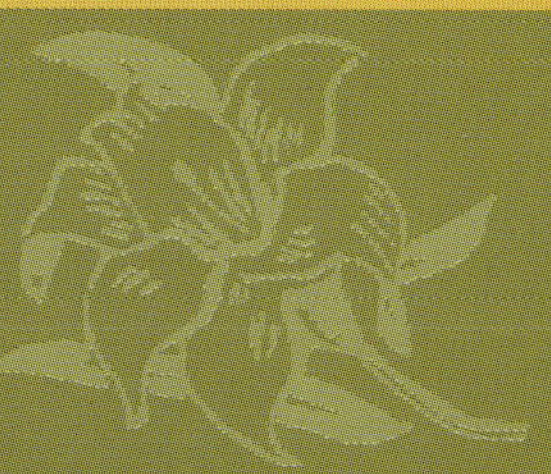

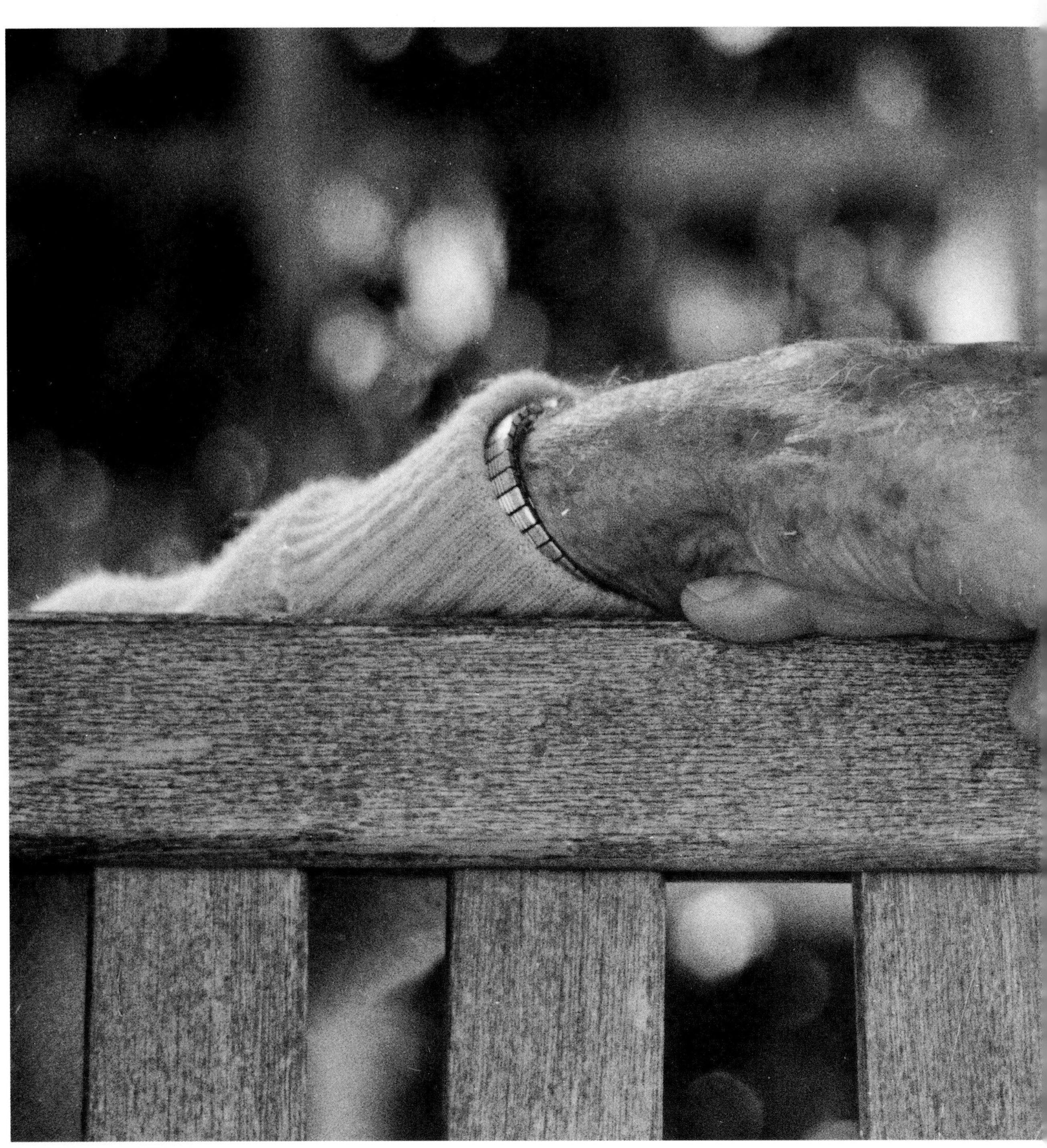

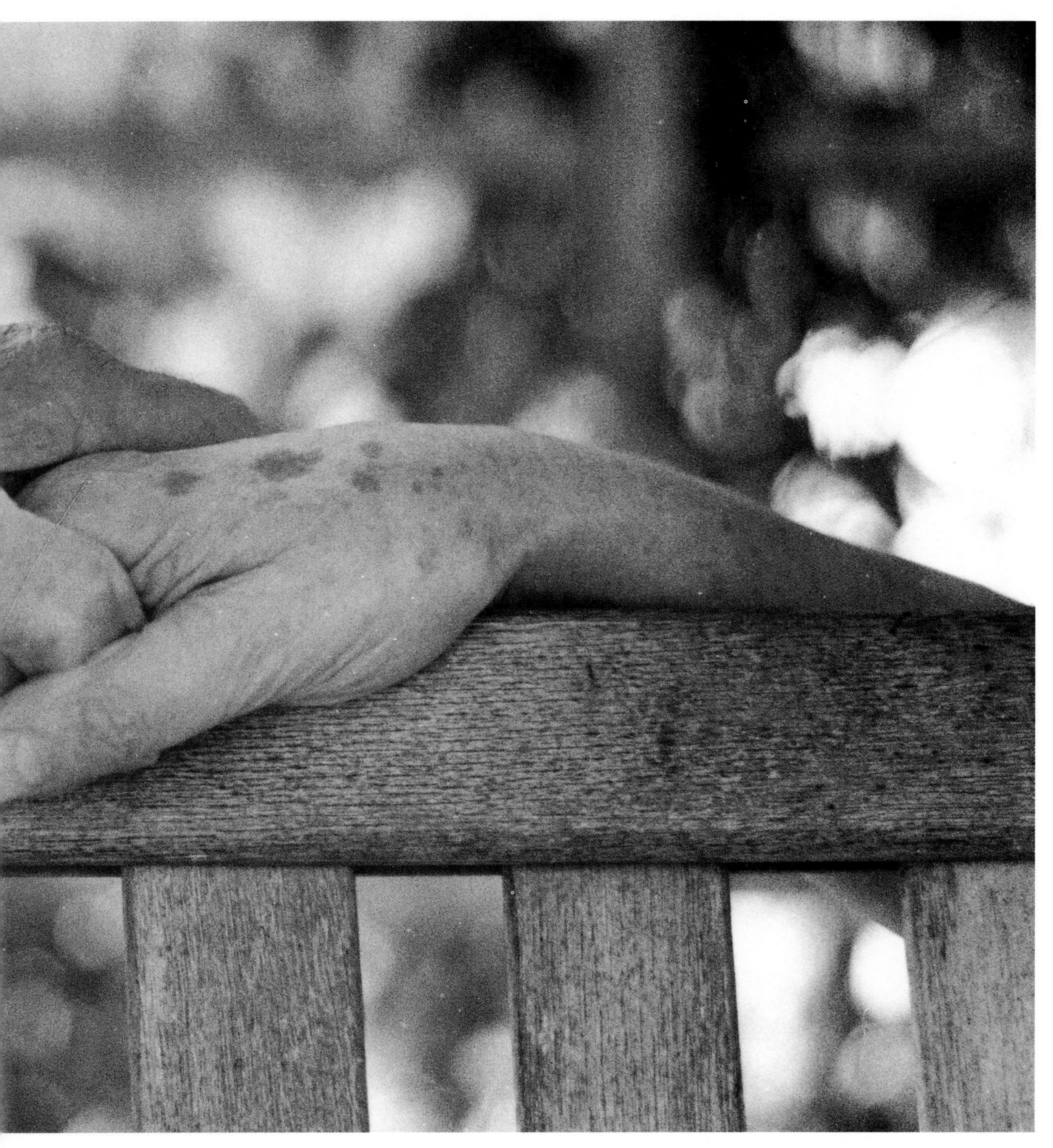

INTRODUCTION

Family picture with
Elizabeth, her sister,
and her mother.
Elizabeth is in
her mother's lap.

As she saw it, Elizabeth Layton had two choices. The 68 year-old Kansas grandmother could act on her sister's suggestion by taking an art class. Or, she could end her life.

It wasn't that Elizabeth Layton wanted to end her life that fall of 1977. But a 35-year depression, a failed marriage, single motherhood, shock treatments, and finally, the death of one of her children the year before, had crushed her will to live.

This suggested art class seemed like, well, something to do. Her sister in California, who painted pretty pictures in a class each Saturday morning, had been urging her. And besides, her sister had joked with her, "Maybe one or the other of us could become the next Grandma Moses."

Fortunately for thousands of us, Elizabeth Layton heeded her sister's advice. She took an art class. What she became over the next 15 years, however, was not another Grandma Moses. Elizabeth Layton became more than that, she became a wholly original Grandma Layton. It was an unexpected Grandma Layton who drew pictures of herself which defy categorization. It was an acclaimed Grandma Layton whose drawings were shown at museums across the country including the Smithsonian. It was a humanistic Grandma Layton whose drawings empathize with women, the elderly, the homeless, the hungry and the victims of society's tragedies such as racial prejudice, AIDS and terminal illness. It was a triumphant Grandma Layton who, in fact, cured her depression by learning to draw. And it was a hopeful Grandma Layton who showed us that we are all in this together, telling the same stories and feeling the same feelings.

We'll never know all that this Grandma Layton accomplished in her 15 and-a-half year art career which was ended by a stroke at age 83 in 1993. We do know that she inspired many people seeking a new career or a new solace or a new life. Her gift of art, which manifested itself in nearly 1200 self-portrait drawings, was one which she gave to others, to the world. Her big green eyes, whether seen in person or in her drawings, said with humility, "Yes, I understand. Now, let's move on."

All of this was readily seen in messages written to her in an open comment book at her exhibit in the Smithsonian's National Museum of American Art during the spring of 1992.

"Came to Washington to see older, more tempered-by-time art. These rooms of your work have brought me to lots of tears and yelps of laughter."

"I am going through a hard time right now and it takes some effort to remember that it's all a part of life. Your drawings are helping me to do that, and they remind me that other people feel pain and ecstasy, rage and glory. Thank you for celebrating"

"You are a candle to the world."

"You are more than the 'grandmother of us all.' You are our conscience, the voice from within our hearts that reminds us of what is right and good and true."

"Thank you for giving us hope."

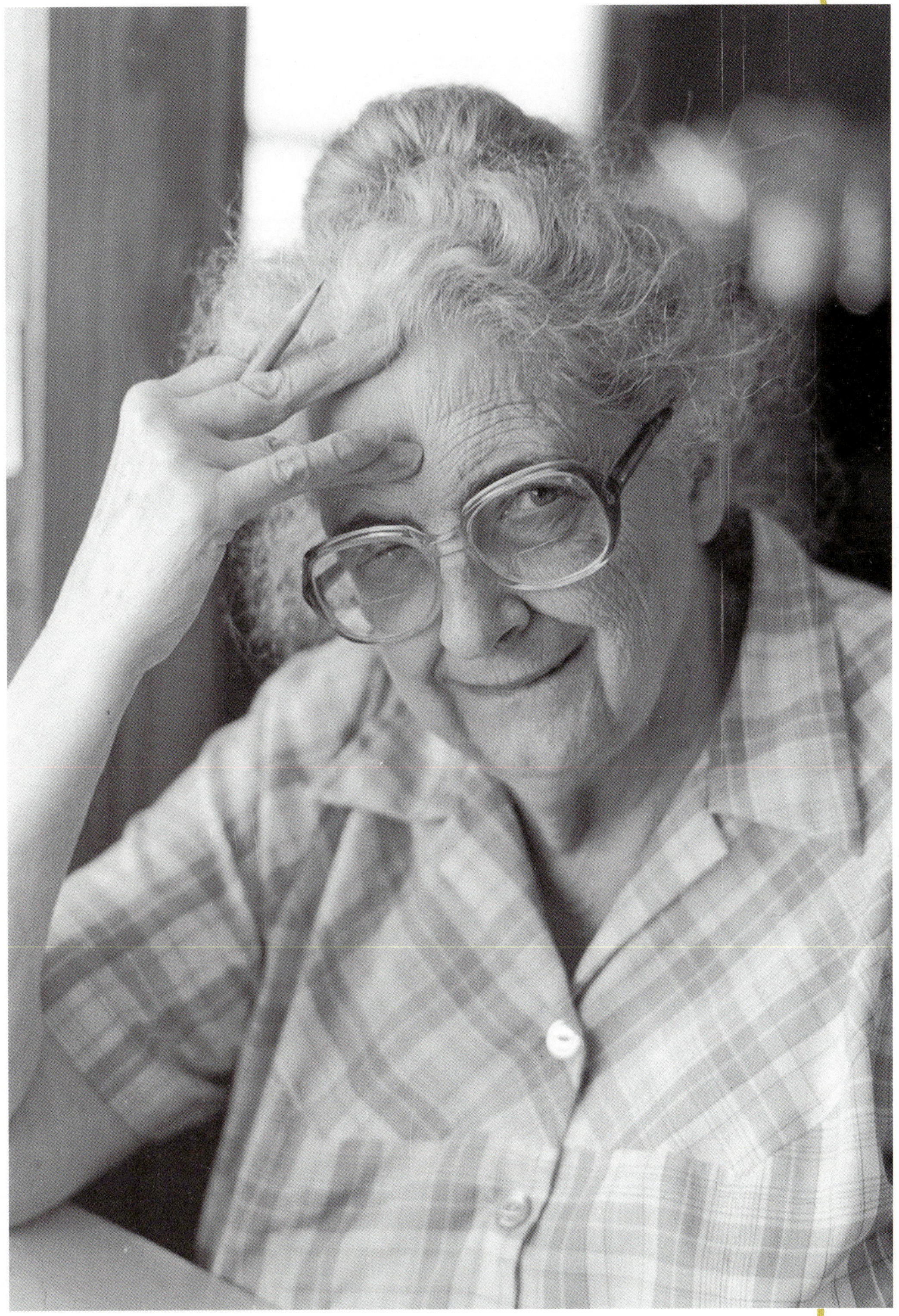

Elizabeth Layton at age 75.

HER STORY

Ͻne evening early in September of 1977, shortly after she'd done the dishes and sent her husband off to a high school football game in their hometown of Wellsville, Kansas, Elizabeth Layton sat down at her kitchen table.

Her purpose was clear and simple: to draw a picture of herself, as had been suggested by her art teacher. The 68-year-old woman was fearful, never having drawn before except that which might be expected from a mother and grandmother. More than drawing, however, it was life itself which brought fear to the woman whose own life had been thwarted by depression for nearly 35 years.

Those fears would have to be set aside that particular evening because she had something to do. Aided by a new found drawing method, drawing supplies from the local drug store, and a mirror, Elizabeth Layton unwittingly began the process of ending her depression and of making a new and meaningful life.

She followed her teacher's instruction to the letter. Pal Wright was the art teacher at Ottawa University, a small Baptist college, 14 miles from Wellsville. He had instructed his class of a dozen 19-year-old freshmen and one 68-year-old grandmother to draw using the blind contour method whereby one looks at the object being drawn, rather than at the paper, while drawing. It is a technique often taught in beginning art classes and one which had been promoted by Kimon Nicolaides at the Art Students League in New York and in his 1941 book, *The Natural Way to Draw*. More recently, it was advanced by Betty Edwards in her 1989 book, *Drawing on the Right Side of the Brain*.

Wright gave his students three pieces of advice for beginning the contour drawing exercise, advice which seemed as apt for life as for art: 1) Draw honest and definite lines, 2) Don't erase—if you make a mistake, if your line strays a bit too far, make it work for you, and 3) Make your drawing fill the sheet of paper, go to the edge.

Elizabeth Layton had gone to the edge. Many times. For half her life she had battled depression and so many other problems she tried not to think about them. Going to that edge, she'd considered plunging over it, ending her own life. There had been times… times when her family, fearful of the possibilities, made sure someone was with her at all times.

Elizabeth had always returned from the edge, feeling hopeful for some kind of restoration but resigned and obligated to the increasingly difficult task of living. She explained, "It isn't that I wanted to die, but I could see no reason to continue living."

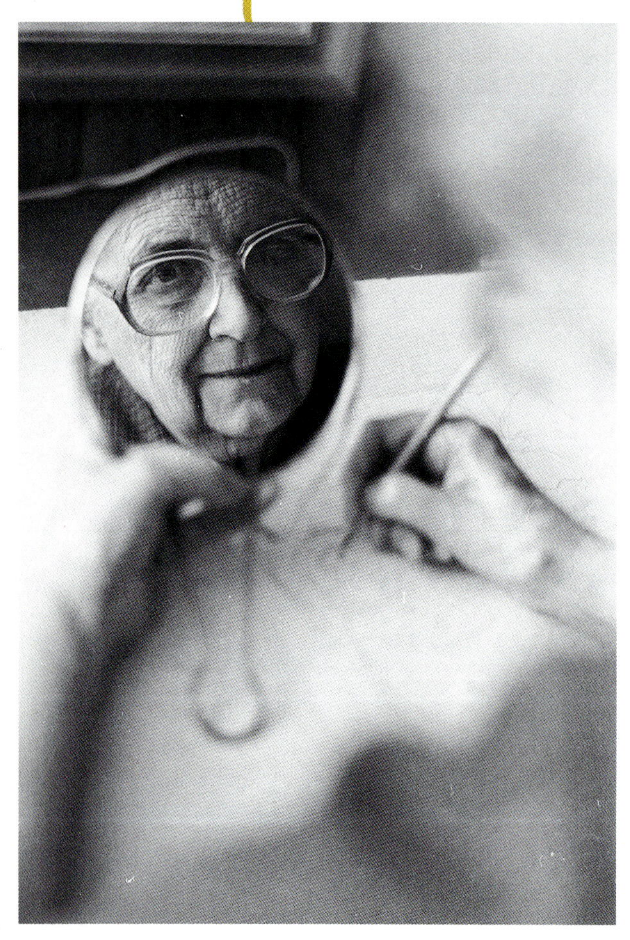

Like most of America during the early 1900s, Elizabeth had grown up with the *Saturday Evening Post* Norman Rockwell covers as weekly guides to what life should be like. Smiling faces, happy families, good times… but that is not what was in store for her.

Elizabeth's parents had wanted her to receive a college education. There was precedent in her family for both men and women to be educated and to achieve. Elizabeth's father, Asa Converse, graduated from Ottawa University and was editor of the Wellsville *Globe* for nearly 45 years. He was also a Republican member of the Kansas House of Representatives from 1935-1942. Elizabeth's mother, May Frink Converse, was chosen by the Kansas Author's Club as Poet Laureate of Kansas in 1926. Her column appeared for years in the weekly *Globe* under the heading, "Conversations." May's twin sister (Elizabeth's aunt) opened a photography studio in Wellsville in 1904. Elizabeth's sister, Caroline, graduated from Stanford University, and their brother, Adelbert, from the US Naval Academy.

Amid this proper background and parental expectations, Elizabeth rebelled. Against her parents' wishes, Elizabeth abandoned her college education at Ottawa University to marry the man of her dreams, Clyde Nichols, in 1929. Not long after the marriage (within months, she once commented) Elizabeth realized that the marriage would not and could not work. Her young husband's alcoholism was more than she could handle. Where could she turn? Her parents would say they'd told her so. Treatment programs were not so readily available then and her once cherished church had lost its meaning.

Five children and that many miscarriages later, she separated from her husband.

Who can say exactly why any marriage fails? In spite of numerous attempts at reconciliation, this one did. It took Elizabeth ten years to finalize her divorce from Clyde Nichols. Later, Elizabeth sometimes talked about how difficult it is to get over rejection and the feeling that one is no longer loved.

To support their children, she managed her father's newspaper following his death in 1942. Without much money coming in (and no child support), she struggled to make ends meet. She worked hard to fulfill her roles as mother and managing editor. Given the times, the circumstances, and the pressures, it seems no surprise that depression would find and bind her.

In the mid 1950s, with her children nearly grown and few obligations to meet, Elizabeth sold the newspaper. She no longer had anything to do with herself. Following a brief psychotic phase, she received 13 shock treatments at a hospital in Kansas City. This was followed by years of prescribed drugs and therapy.

Years later, she described her depression to a friend. "Sometimes it was a tremendous homesickness (for what)? Sometimes it was a great tiredness, when I'd sleep 20 hours out of the day. I couldn't move. Sometimes I'd scream, the top of my head hurt so bad. Years ago, I'd try one way or another to die. Sometimes just listless, I never got happy or excited. My brain spun round and round. I used to beat my head and yell! You're Stupid, You're Stupid, to myself. Sometimes I'd get panicky and hide in the closet. When I felt this way I often hated the town and everybody in it. Frustration, I expect. No sleep. Then I used to throw away all but one or two of my clothes because I didn't deserve them, anything good or bad. I lived quite a few years on amphetamines (this is

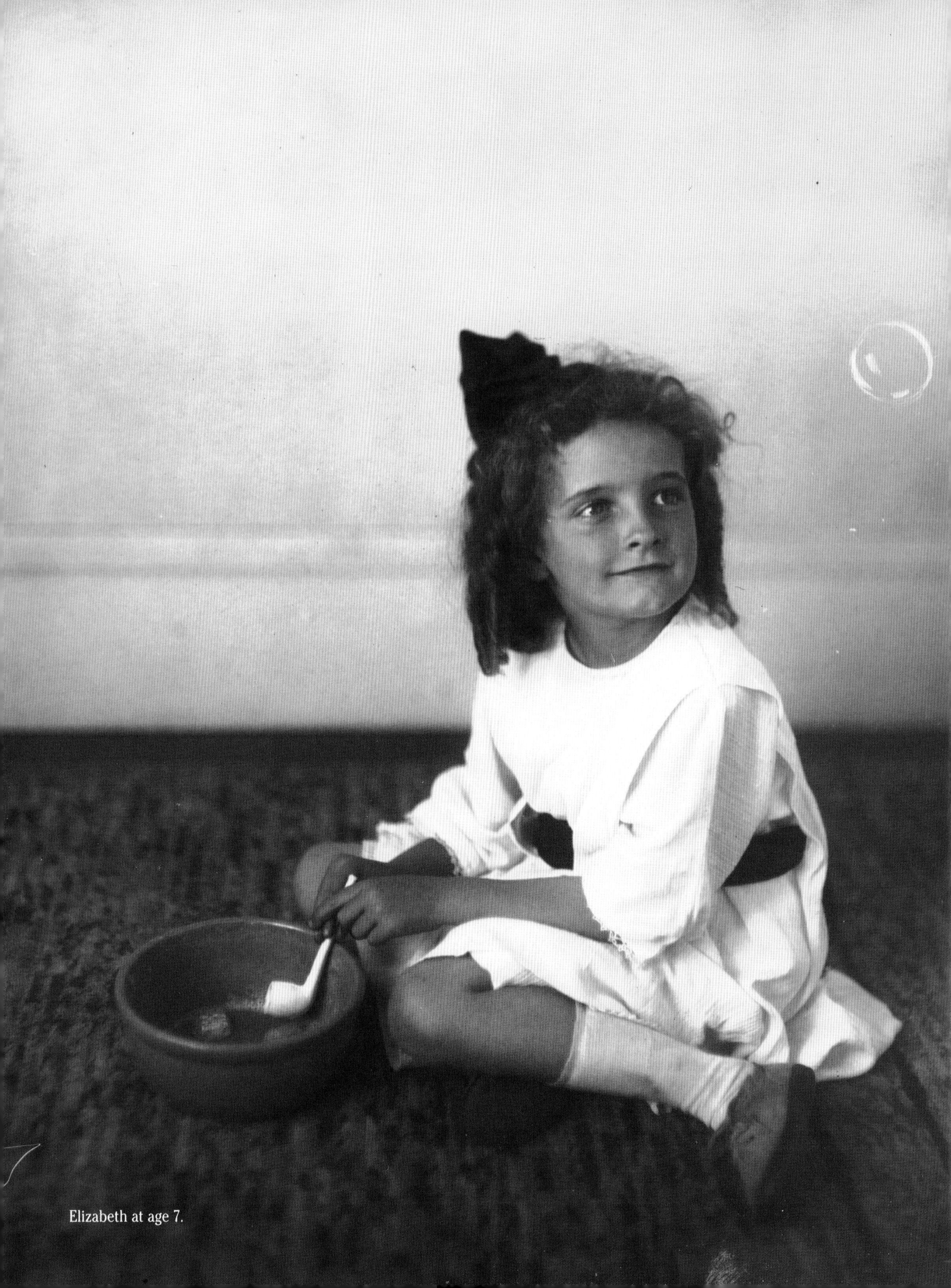

Elizabeth at age 7.

before effects became known and were doctor prescribed.) Then I got to taking downers, too… I feel that I inherited a lot of this depression and that I passed it on to my kids… It wasn't that I longed for death, it was that I felt unworthy for life."

Even a new marriage in 1957 didn't pull Elizabeth from the edge. Glenn Layton, a widower whom she'd known for years courted and wed her amidst the shock treatments. He tried valiantly to retrieve her.

Elizabeth reached the edge again in 1976 with the death of one of her sons from liver problems due to alcoholism. Elizabeth thought he'd inherited the depression from her and the alcoholism from her first husband. Her own depression, grief, pain and guilt were renewed.

It was at this time that Elizabeth's older sister, Carolyn Misselwitz, came to her rescue. A photographer, former missionary in China, and wife of a writer, Carolyn had taken up oil painting during her retirement. On Saturday mornings she joined other retired women in art classes on the West coast. They all painted "pretty" pictures, mostly of flowers and the mountains. Carolyn suggested that it might do Elizabeth some good to get out of the house and try her hand at oil painting.

Elizabeth had hoped to paint pretty pictures like her sister did. But she realized that before she learned to paint, she should learn to draw. She enrolled in a class titled, "Contour Drawing" in the fall semester of 1977 at Ottawa University. The same university where she'd spent two unhappy years as a young woman prior to her first marriage 50 years earlier.

By that evening in September, 1977, Elizabeth had already tried the contour method of drawing. Instructor Pal Wright had set up still life scenes in class for the students to draw. Elizabeth, participating along with the 19-year-olds, seemed uneasy about signing her name to her first drawing. A fellow student made the off-hand suggestion that since she was the only "Grandma" in the class, that is how she should sign the drawing. Assuming the only role in which she felt comfortable, Elizabeth signed her first drawing, "Grandma Layton."

After a few sessions of drawing the classroom still life scenes, Wright encouraged the students to take their paper and pencils home to draw in the contour method. They could draw whatever was familiar to them — salt and pepper shakers, the front porch swing, anyone else living at home. "And if you run out of things to draw, Wright added, draw yourself." Elizabeth did at least two drawings in the contour method at home.

Looking into the mirror that September evening and not looking at the paper, she slowly and carefully drew the outline of one green eye. It was sad, bleak. Then the other eye, slightly smaller. Around the eyes, she filled in the lines of pain and joy which had attached themselves. She drew a stare which went both inward and outward: inward to her soul and outward back at her. She drew the nose, strong and slender, almost a caricature. A mouth, tight and pinched, bearing no trace of its former ripeness. More lines across the forehead, darkened and deepened by inexplicable headaches. A jaw line, once firm, dropped and drooped. Age spots and liver spots which were to become unconscious trademarks.

Looking into the mirror, she drew herself. What is was like to be Elizabeth Hope Converse Nichols Layton. What it was like to grieve a child's death that seemed to destroy her world and being. What it was like to stand helpless as the aging process spoils one's femininity and sexuality. What it was like to feel only the black aloneness of depression. What it was like to no longer be able to wear society and family's expected faces. What it was like to feel the struggle of a woman in a man's world, of forgotten humanity in an uncaring universe.

Looking into the mirror, she drew herself as Eve fleeing the harshly male-dominated Garden of Eden, herself as Lady Macbeth feeling the guilt of society's sins, herself unable to carry out the advice of her Weight Watcher's menu tacked to the wall, herself watching as her son dies on a hospital bed, herself going through the motions of cooking in front of a sign feebly announcing the 50th anniversary of women's suffrage.

Looking into that mirror, hour after hour, sometimes for as long as 12 hours a day, Elizabeth drew herself to wellness. What shock treatments, drugs and therapy had not been able to do, she did herself with crayons, colored pencils and sheets of poster paper she'd purchased for 17 cents apiece at the local drug store.

"I didn't think about it, I just did it," she explained years later. "Here was this space and here was this thought or thing which seemed to fit exactly into that space… I just did what I needed to do."

Within a few months of when she began drawing, she realized that the gripping depression was loosening. It was coming out onto the paper, along with many other feelings she'd so desperately kept to herself. Once on the paper, those feelings could be examined. The drawing, along with the particular feelings it represented, could then be put away — under the bed or in the closet. Even when the drawing was revisited the feelings stayed with it rather than triggering a depression within the artist. Thus, tucked away, each drawing allowed Elizabeth to move on to the next drawing, the next issue, the next struggle, as she not only reclaimed herself but reflected shared feelings of the human race.

Apparent in each of the drawings, even those most devastating, was a message of hope. There were rainbows, hands reaching out, eyes pleading for understanding, and eyes indicating acceptance.

Elizabeth Layton — one woman on the verge— suddenly, serendipitously, miraculously able to turn her life around and spread a message of hope. A message she expressed with common threads of anguish, fear, rage, wisdom and joy. All of this by following her teacher's simple advice of drawing honest lines, of not erasing and of going to the edge.

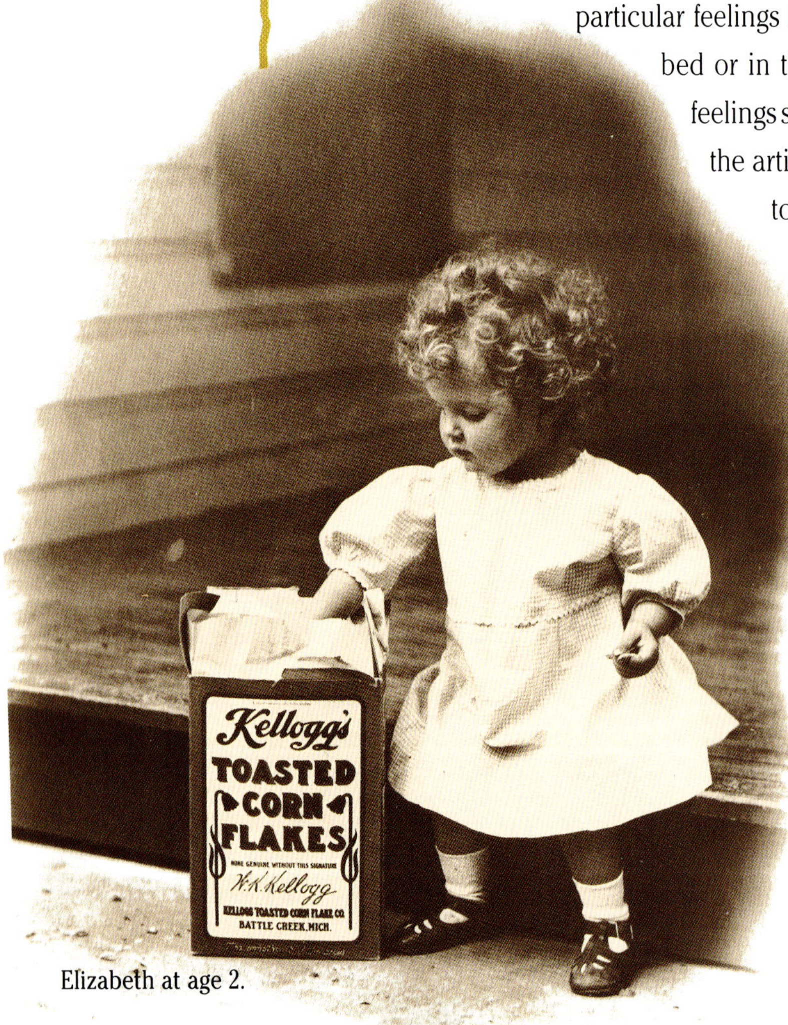

Elizabeth at age 2.

DISCOVERY

My role in Elizabeth Layton's story is difficult to describe in a few words. She and I were never able to find that exact one word. "Agent" didn't work because it implies making money, which I never did, at least not much. When an artist does not sell her work, there are no commissions to be made. "Promoter" does not indicate the depth of our relationship. So, the word we both used was "friend."

In this chapter, I'll explain how I "discovered" Elizabeth Layton, along with how she got from Point A, a depressed grandmother with a handful of drawings under the bed, to Point B, a grandmother with a Smithsonian exhibit and a national following. And I'll point out how dozens, probably hundreds along the way, helped with her journey.

One thing that should be pointed out is that Elizabeth Layton never intended to be an artist, let alone a famous one. She began drawing as a desperate, last-ditch effort to do something that might bring a purpose to her older years. Once the drawings came and brought with them her relief from depression, that was enough for her. She called it a miracle. Thus "cured," she would have been content to leave her few existing drawings under the bed and in the closet.

But when the piecemeal "discovery" came, she realized there must be a larger purpose to her drawings and to her life. She complied as that purpose unfolded.

In no way did she want or seek any degree of fame. At the same time, as she saw the cathartic effect her drawings were having on some people, she realized the need for her drawings to be known. For her gift of art to be given to others, some exposure would be necessary. She understood, she consented, she never complained. It was all part of the purpose.

That I was the one to "discover" and promote Elizabeth Layton is something I, too, never sought. But when the time came, I accepted the role and gained a friend like no other.

As a 27-year-old reporter for a small town daily newspaper, the *Ottawa Herald* in Ottawa, Kansas, I was always looking for a good story. Little did I realize that I was about to find the story of my career.

It was in the student union at Ottawa University late in 1977 that I first saw Elizabeth Layton's drawings in a col-

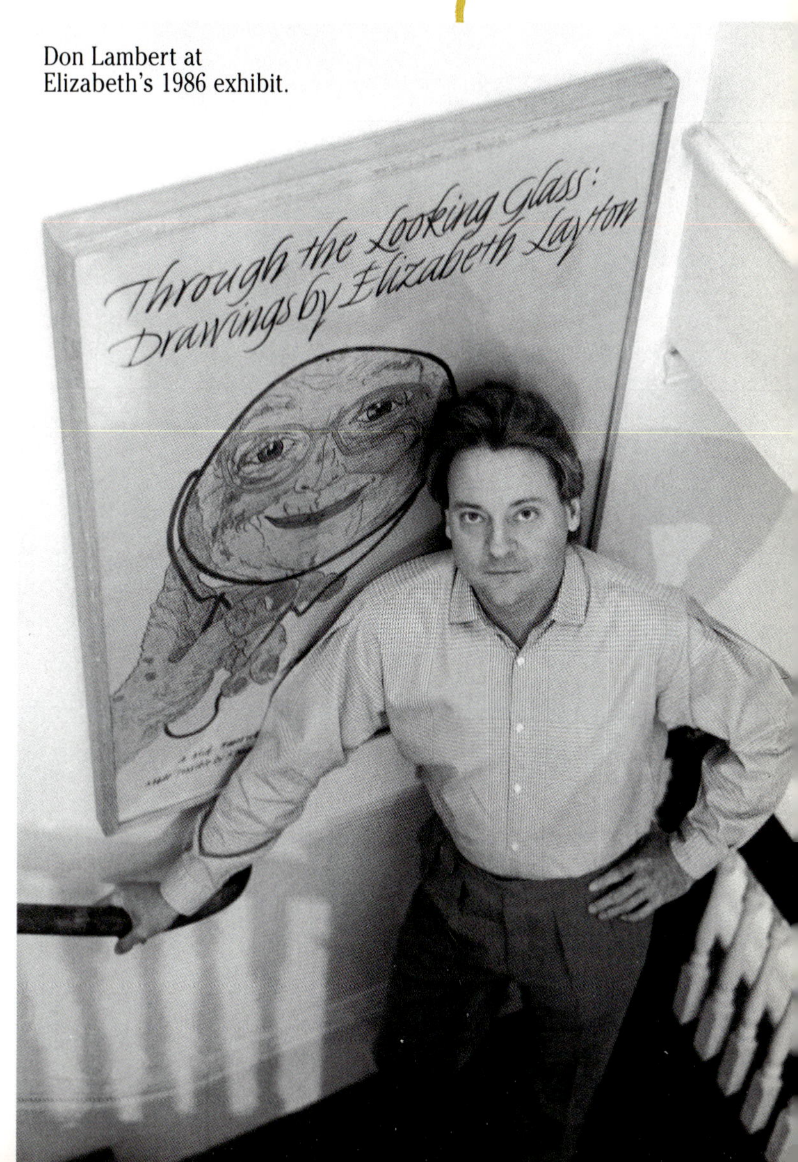

Don Lambert at Elizabeth's 1986 exhibit.

lege freshmen drawing show. There were the usual muddy still lifes. Among them, however, were two drawings like I'd never seen before.

They were drawings of an old woman, I don't remember which specific drawings they were. But, I do remember green eyes, so sad, so pleading.

I dashed out of the student union and to the art room. More for myself than for a story, I had to know who did the strange drawings. The art teacher was Pal Wright, on whom I'd done a story a few years back. He told me the astonishing news—that the drawings were by Elizabeth Layton who had just completed her first art class at age 68. When I asked him what he thought of the drawings, he scratched his head and relayed what he'd told her, "I don't know what you're doing but keep doing it."

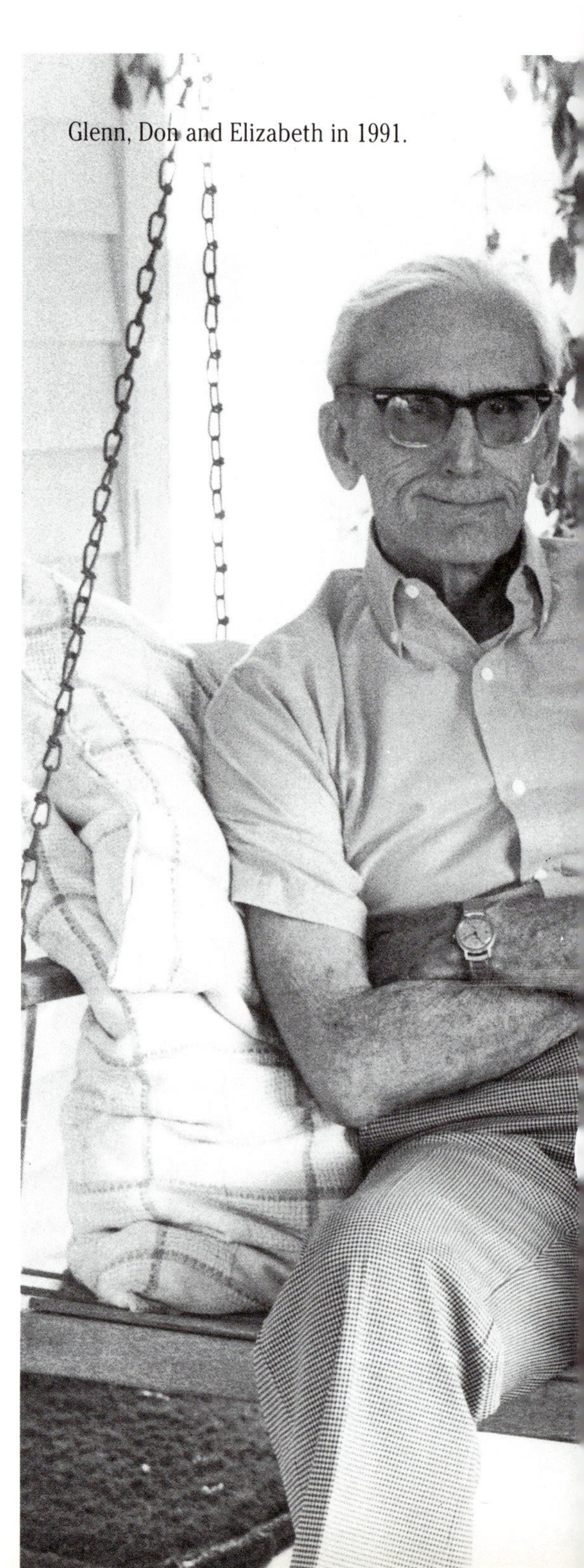

Glenn, Don and Elizabeth in 1991.

Returning to the student union, I looked again at those troubled and troubling drawings. Not long ago a friend told me that he remembers, as an Ottawa University student, saying something to me at that time. Mesmerized by the drawings, I didn't hear him.

Upon returning to the newspaper office, I called this Elizabeth Layton in Wellsville to set up an appointment to interview her for a story. I envisioned the headline, "Granny Takes Art Class." Imagine my chagrin when she declined my offer! A few days later, however, her letter to me arrived at the newspaper office. It offered a compromise. I could write a story about her art but not about her. I agreed to her condition.

The weather had just turned cold prior to my first visit. In my blue Volkswagen (my first car), I found her address, 3-4-5 West Third. I learned only later that houses in Wellsville have no numbers on them. They are not needed since everyone already knows where everyone lives. Afraid that I wouldn't be able to find her house (in a town of fewer than 2,000 people), Elizabeth had that morning painted the numbers onto the front of her house. She also told me later what a formidable sight I was, with long blond hair blowing in the wind, a moustache, and a huge black coat that went nearly to my ankles.

She, on the other hand, in a sleeveless house-dress, with frizzy hair gathered into a bun atop her head, looked much like anyone's grandmother. She'd been waiting for me. After a brief chat during which she revealed quite a knowledge about my newspaper and about my stories, she led me upstairs to a bedroom she'd confiscated as a studio. There, she pulled one drawing after another from under the bed and in the closet. Each drawing was matted and wrapped with acetate.

She explained that all the drawings were done with the blind contour method and that all were self-portraits. There were at least two dozen of them. When I asked what she intended to do with them, she said she hoped she might have a show of them some day at the local nutrition center where "the old people go to eat." I asked if I might show some of them to friends and if I might

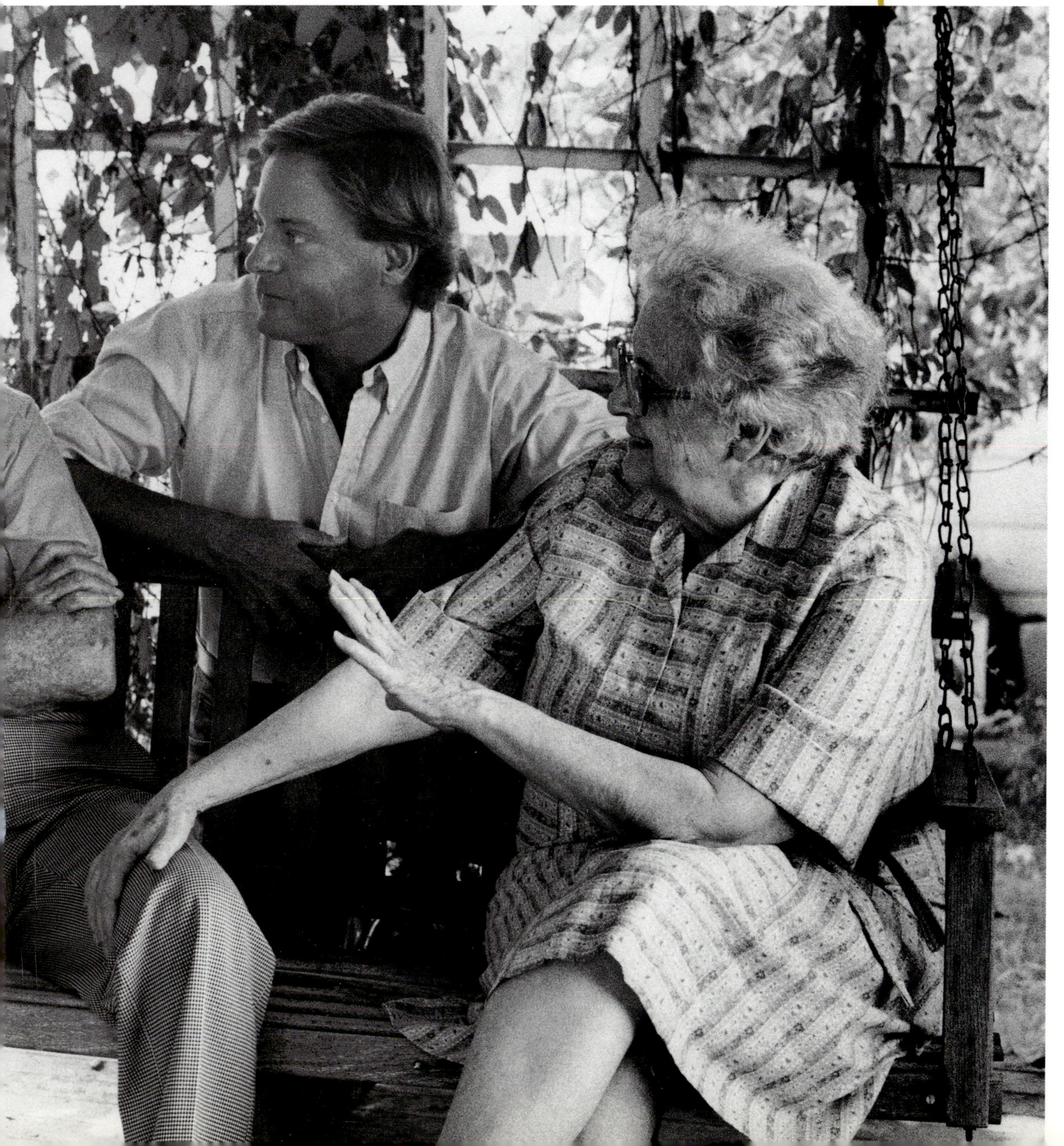

organize a display of them at the Ottawa Library where my volunteer job was to hang monthly shows by local artists. While she didn't understand why this young, male reporter would be so interested in drawings of an old woman, she said I could take the drawings with me. I chose eight. She followed me to the front porch, waving as I drove away with my "find" in the back seat of my Volkswagen.

Back at the newspaper office, I proudly placed the drawings against a wall and rounded up my co-workers to get their reactions. To my surprise, they were baffled, shocked, belittling. The kindest comment was, "I wouldn't want one of these things hanging in my house."

Thus, I'd had my first indication that not everyone would be as enamoured by the drawings as I was. Undaunted, I made appointments to show the drawings to "experts" at three nearby places—the Nelson-Atkins Museum of Art in Kansas City, the Spencer Museum of Art in Lawrence, and the Public Library in Topeka. People at all three places agreed that they'd never seen anything like these drawings but didn't think their institutions would be interested in showing them. Nor did they have any idea what should happen with the drawings.

I was confused, disappointed. I had found some drawings which I knew were extraordinary. Yet, they'd been ridiculed by my peers and ignored by the "experts." What could I do? Knowing that the drawings would somewhere find acceptance, I decided that I'd simply have to look elsewhere. Where that would be, I did not know.

Against the wishes of the local librarian, I hung my eight drawings in the library and wrote a story about them. Within a few days, the librarian, Barbara Dew, called to ask if the drawings might be displayed longer. Far from reacting negatively, patrons seemed fascinated by them. There was something going on in these drawings, she admitted, even if she couldn't explain what it was.

As I look back on that first newspaper story, I continue to be amazed by its perceptions. The story indicates that Elizabeth was well on her way to understanding the drawings and I was on my way to deciding it would be up to me to promote them.

About that time, I moved to Topeka to become director of the Arts Council of Topeka. The importance of that move, it now seems, was that it allowed me access to the Kansas art scene. I soon discovered that there was no mechanism to get an artist "discovered." At least, not yet. The Kansas Arts Commission, which is the State's official conduit for state and federal monies to be distributed throughout Kansas, was organizing a new program, the "Traveling Visual Arts Program," for the exact purpose of putting together exhibits of art by Kansans which could be shown at museums across the state.

Having heard that the Wichita Art Museum often champions works by Kansans, I got an appointment with its director, Howard Wooden. Immediately, he stated the desire to assemble an exhibit of Elizabeth's drawings and said such a task would be easier with the newly formed TVAP program which his museum would be administering for the Kansas Arts Commission. Through the melding of these organizations, such an exhibit was organized. Two people on their staffs should here be mentioned. Wichita curator Howard Spencer asked Elizabeth to record her comments about each drawing, comments which were transcribed and placed on labels displayed beside each drawing. This idea, rather unorthadox at the time, proved most helpful to the public in understanding the drawings. And, Elizabeth's comments proved to be nearly as witty as her drawings. Joan Wingerson, program coordinator of the arts commission, made sure the exhibit was successfully organized as the State's first sanctioned touring art exhibit.

Titled "Through the Looking Glass, Drawings by Elizabeth Layton," the exhibit opened in Iola, Kansas in September of 1980. It then went to Lawrence, Kansas City, Topeka, and nearly two dozen towns across Kansas. People were astonished, the show was a success.

In what soon became weekly visits to Elizabeth Layton's home where I was also befriended by her husband Glenn, I gradually learned more about her. Foremost was her struggle with depression. During one visit, shortly after I'd moved to Topeka, she asked whether I knew any art therapists. Might there be one at the Menninger Foundation? I'd heard of one, Robert Ault, whom I later learned was one of the founding members in 1969 of the American Art Therapy Association.

Ault later told the story that when I called, asking him to look at Elizabeth's drawings, he agreed only reluctantly. He had to look at patients' works all day. But, he agreed in order to meet the town's new Arts Council director. He could not have been more taken with her work. Not long afterwards, I drove him to Wellsville to meet Elizabeth, the first of dozens of people I'd take on that hour-long drive.

The two of them concluded that Elizabeth's inklings might be well-founded. Indeed, she might have cured her depression by learning to draw.

Ault later wrote, "Elizabeth Layton had gone through the whole course of modern psychiatry over 30 years and it hadn't really changed her life. Then she takes up drawing and cures herself."

Ault would meet with Elizabeth many times as she explained to him her process of self-portraiture. He documented her techniques and then taught them to his students for use with their patients. Each semester for his students would include an afternoon with Elizabeth Layton, a master art therapist.

Elizabeth's reluctant burst into the public spotlight happened a few months before the opening of her traveling exhibits. It was the spring of 1980, I'd entered two of her drawings in a competition in Kansas City called the Mid-Four Annual Juried Exhibit sponsored by the Junior League. Elizabeth's two drawings were among some 600 entries that year.

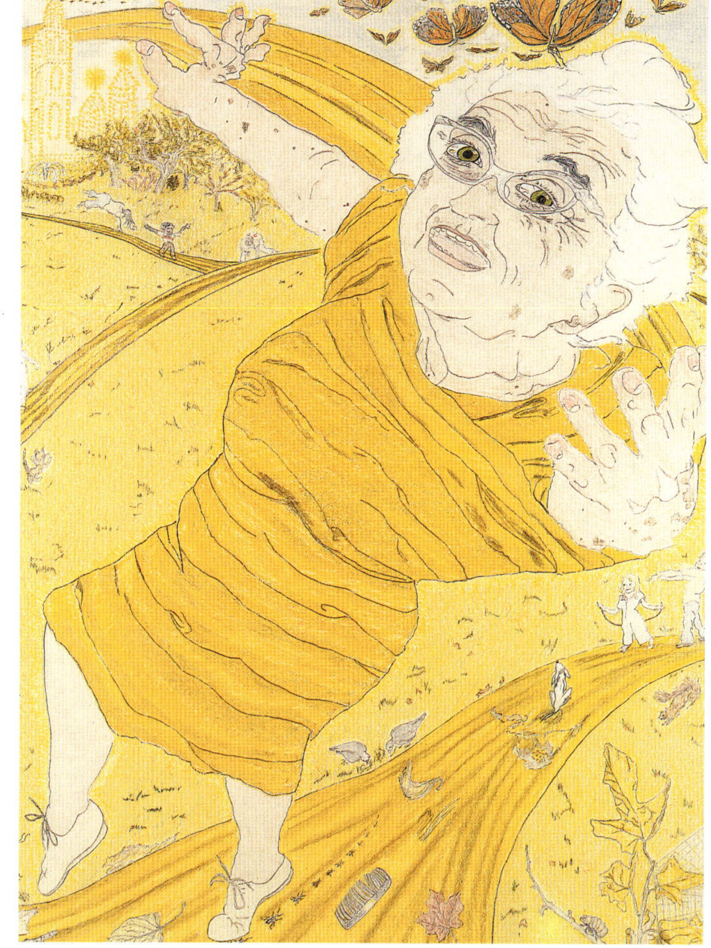

Skipping Down Christo's Walkway

Imagine Elizabeth's surprise (and the Junior League's) when the three judges agreed that the first prize would go to Elizabeth for her drawing, "Skipping Down Christo's Walkway." From reading in the *Kansas City Star* about Christo's wrapping of sidewalks in Kansas City's Loose Park, Elizabeth sensed how "wrapped up" some people were in the project. Thus, she drew herself "wrapped up" in the golden fabric that Christo used. The fabric had become a cocoon, her feet, arms and head emerging so she can join the butterflies above.

Juror Cathleen Gallender said the drawing has "real spontaneity, real energy." Franz Schulze, juror and Chicago art critic, called the drawing "Unaffected, unsophisticated, honest." And Graham Beal, then curator at the Walker Art Center in Minneapolis, Minnesota, commented on the drawing's "absolute joie de vivre…odd kind of sophistication — which the artist probably does not know about in an academic sense…kind of like Chagall at his best in 1913, has that kind of magic charm and dream-like quality."

When I showed the comments to Elizabeth, her response was, "Fine. But who was Chagall?" It didn't take her long to learn.

The opening reception for the Mid-Four exhibit was the first of only about a half-dozen public appearances Elizabeth would make. I joined Elizabeth, accompanied by Glenn and a carload of family members as she looked at the 40 other works which had been included in the exhibit. Well-heeled Junior League members were genuinely thrilled by the 70-year-old "discovery" they had made. In fact, they walked proudly beside the newly acclaimed artist who was wearing her best cotton housedress bought down the street for $12.95.

The Mid-Four exhibit was seminal to Elizabeth's artistic career. Ironically, the exhibit was at the Nelson-Atkins Museum of Art, the Kansas City museum to which I first showed Elizabeth's drawings just a few months after she began drawing. Then, and repeatedly since, the staff refused to acknowledge the drawings. As on curator quipped, "I won't look at anything by a primitive."

Even though Elizabeth donated the joyous "Christo's Walkway" to the Nelson in 1984, the drawing remains in the basement.

Thus, the Nelson has maintained its non-recognition of Elizabeth Layton for 17 years. The result is a profound loss to Kansas City and to a larger community.

During the early 1980s, as Elizabeth's drawings were gaining wider acceptance in Kansas, I became more confident that this art and this story merited national attention. But how could that be obtained? I realized that my knowledge, skills and contacts were limited. But I had a story and a stack of art bigger than I was. With a sense of urgency, wanting to get Elizabeth's drawings "discovered" on a national level while she was able to enjoy it, I realized it would be up to me to make the media contacts, learn about contemporary art, and make the art connections. From New York to San Francisco, I beat the pavement, always hoping for that big break. It didn't come, at least not when and where I'd hoped it might.

Everywhere I went, reaction was the same. Art magazine people were not impressed with any art that wasn't Picasso or whatever was "hot" in New York. Curators were mostly indifferent. The response I remember most vividly was from a 35 year-old art history graduate. After I'd shown her one heartfelt drawing after another, her comment was, "Like, I don't relate, you know?"

The rejections made me more persistent. I didn't have a plan, I didn't really think about one. I did what had to be done. I found people who did respond to Elizabeth's drawings, wonderful people around the country.

The "Through the Looking Glass" exhibit, after being shown in 20 Kansas towns, was taken over by the Mid-America Arts Alliance in Kansas City which prepared the exhibit to go national. (Ironically, this organization had originally rejected the idea of touring Elizabeth's drawings, saying the public wouldn't like them. The organization changed its mind after seeing the response in Kansas. Since then, it and a second touring exhibit of Elizabeth's drawings, "Drawing on Life" have become the organization's most successful exhibits.)

The exhibits went coast to coast — the Honolulu Academy of Art, the Phoenix Art Museum, the Chicago Public Library Cultural Center, the Grand Rapids Art Museum, the Joslyn Museum in Omaha, and the National Council on the Aging in Washington, D.C. The exhibit in Phoenix was the most popular in ten years, the one in Chicago drew 45,000 visitors. There were nearly 200 other locations. Places like Lubbock, Texas where the show was as successful as in Chicago and Phoenix.

National media attention was happening, stories in *People, Life* and *Parade* magazines. Interviews on National Public Radio, NBC News, ABC's "Incredible Sunday" and CBS's "Good Morning America."

A major boost was the 1984 publication of a 64-page exhibit catalog called "Through the Looking Glass" by the Mid-America Arts Alliance and its visual arts wing, Exhibits USA. Through the generosity of the late William N. Deramus III, chairman of Kansas City Southern Industries, people could have with this catalog the same experience they'd had seeing Elizabeth's exhibit. Text for the catalog was by Lynn Bretz, photography by Suzanne Robinson.

Frequently, I'd travel on Elizabeth's behalf to her exhibits where I'd lecture about her and teach how to draw like she did. I was often accompanied by Elizabeth's youngest daughter, Julia Nichols.

At a time when federal and state support for the arts has been called into question, the profound importance of that support on Elizabeth's career can not be underestimated. Without that support, as Elizabeth understood well, her exhibits would not and could not have come to fruition. It was state and federal money (our tax dollars) which made Elizabeth's exhibits a reality and inspiration.

The big break finally came, a call in 1990 from the director of one of the Smithsonian museums, the National Museum of American Art, saying the museum would exhibit Elizabeth's drawings for three months, April, May and June of 1992.

Director Elizabeth Broun was not unfamiliar with Elizabeth's drawings. She'd been a curator at the Spencer Museum of Art in Lawrence, Kansas at the time I was beginning to show the drawings. She had also met Elizabeth then and had said to me, "Someday, I'll do something with Elizabeth's drawings." Her call came 12 years later. I'd also apprised her of my dealings with a previous director at her museum.

One of the first appointments I had with a "big" art person was in the winter of 1980 with Dr. Joshua Taylor, longtime director of the National Museum of American Art. I'd carried Elizabeth's actual drawings with me to show to him. He agreed that the drawings were wonderful. We planned a late spring visit to Kansas for him to meet Elizabeth and to plan a show of her drawings at the museum. His unexpected death just months after our visit ended those plans.

Preparing for a Smithsonian exhibit was a challenge. I realized that with this "hook," much media attention could be generated, particularly in areas with interests overlapping Elizabeth's—women's rights, mental health, aging, etc. Stories about the Smithsonian exhibit appeared in Time, *Christian Science Monitor, Mother Jones, USA Today,* and *Ms,* (a magazine I'd been talking to for ten years.) Stories I'd written were in *American Artist,* the *Humanist, Arthritis Today,* the *University of Kansas Alumni Magazine* and *Press Woman.* Notices were carried in journals of the American Psychiatric Association and the American Psychological Association. And, of course, there was much attention in the local media, stories like one from the Associated Press headlined, "Artist, 82, skips debut of show."

And a front page banner headline in the Wichita Eagle proclaiming, "Enthusiasm over Kansan's art takes Smithsonian by surprise."

The guage to the success of Elizabeth Layton's Smithsonian show was a five-inch thick book of messages written to her from new and old fans. Curators at this museum have such a book for all of their exhibits. They were surprised by the emotional depth expressed in so many of the comments.

Elizabeth and Glenn did not attend the Smithsonian exhibit. They chose, instead, to enjoy the show vicariously, from their home in Wellsville. Elizabeth explained, with her usual modesty, "It's wonderful, and, yes, I'm impressed. But I'm just as impressed if the exhibit goes to the hometown library because people will see it there, too."

> **" It's wonderful, and yes,**
>
> **I'm impressed. But I'm just as impressed**
>
> **if the exhibit goes to the**
>
> **hometown library**
>
> **because people**
>
> **will see it there, too. "**
>
> — Elizabeth "Grandma" Layton

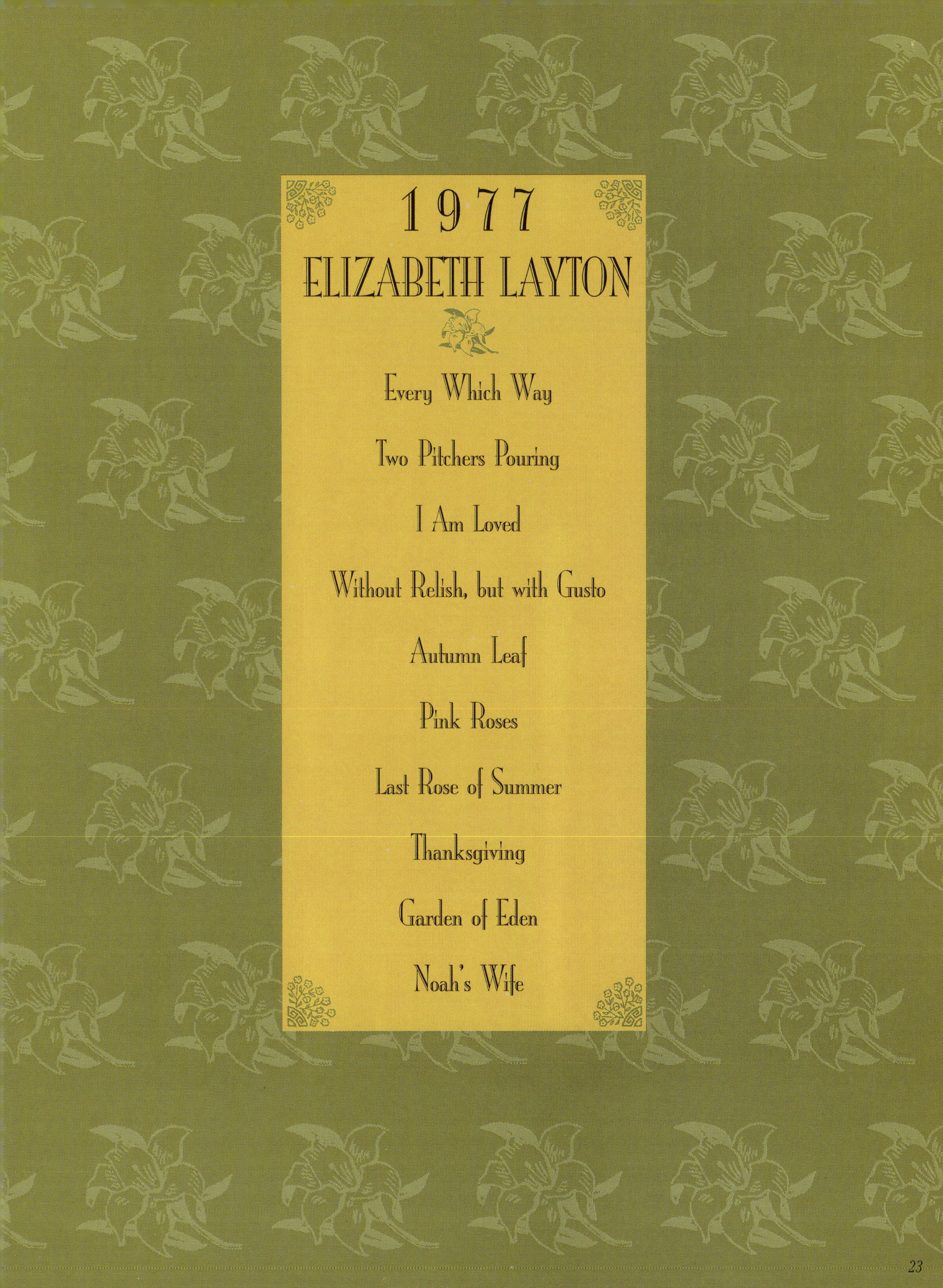

1 9 7 7
ELIZABETH LAYTON

Every Which Way

Two Pitchers Pouring

I Am Loved

Without Relish, but with Gusto

Autumn Leaf

Pink Roses

Last Rose of Summer

Thanksgiving

Garden of Eden

Noah's Wife

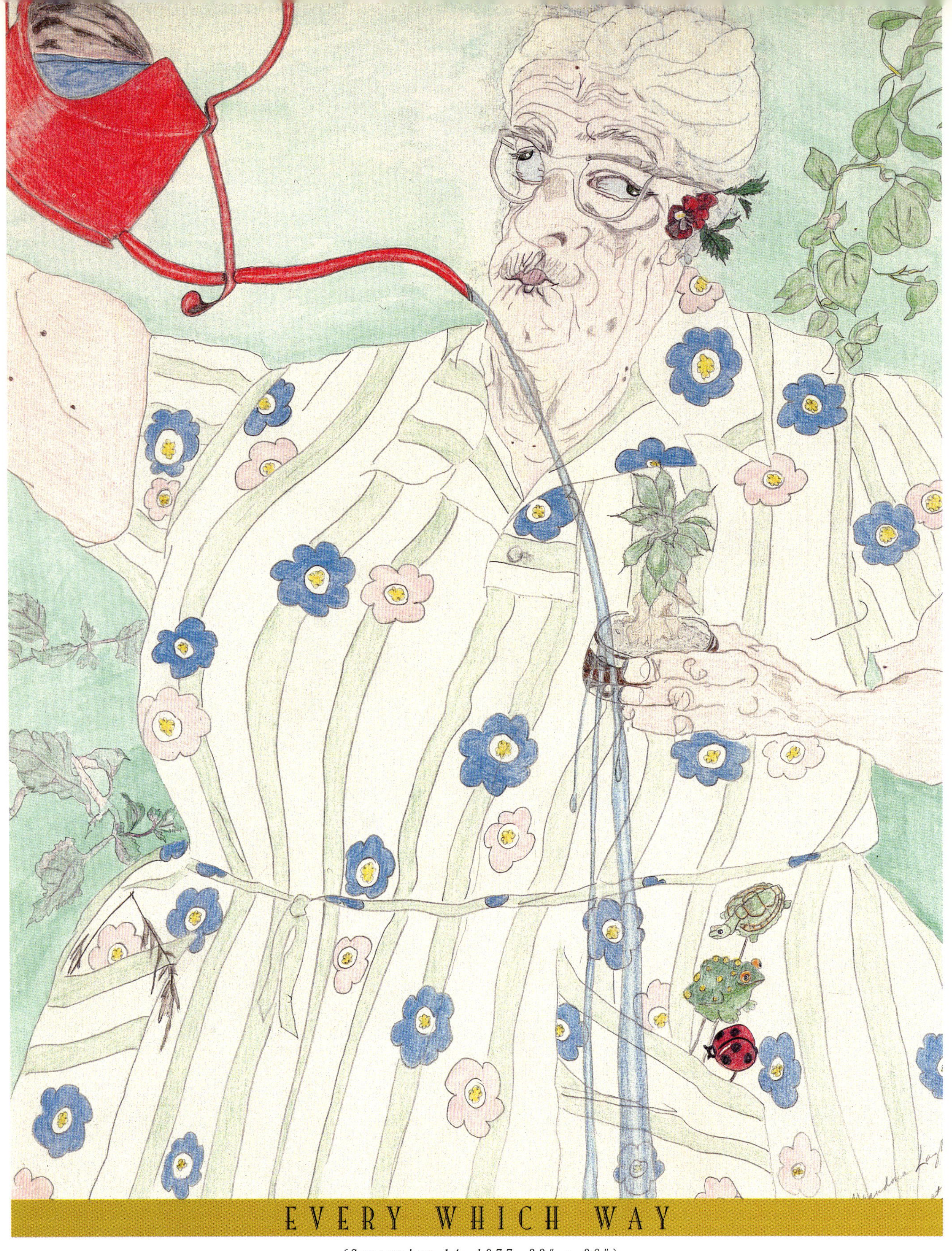

(September 14, 1977, 22" x 28")

"*People see you on the street and they're used to you being thin, and one woman came up behind me and said 'You're too fat!' and I came home weeping. It really gets to you… but this drawing is just watering the flowers…I missed the flowers.*"

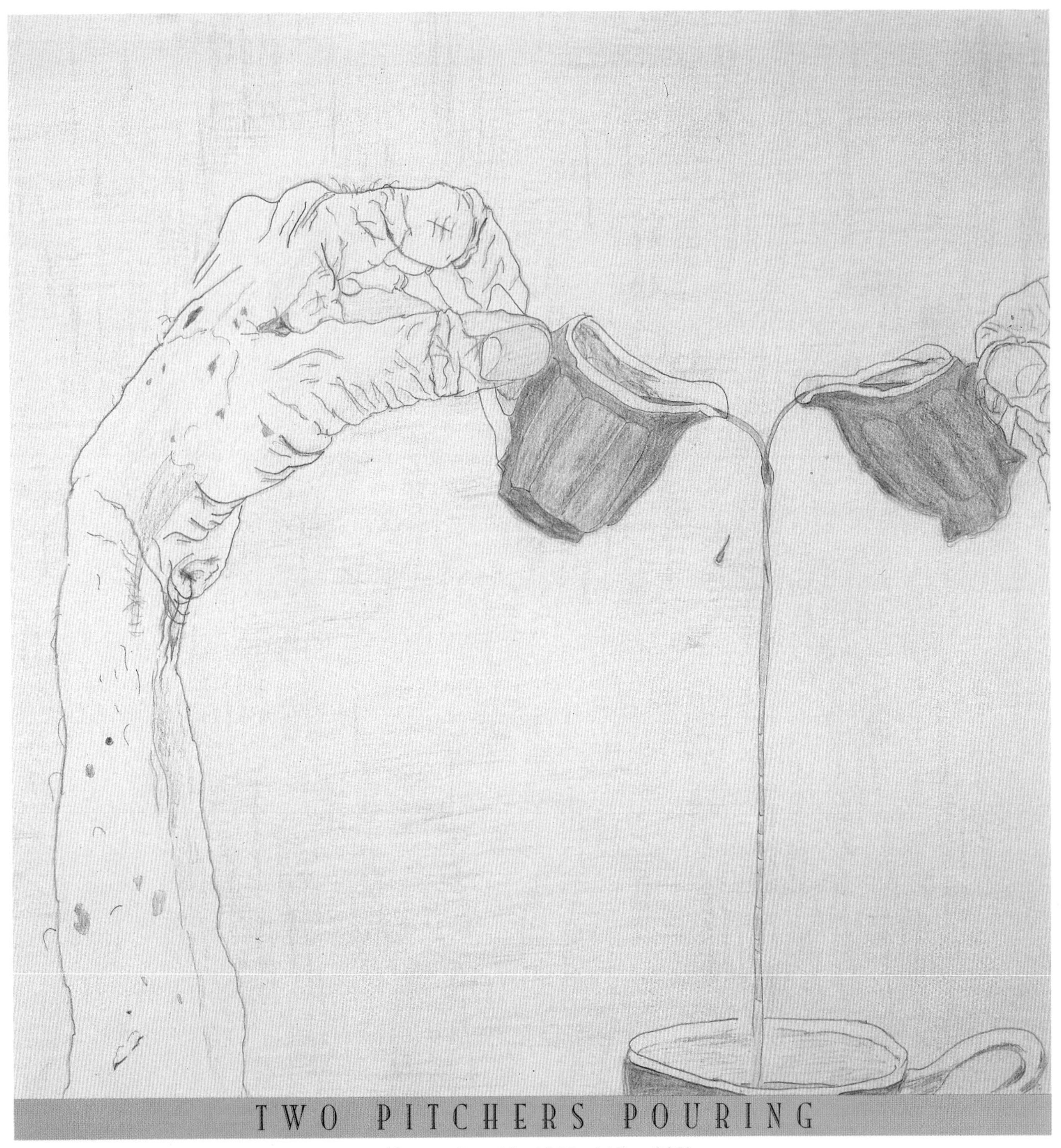

TWO PITCHERS POURING

(September 18, 1977, 14" x 22")

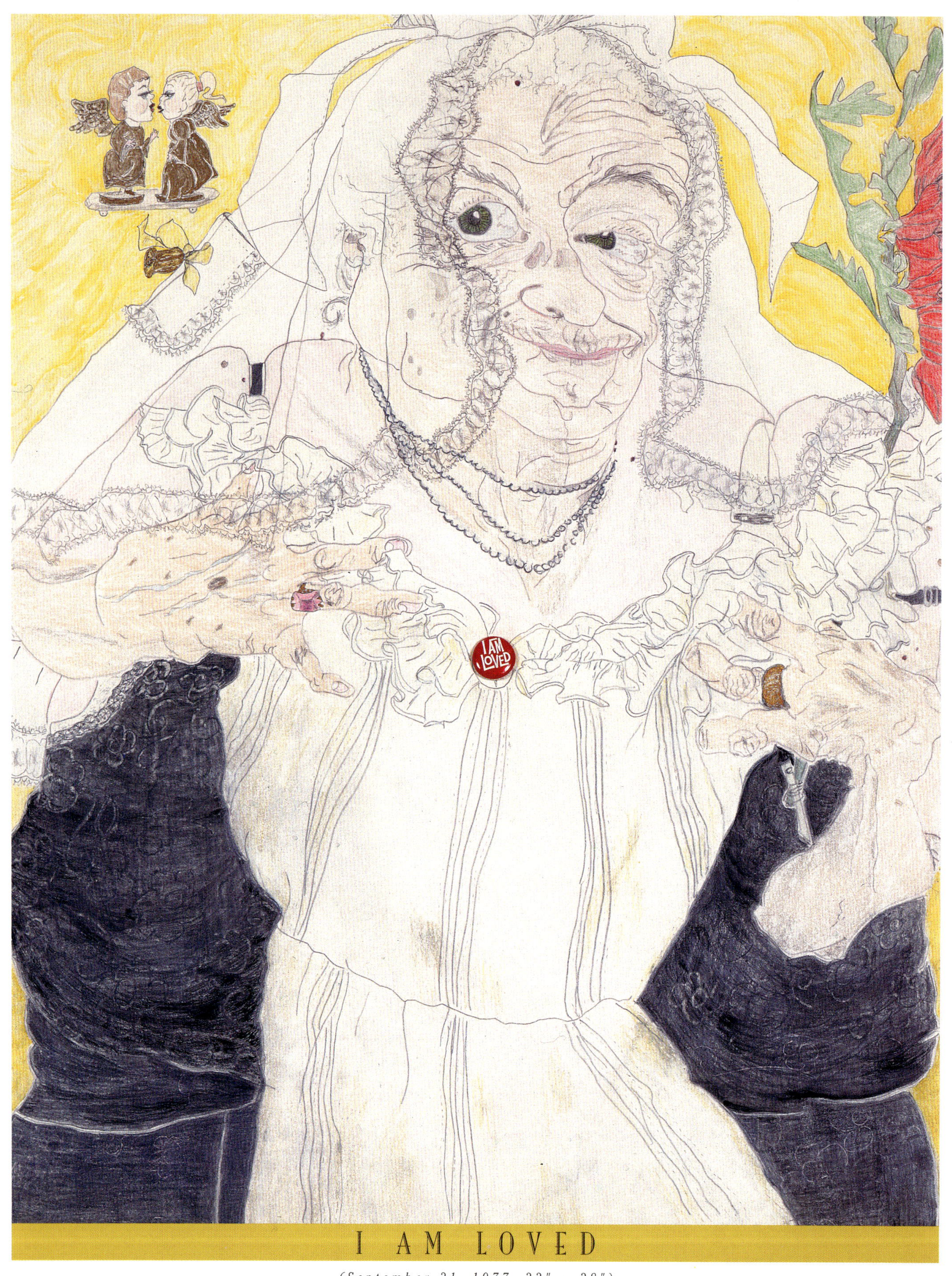

I AM LOVED

(September 21, 1977, 22" x 28")

"*This is her wedding dress… she is holding it up to her.***"**

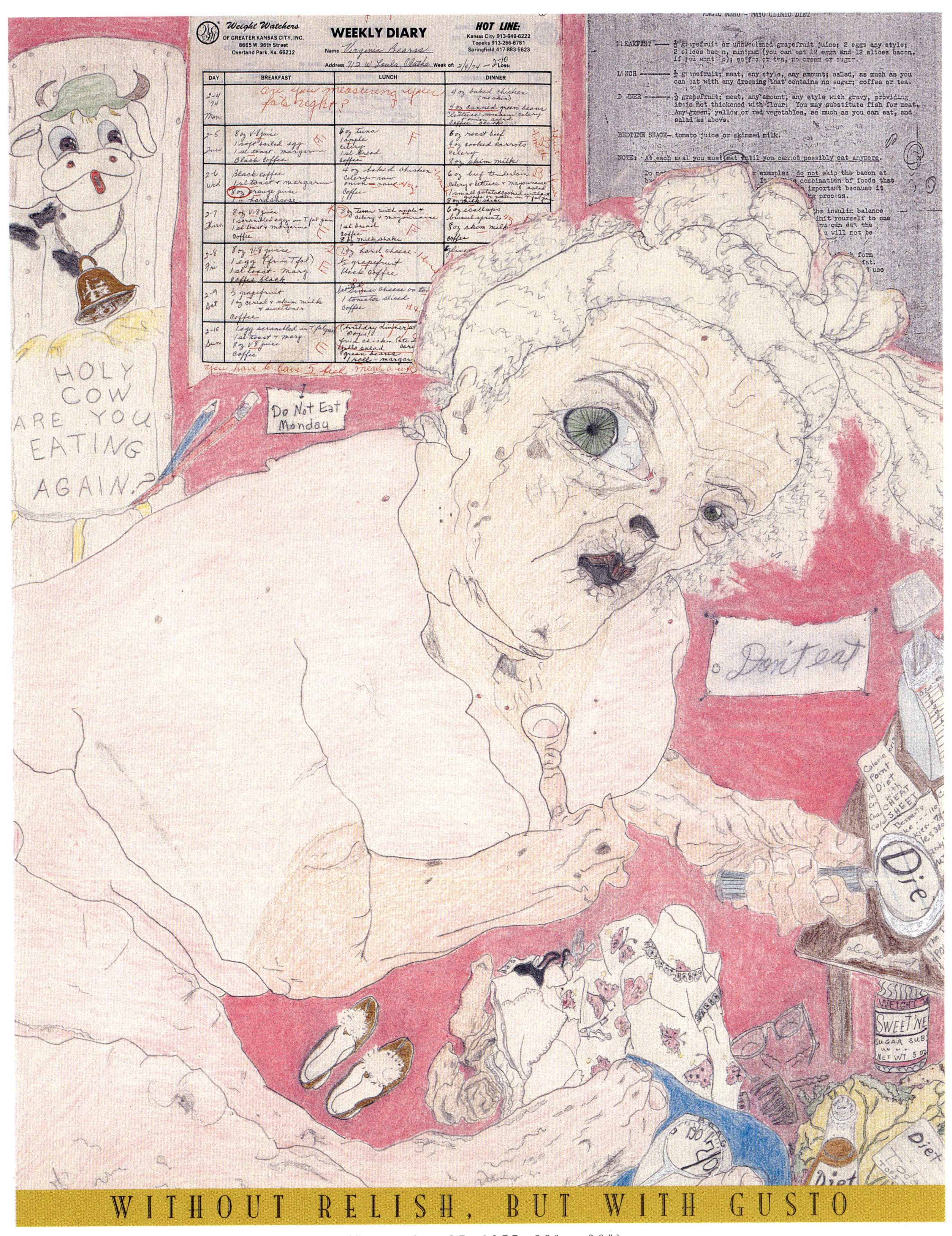

WITHOUT RELISH, BUT WITH GUSTO

(September 27, 1977, 22" x 28")

> ❝*I am standing on the scale. I had the magnifying glass so I could see what the scale said… and this magnifying glass is showing through… it's supposed to say diet, but all you get is die. If you don't diet you are going to die.*❞

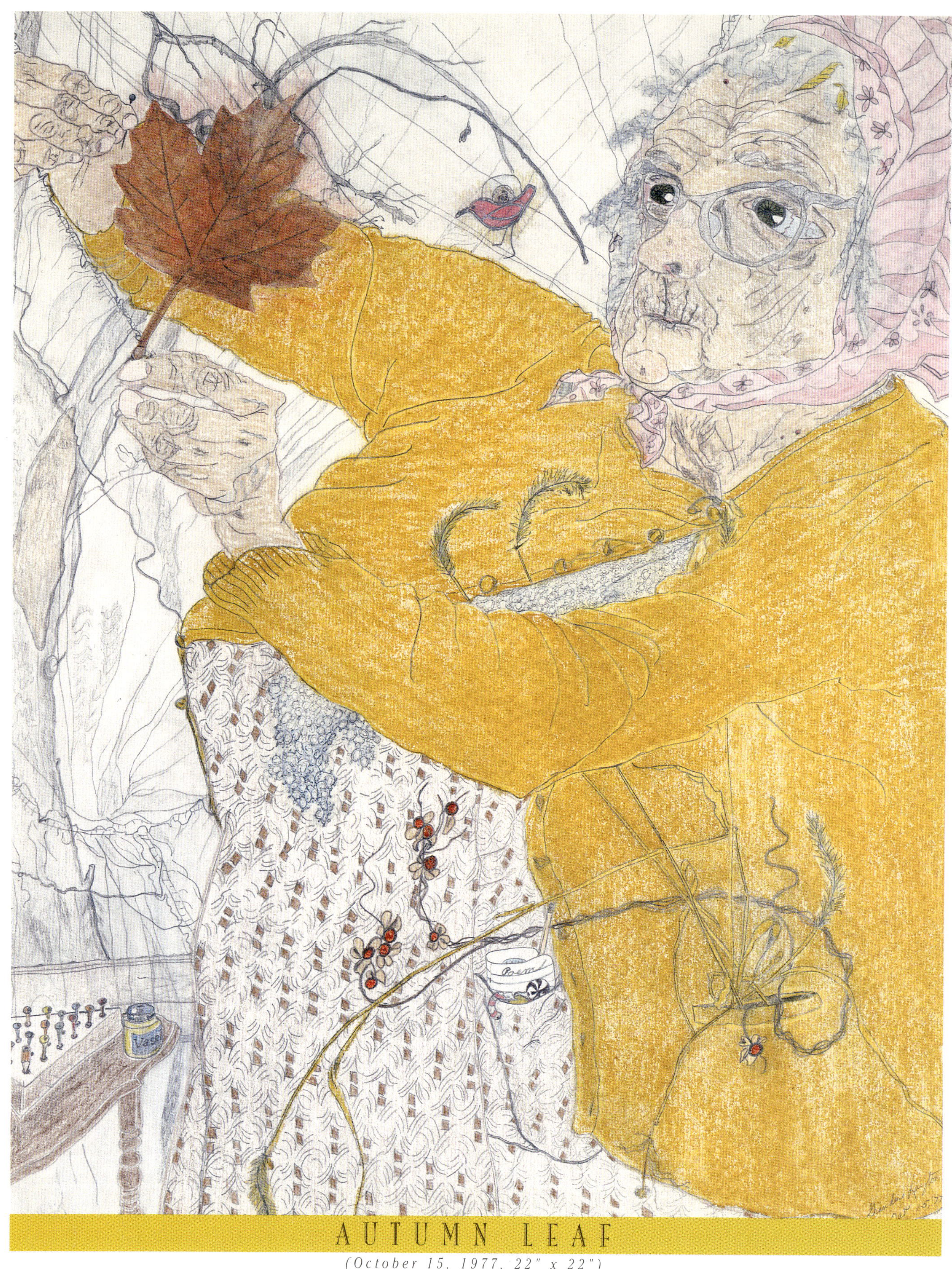

AUTUMN LEAF

(October 15, 1977, 22" x 22")

> "*My mother wrote a poem. I can't remember how it went, but she brought the leaf in to flaunt against window's frost. You bring this autumn leaf in, put vaseline on it, and pin it on a curtain.*"

28

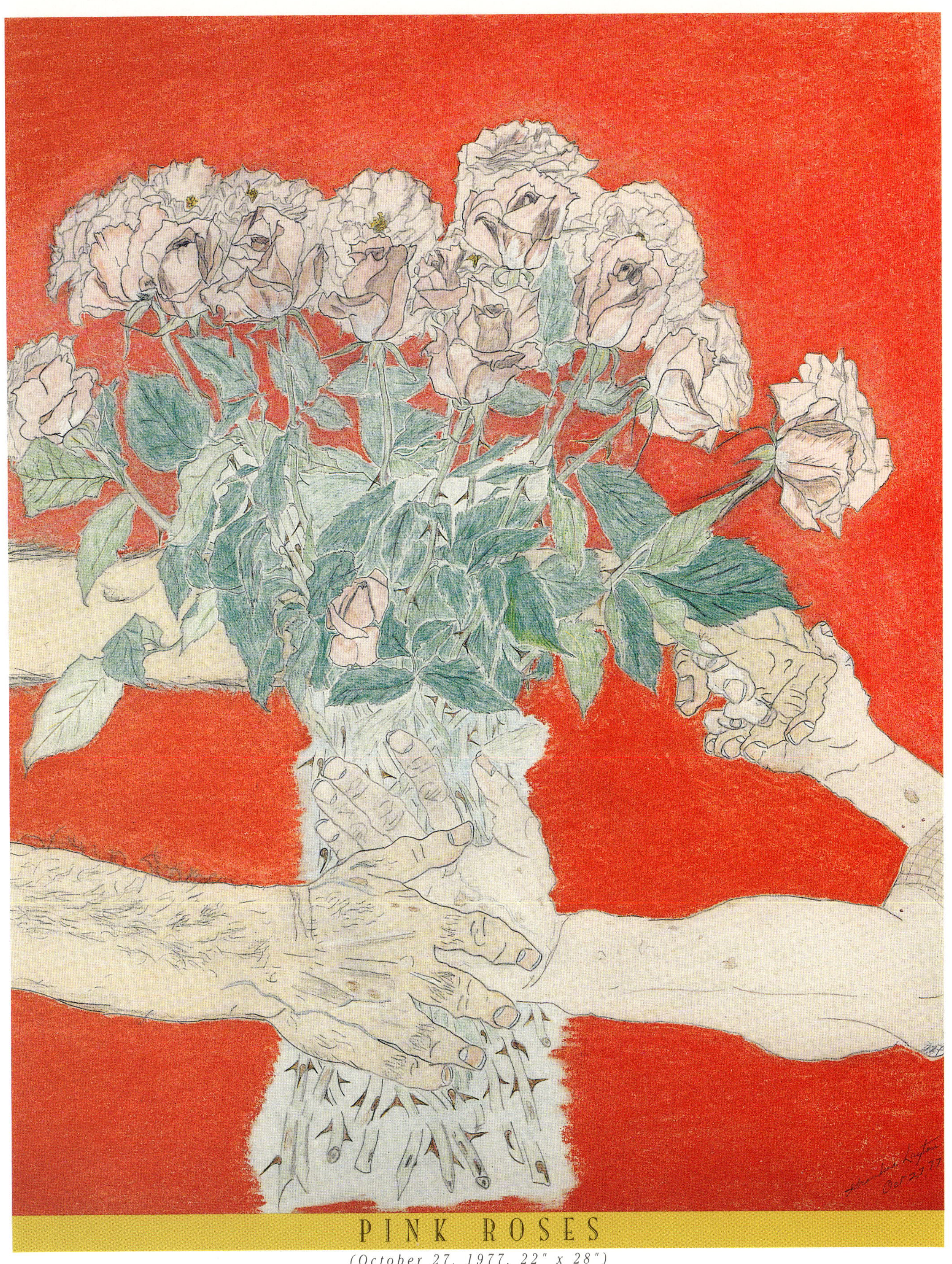

(October 27, 1977, 22" x 28")

"*These were birthday roses I set on my desk and drew. I never moved the glass pitcher but drew the roses a week later after they had opened out. One never opened. I call this comfort.*"

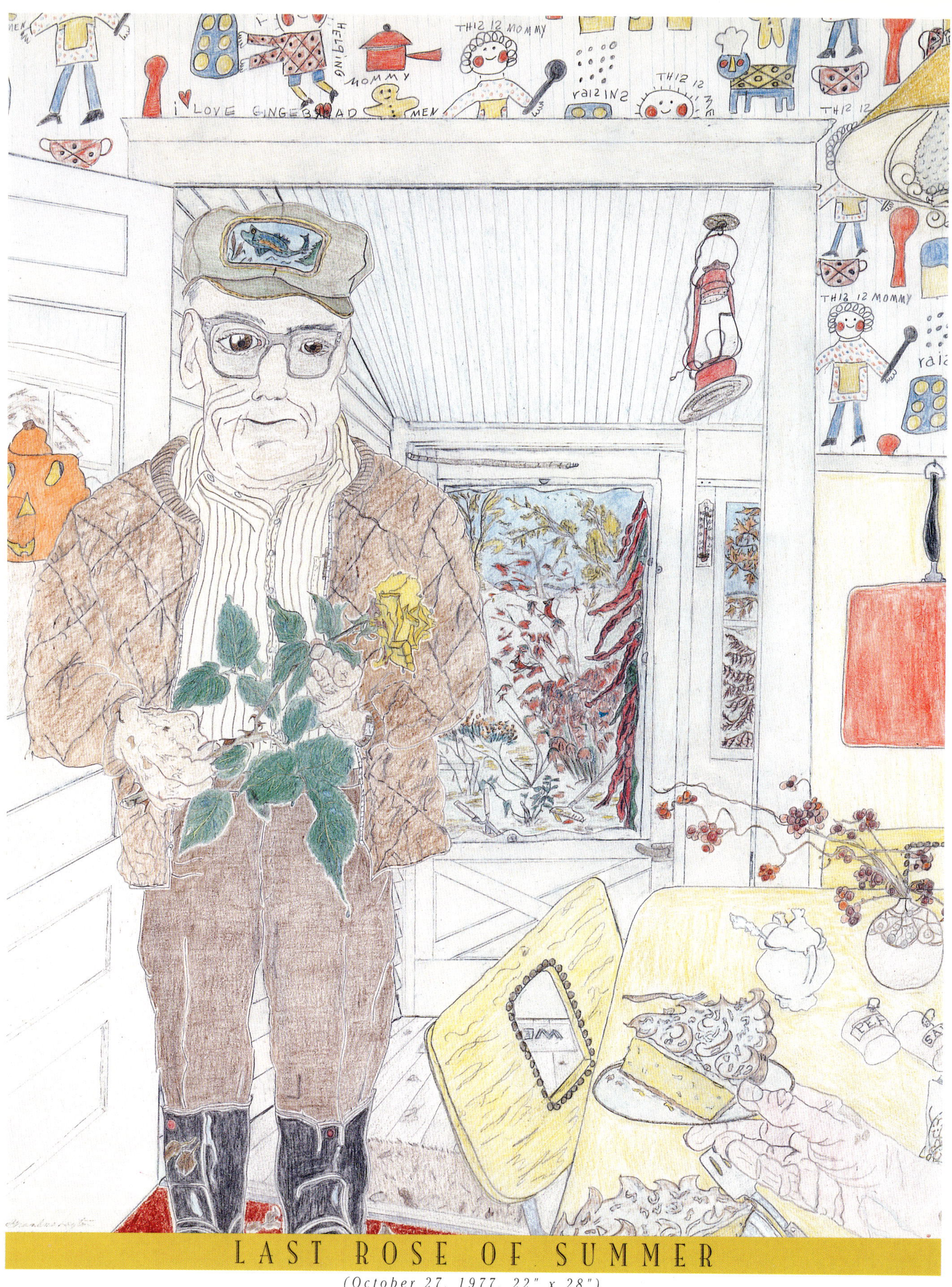

LAST ROSE OF SUMMER

(October 27, 1977, 22" x 28")

"*Glenn came in one morning with this yellow rose. It was like marriage. You give and you take.*
And that is why I was offering him the pie."

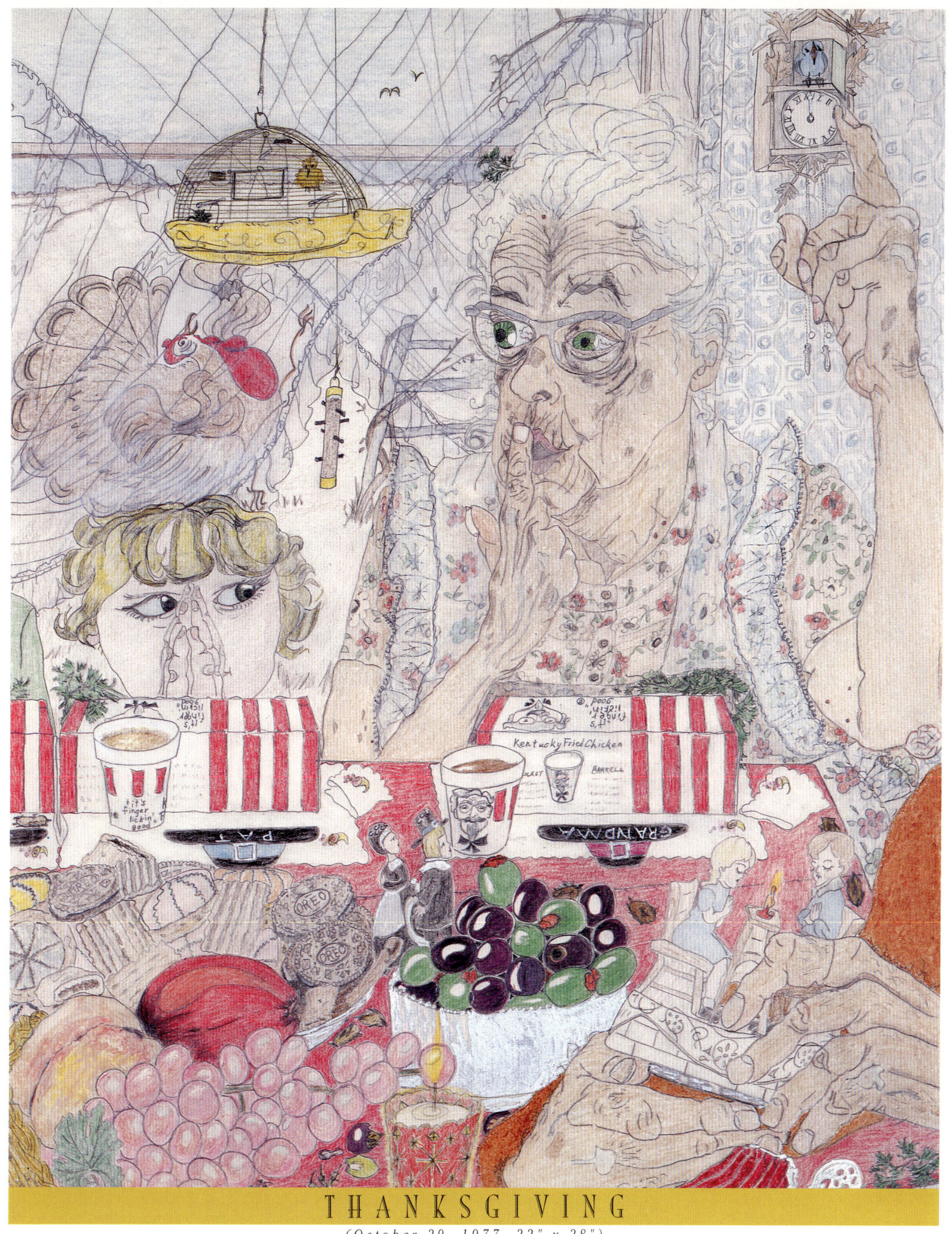

THANKSGIVING

(October 29, 1977, 22" x 28")

> **"** *I hate to cook, so this is my Thanksgiving, because we have Kentucky Fried Chicken and Oreo cookies, and I didn't have to work at it. I have cooked I don't know how many family dinners. I've given up. So the turkey is outside there, strutting because he didn't get killed. See, it's better for everybody.* **"**

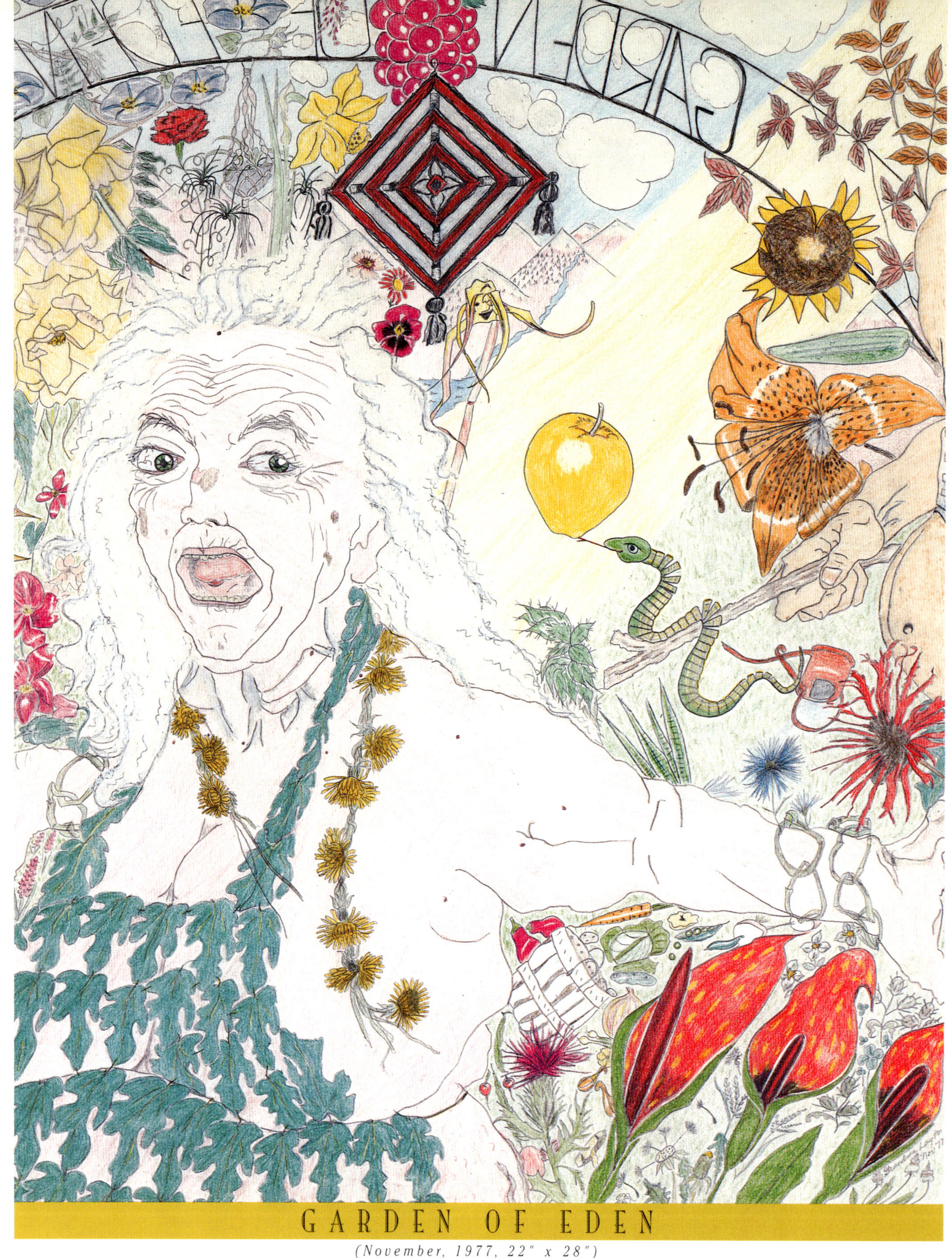

GARDEN OF EDEN

(November, 1977, 22" x 28")

“*Women have had the blame all through the ages for everything. You know that's not right. Now a woman would not listen to a snake, she'd run, wouldn't she? This is Adam, he's got a Band-Aid where his rib came out. This was my first E.R.A. picture. I was just objecting to being blamed for all of the sin of the world.*”

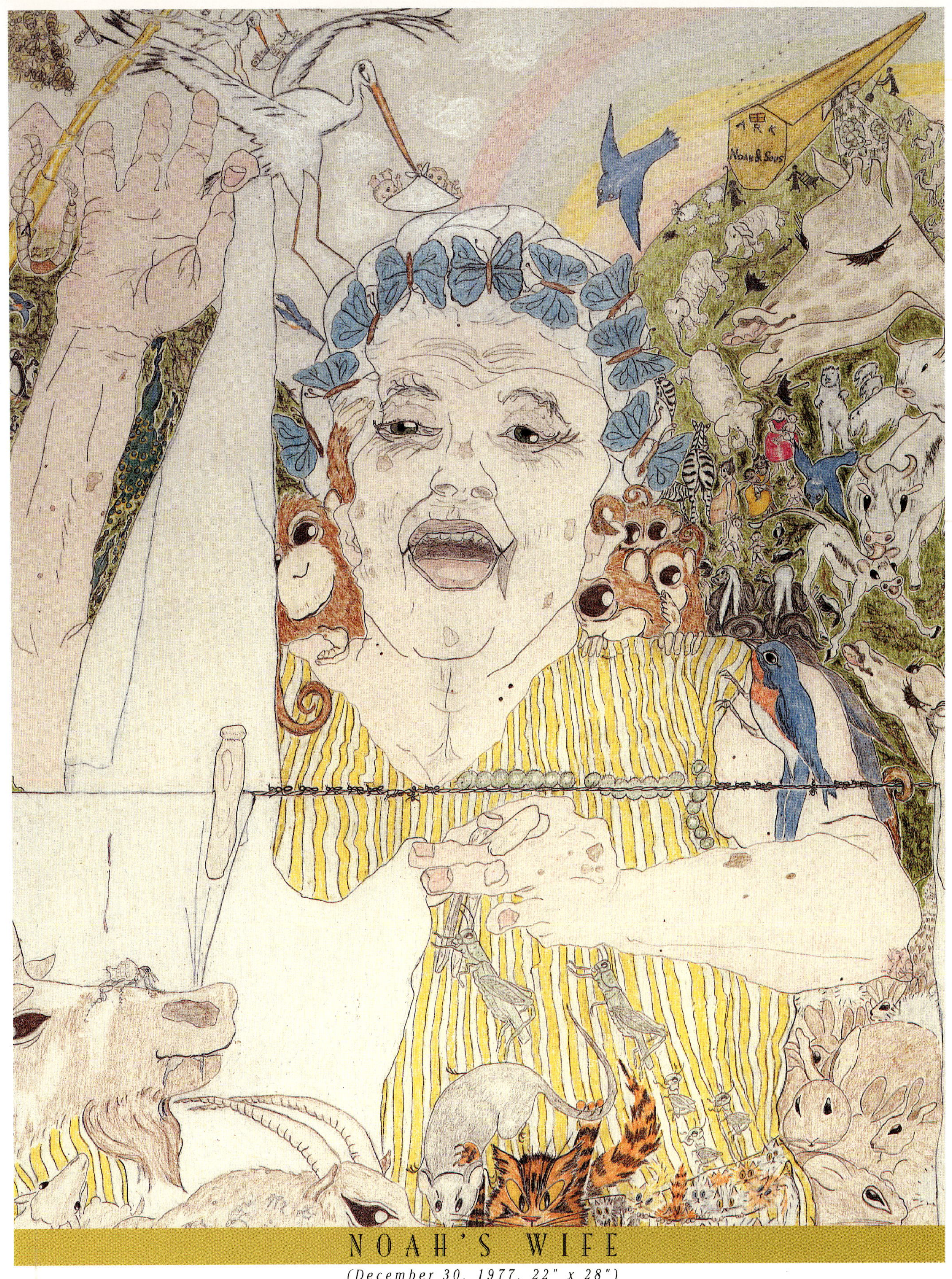

NOAH'S WIFE

(December 30, 1977, 22" x 28")

"*Oh, My! Wasn't Noah's wife glad to hang the freshly laundered wash outdoors after all those days of drying the diapers and Noah's underwear on lines strung in the kitchen of the Ark. Noah, himself, has gone fishin'.*"

1 9 7 8
ELIZABETH LAYTON

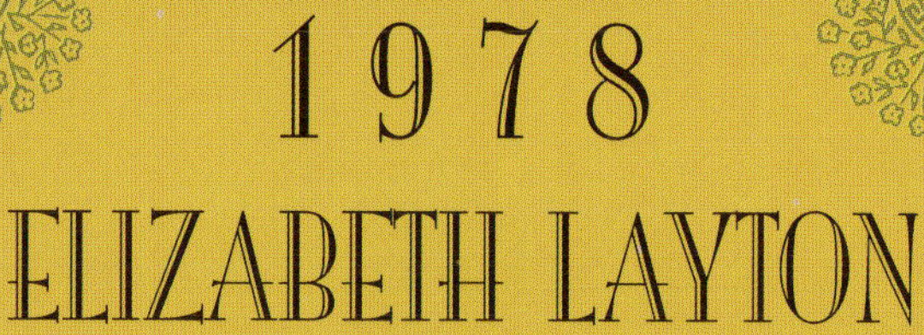

Mountain Climbing
Intensive Care Room
The Sneeze
American Gothic
Warning: The Surgeon General
All Dressed Up and Going Out
The Pedestal
Masks
Mona Lisa
Pushing Up the Daisies
Void
Light
ERA
Carry Nation
Stroke
Cat in Refrigerator
Gold Star Mother
Wreck of the Hesperus
Jonestown
Skipping Down Christo's Walkway
Amaryllis

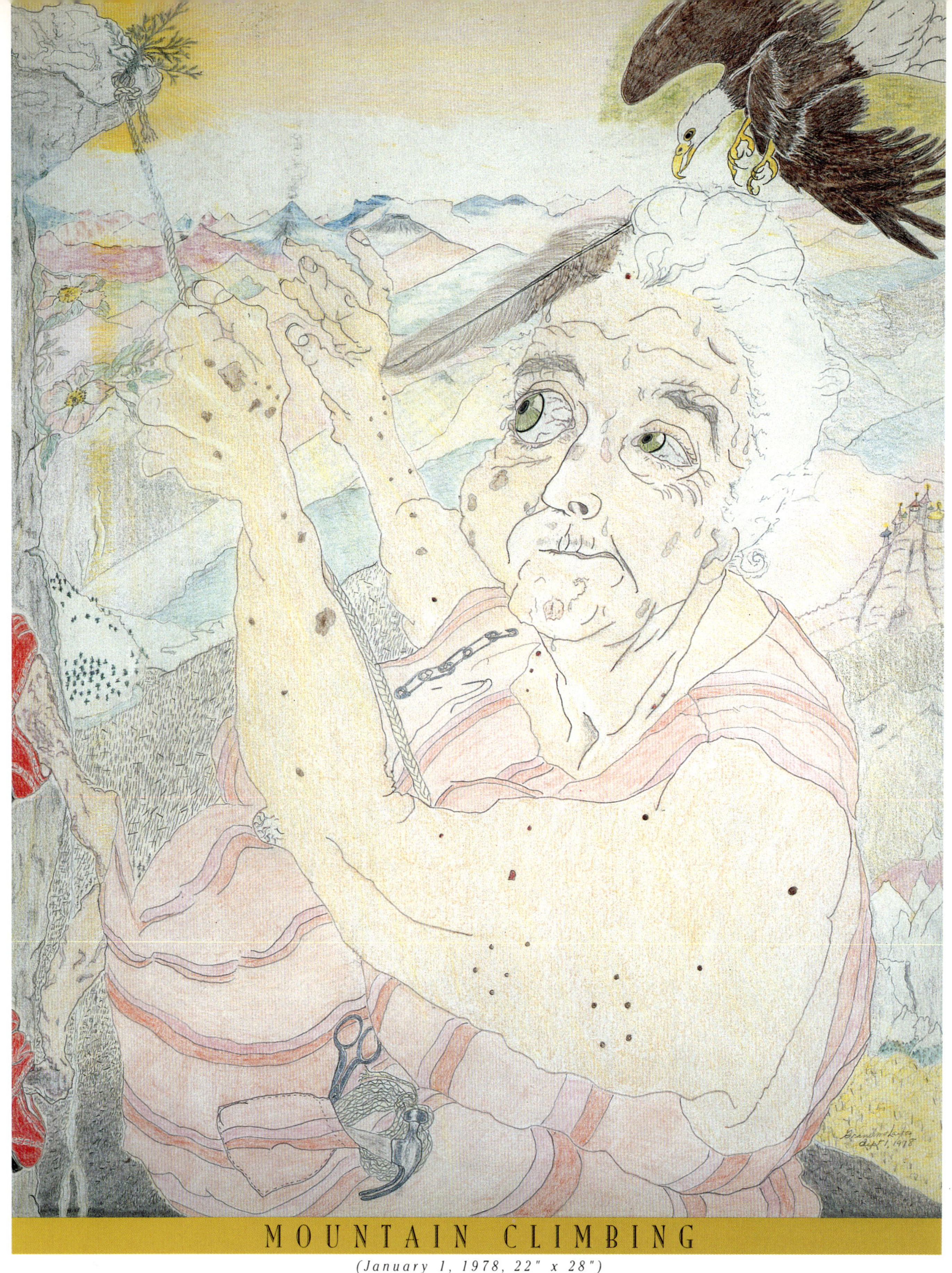

M O U N T A I N   C L I M B I N G

(January 1, 1978, 22" x 28")

*"She is determined to make it to the top, though the odds might seem stacked against her.
She picked up a shed eagle feather along the way, and stuck it in her hair."*

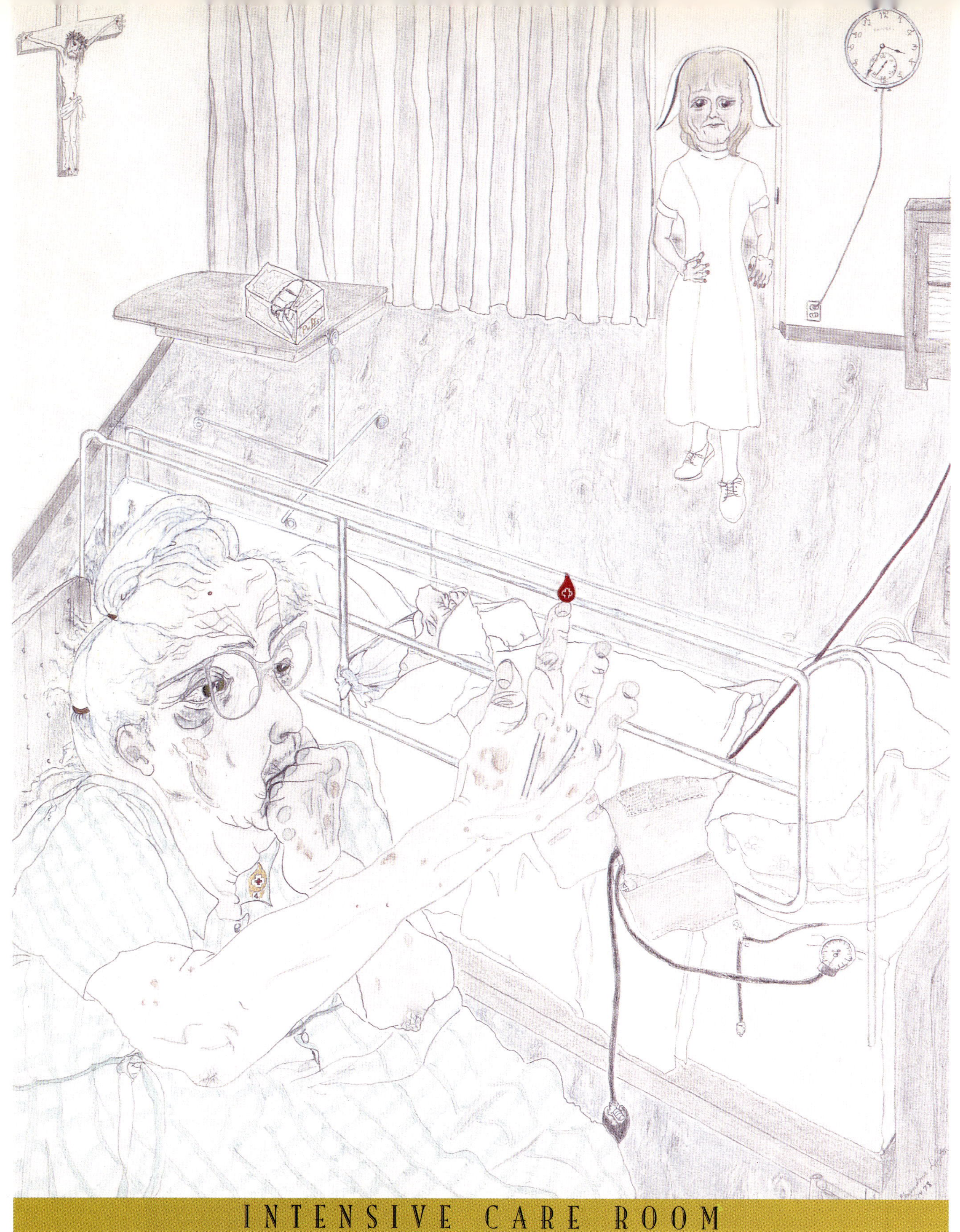

INTENSIVE CARE ROOM

(January, 1978, 22" x 28")

"*This is the room where my son died. They had all these tubes… you know, terrible. There was always blood coming down. I couldn't draw the face, so I put the pillow there. They gave him four gallons of blood. I had always given blood and I couldn't wait till I could go again and give for somebody else. They wouldn't take me because I was taking a medicine for high blood pressure. I felt so helpless.*"

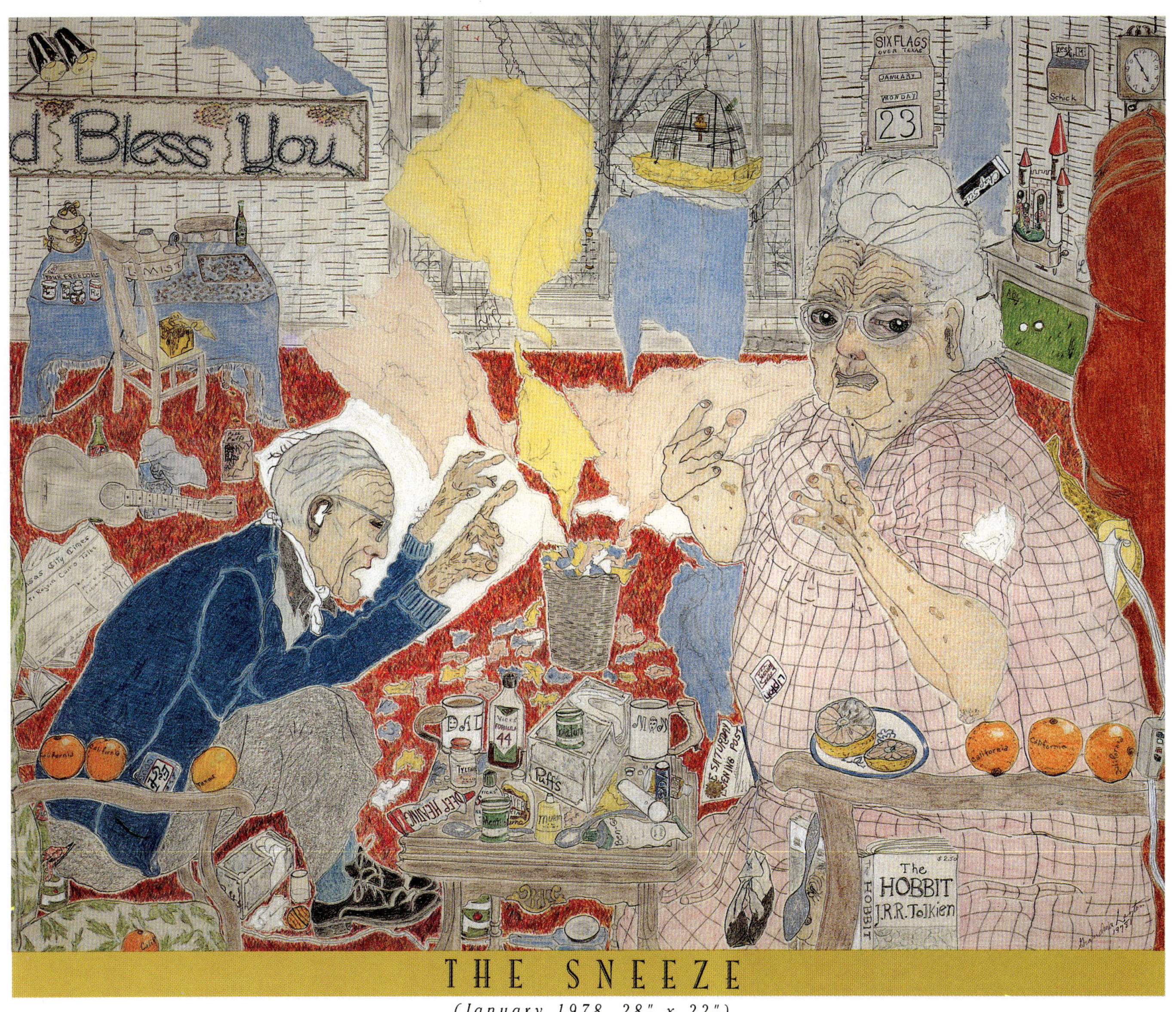

THE SNEEZE

(January 1978, 28" x 22")

"*It was that minus 0 degree winter when this old woman boycotted Florida oranges and Florida orange juice.*"

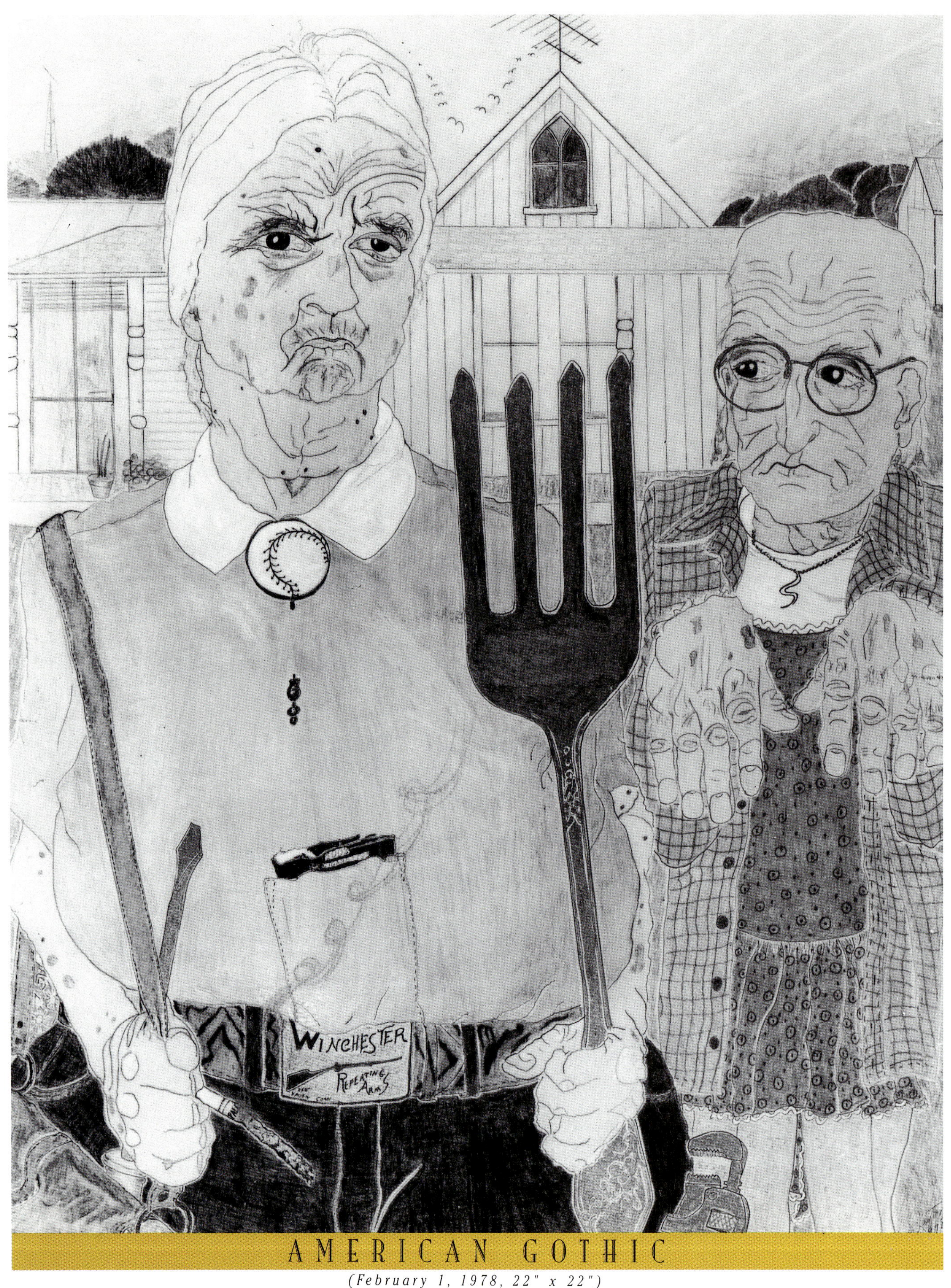

AMERICAN GOTHIC
(February 1, 1978, 22" x 22")

"*Everybody does a take-off on Grant Wood's wonderful bit of Americana, so I did one, too.*"

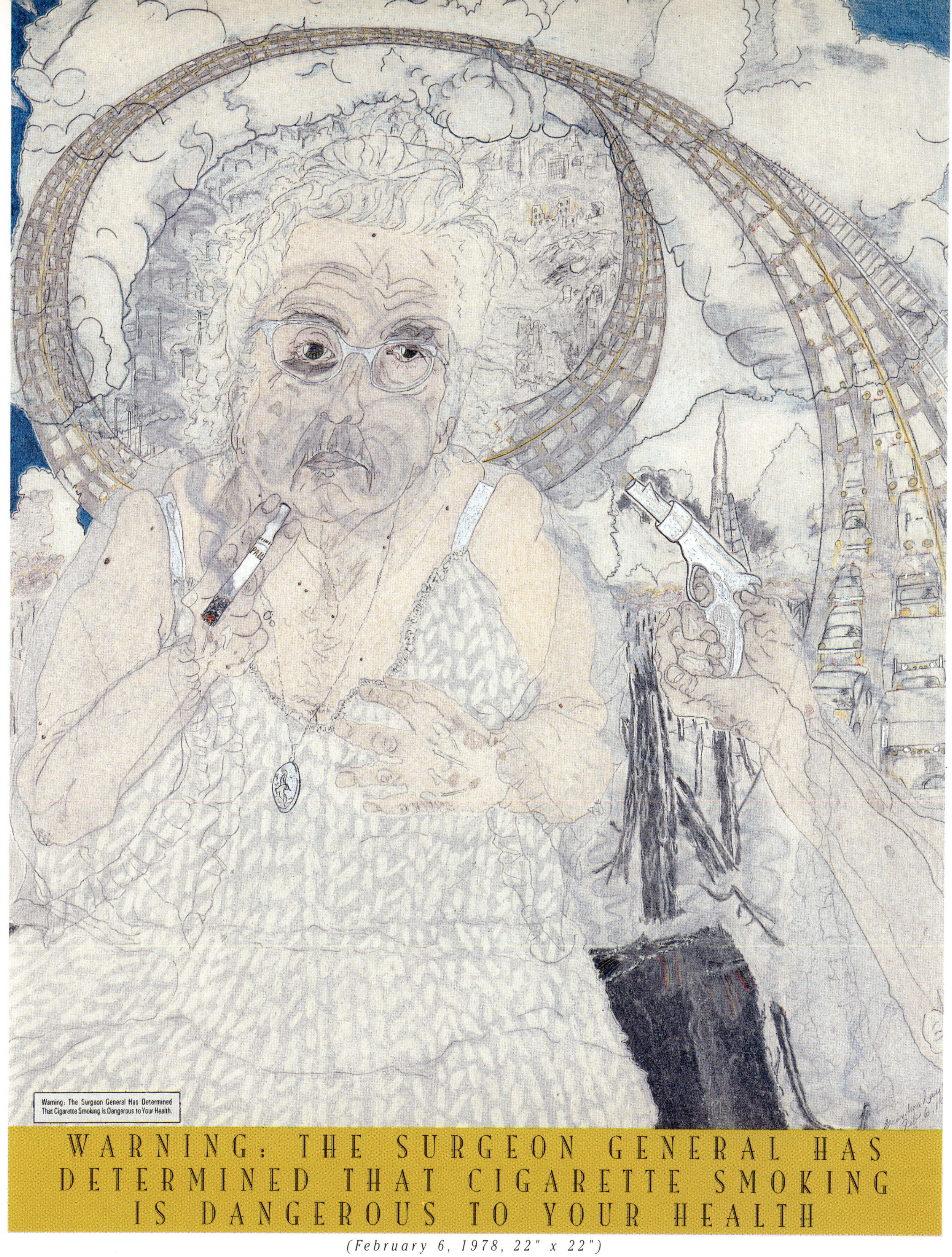

**W A R N I N G : T H E S U R G E O N G E N E R A L H A S
D E T E R M I N E D T H A T C I G A R E T T E S M O K I N G
I S D A N G E R O U S T O Y O U R H E A L T H**

(February 6, 1978, 22" x 22")

> **❝**Cigarette smoking is dangerous to your health. And we know it, but placing a small, inconspicuous warning label at the bottom of advertisements is not any way to prevent it. There is all this other pollution that is also dangerous to our health. Burning things constantly, cars smoking, smoking guns, industries. Oh, how we smoke! Slums burning, nuclear bomb, mushroom cloud.**❞**

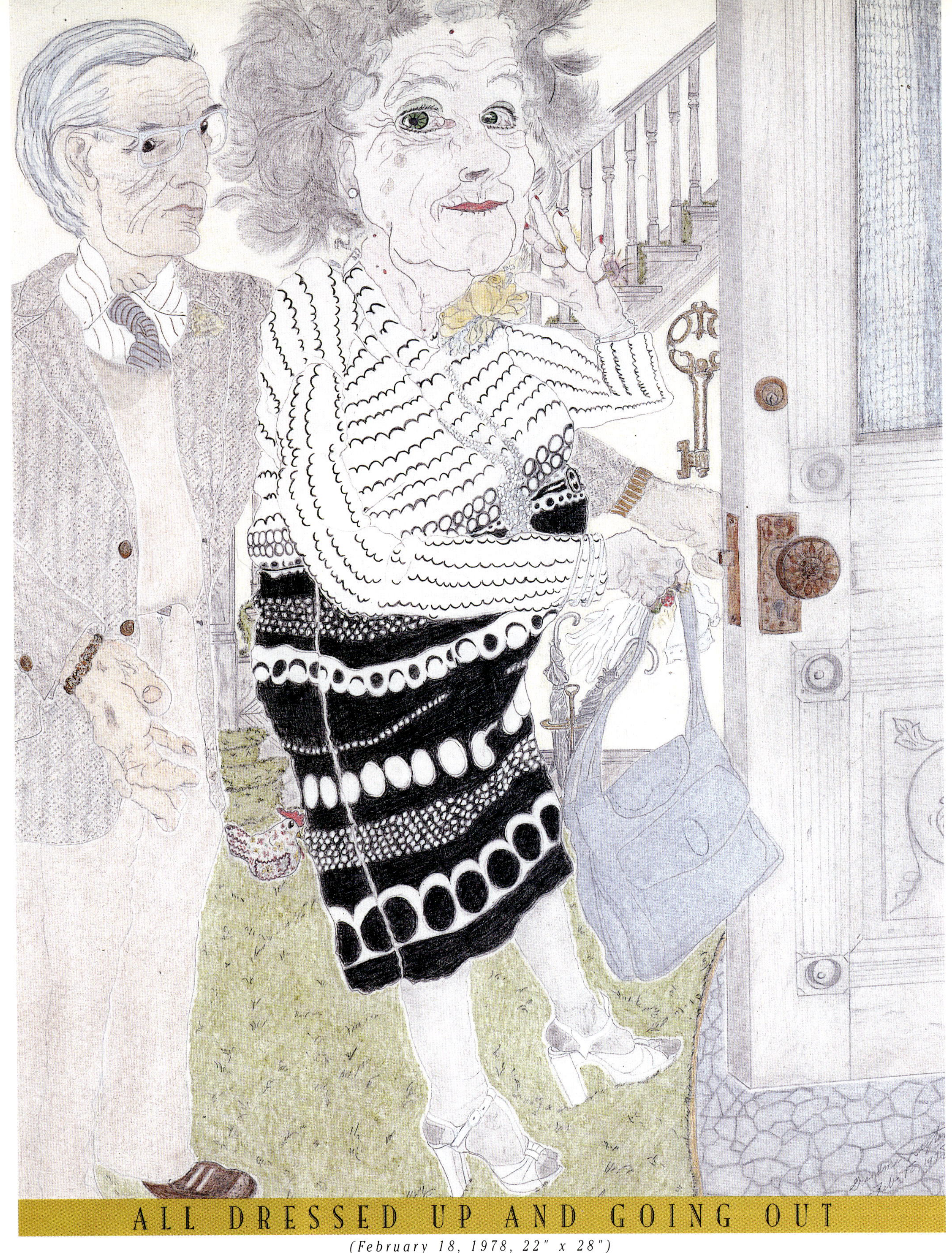

(February 18, 1978, 22" x 28")

"*Glenn bought that dress for me and I love it, but I can't get up nerve enough to wear it. I have to have a dress for at least two or three years before I can get up the nerve enough to wear it. I can't wear high heels, but this is what we people wear, it's terrible.*"

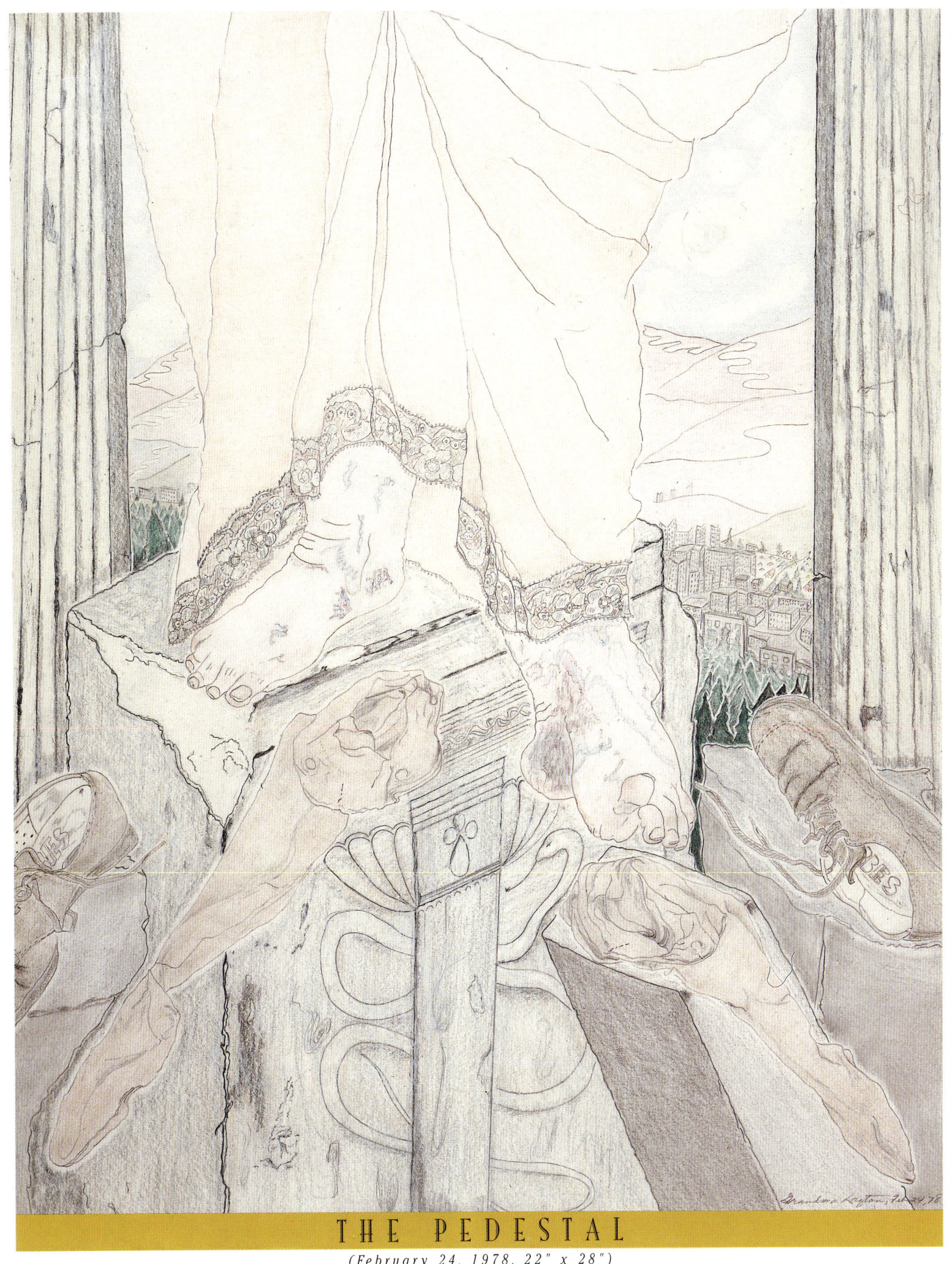

THE PEDESTAL
(February 24, 1978, 22" x 28")

Collection of the Wichita Art Museum, Wichita, Kansas

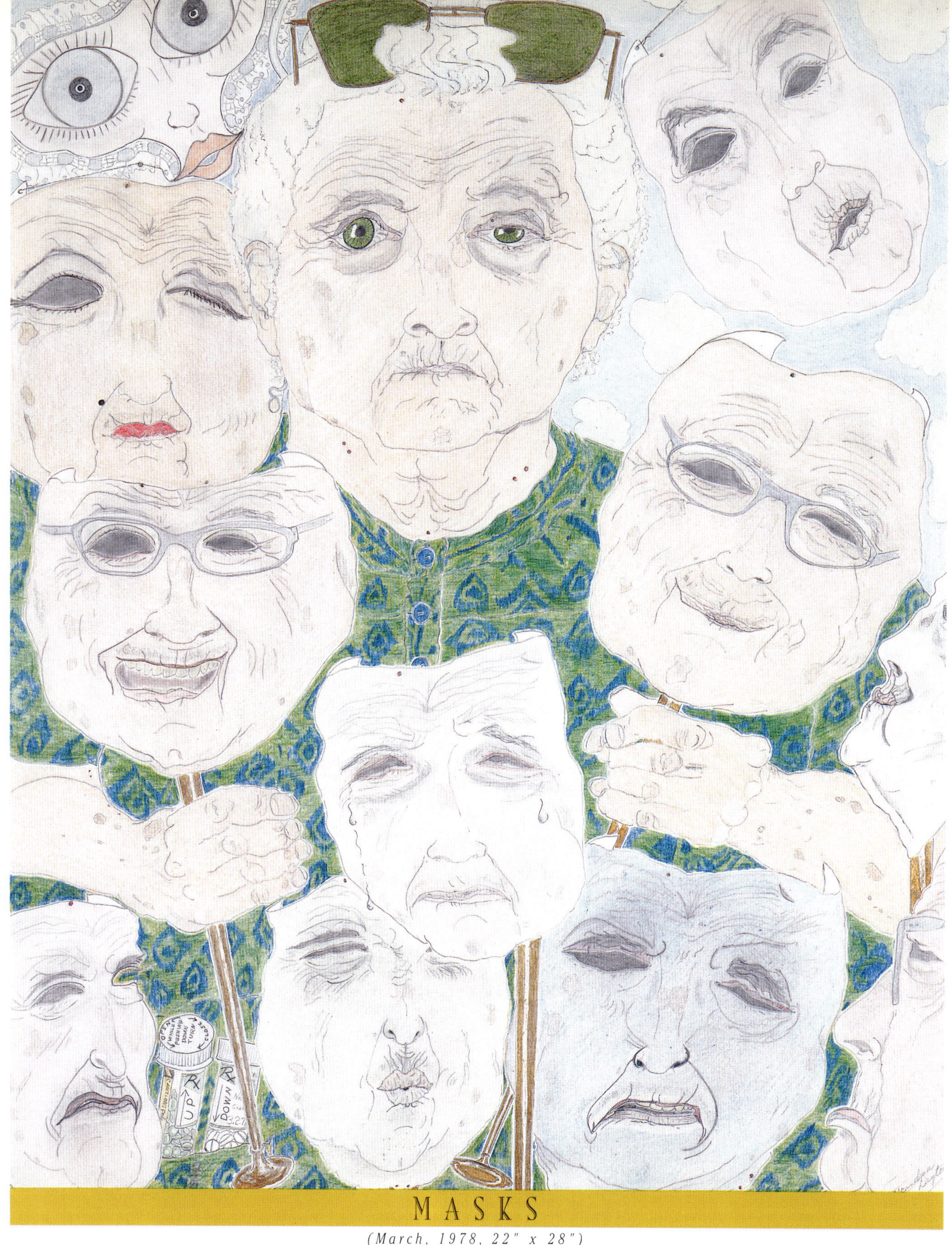

MASKS

(March, 1978, 22" x 28")

"What I had in mind was… all of these emotions you have through your life. There are muscles in your face and each one reacts to every emotion. Say you're real happy for a minute, and you put on that mask and that's going to make an indention in these muscles to a certain extent. I think it's the various emotions you have had that causes the lines and wrinkles in your face."

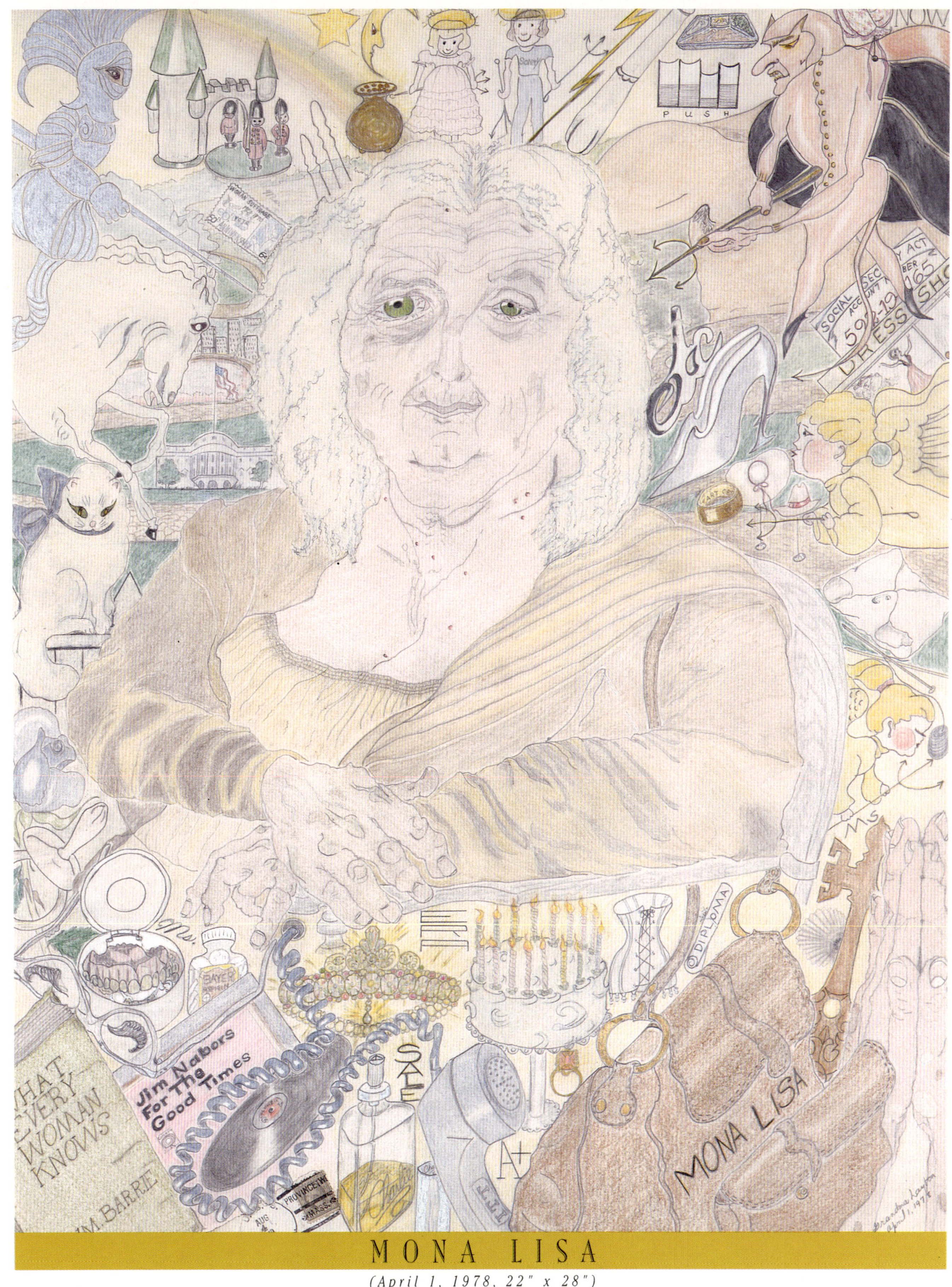

M O N A   L I S A

(April 1, 1978, 22" x 28")

66 *These are some things that the Mona Lisa, when she lived to be an old woman,*
probably would have been thinking about. **99**

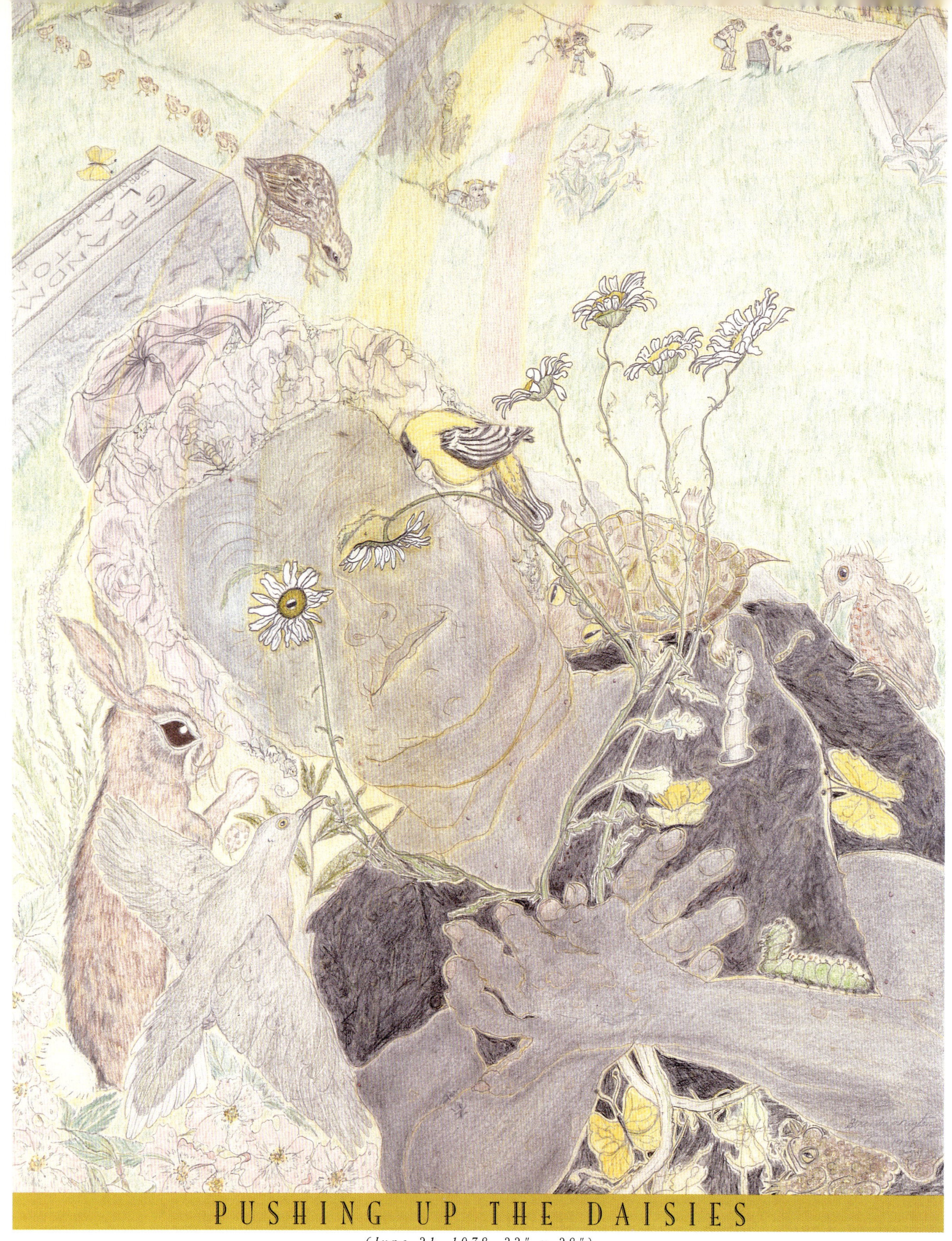

P U S H I N G   U P   T H E   D A I S I E S

(June 21, 1978, 22" x 28")

"*This is my grave. It doesn't make any difference after you're dead what color your skin is so I drew my skin black. People of other colored skin have the same feelings. I think we all have the same feelings. This is my gravestone. Some child has pulled some daisies and laid them there on the grave. See, she's winking. She knows what's after this world. It's a hopeful picture.*"

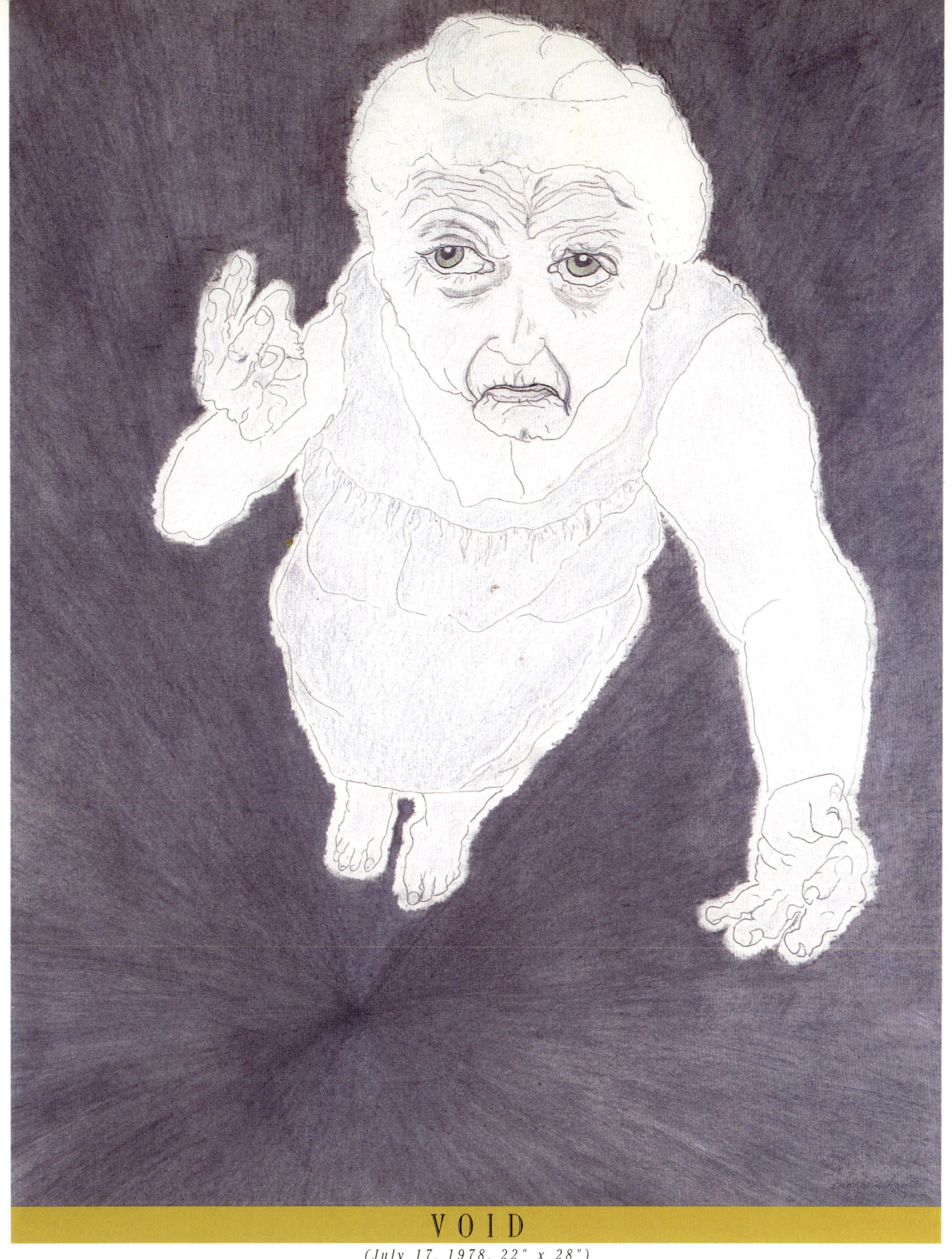

V O I D

(July 17, 1978, 22" x 28")

"*I had this feeling that I was out in the middle of nowhere… absolutely nothing…
and it was such a lost feeling. I was lit up by a white light, but I didn't light up the black.*"

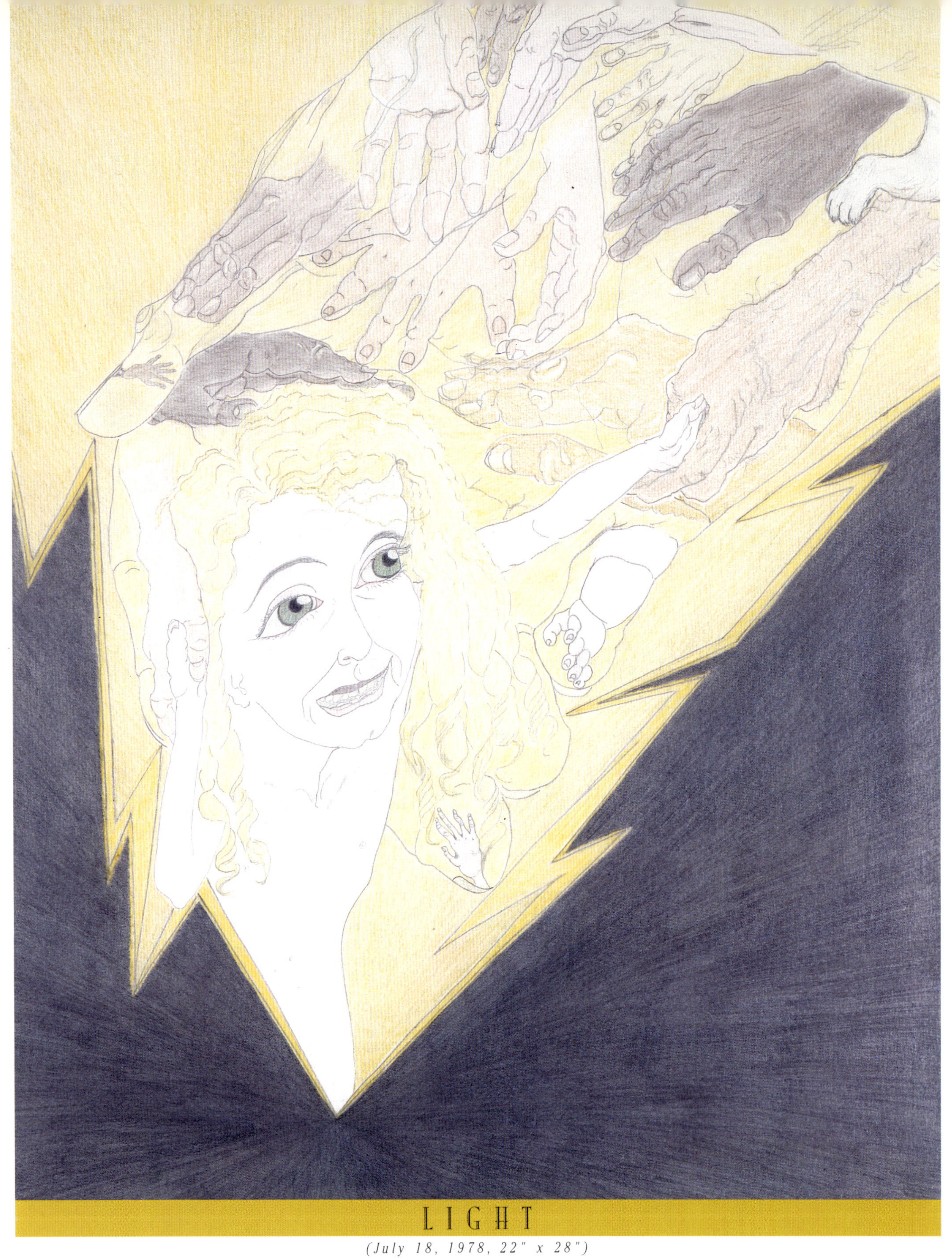

L I G H T

(July 18, 1978, 22" x 28")

"*I keep changing my religion, constantly. I get a new one every day, a new idea. Here was all these people
wanting to help her figure up out of that void. I think we need to keep an open mind. There's this life,
life is one thing, and the life that's in you and the life that's in me is all the same thing. And it's going to go on and on.
It is just this body that the life happens to be in, or whatever, a plant. It is part of one life. Who knows?*"

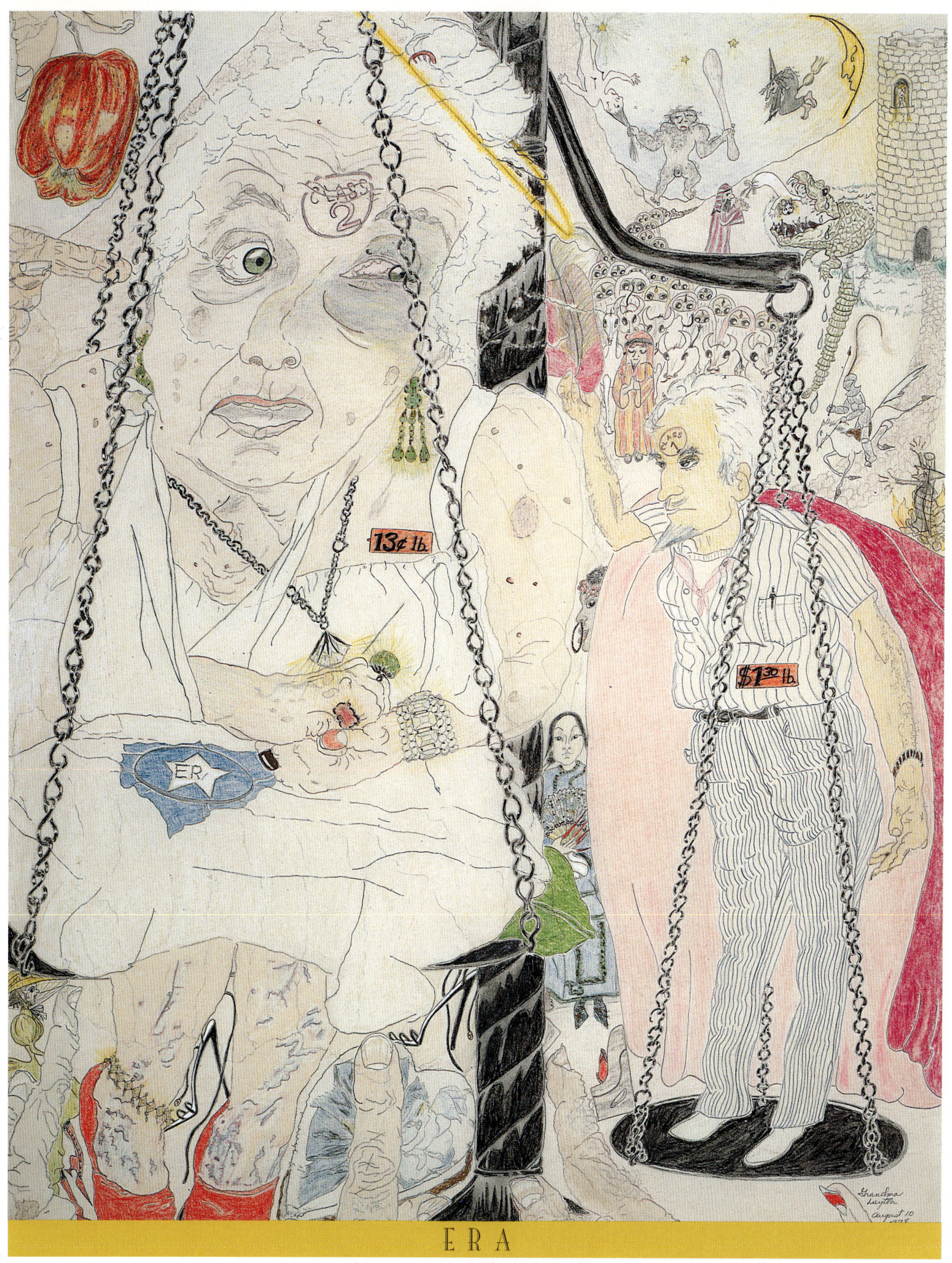

E R A

(August 10, 1978, 22" x 28")

"*Still she works on her embroidery.***"**

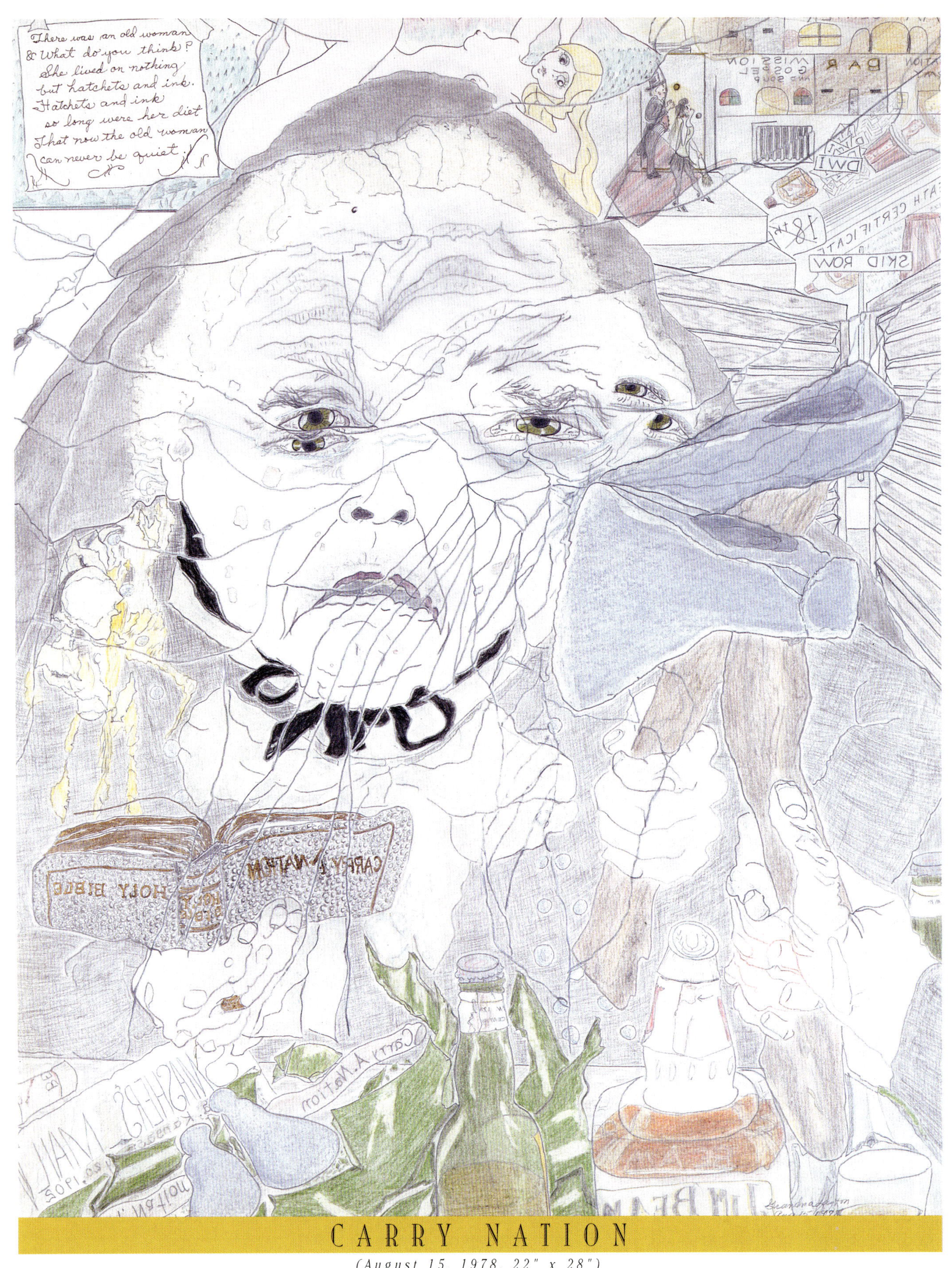

CARRY NATION

(August 15, 1978, 22" x 28")

 I would probably have made a good Carry Nation. But the idea, really, is that if you're angry, you're going to destroy yourself and probably not destroy what you are after. And she was destroying herself… or if I am angry, I destroy myself.

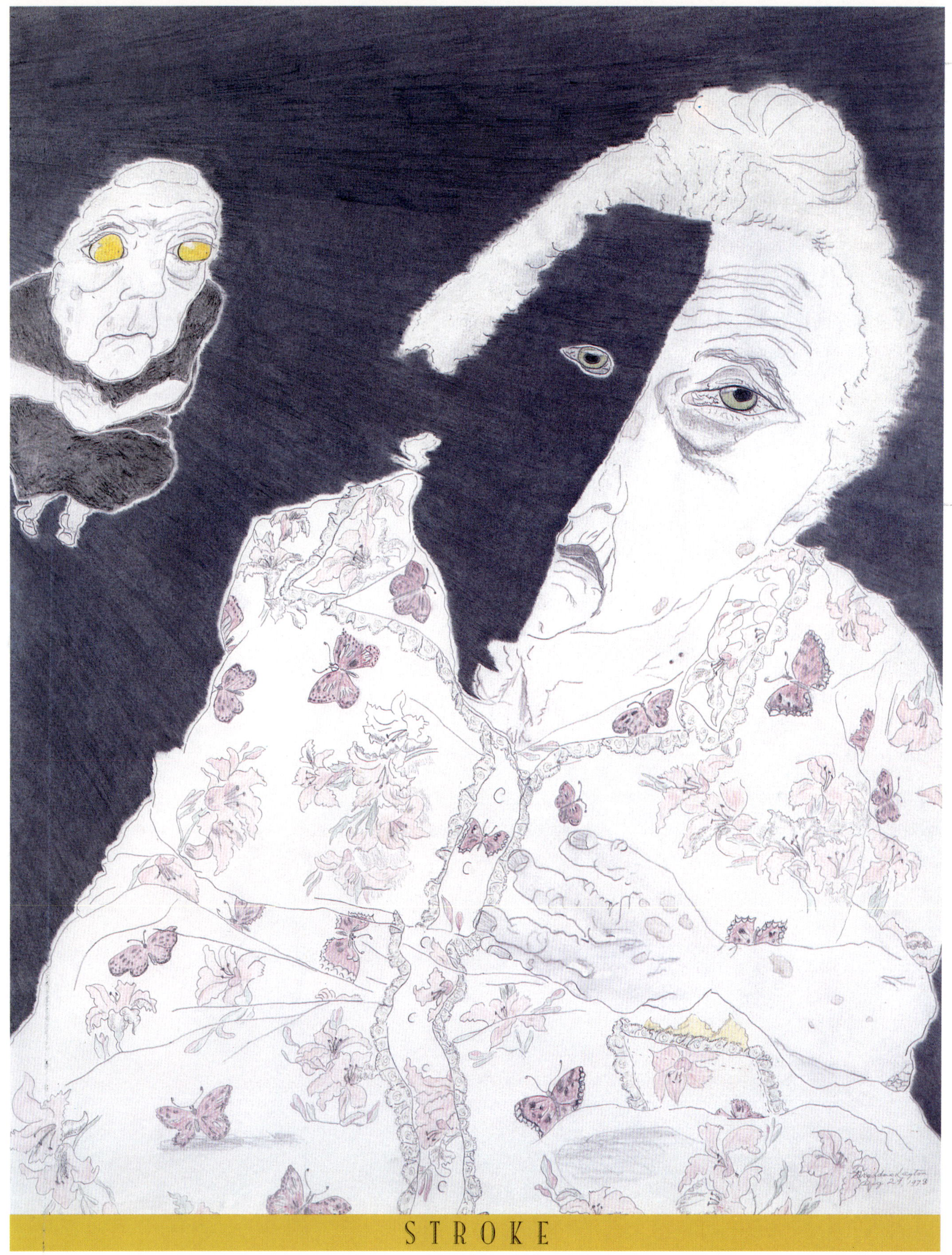

STROKE

(August 28, 1978, 22" x 28")

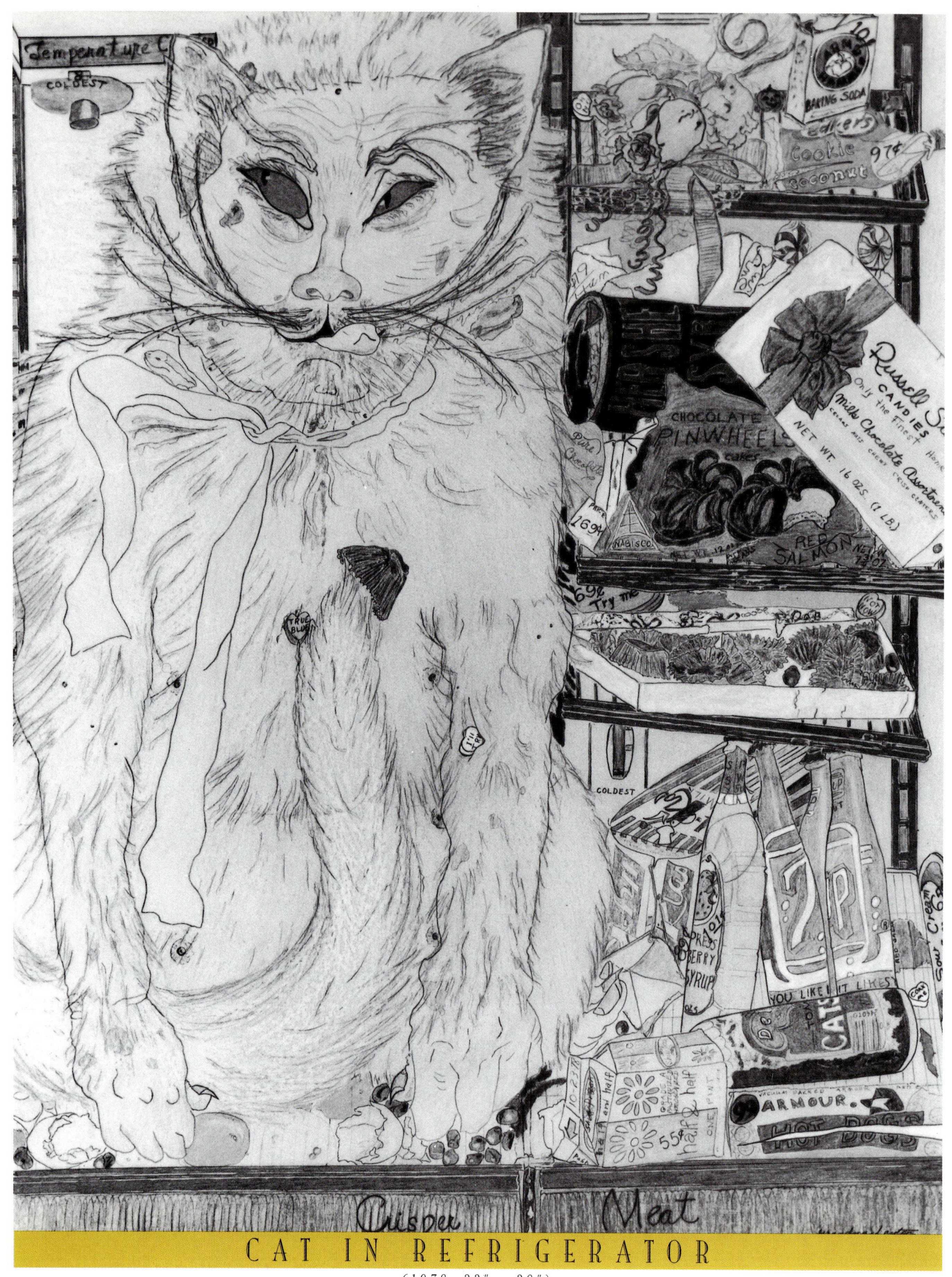

CAT IN REFRIGERATOR

(1978, 22" x 28")

Collection of Mulvane Art Museum, Washburn University, Topeka, Kansas

"One of our family stories is about when the cat got shut in the refrigerator. When someone finally opened the door, the cat had devoured the goodies, causing this wickedly satisfied expression."

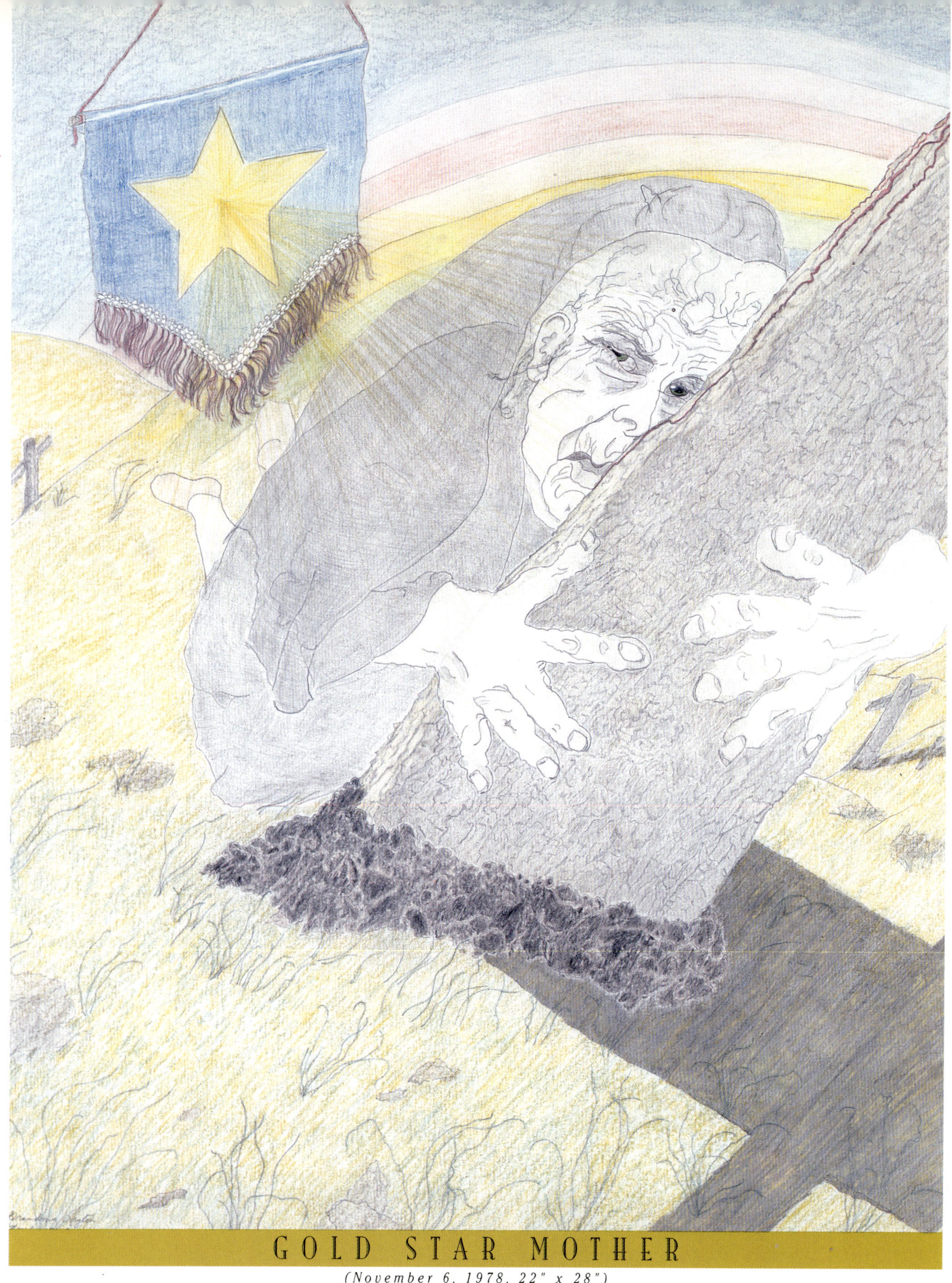

GOLD STAR MOTHER

(November 6, 1978, 22" x 28")

"*When a person was killed in the service, the parents were given a cloth gold star to hang in the window. I used the crucifixion because that's a symbol that everybody knows. You hang somebody on a cross, and they die. So this is Mary, only it's the gold star mother. Mary at the cross, how she must have felt. But any woman would have these same feelings, were her son dead. When something gets too hopeless, I put a rainbow in. There is always hope.*"

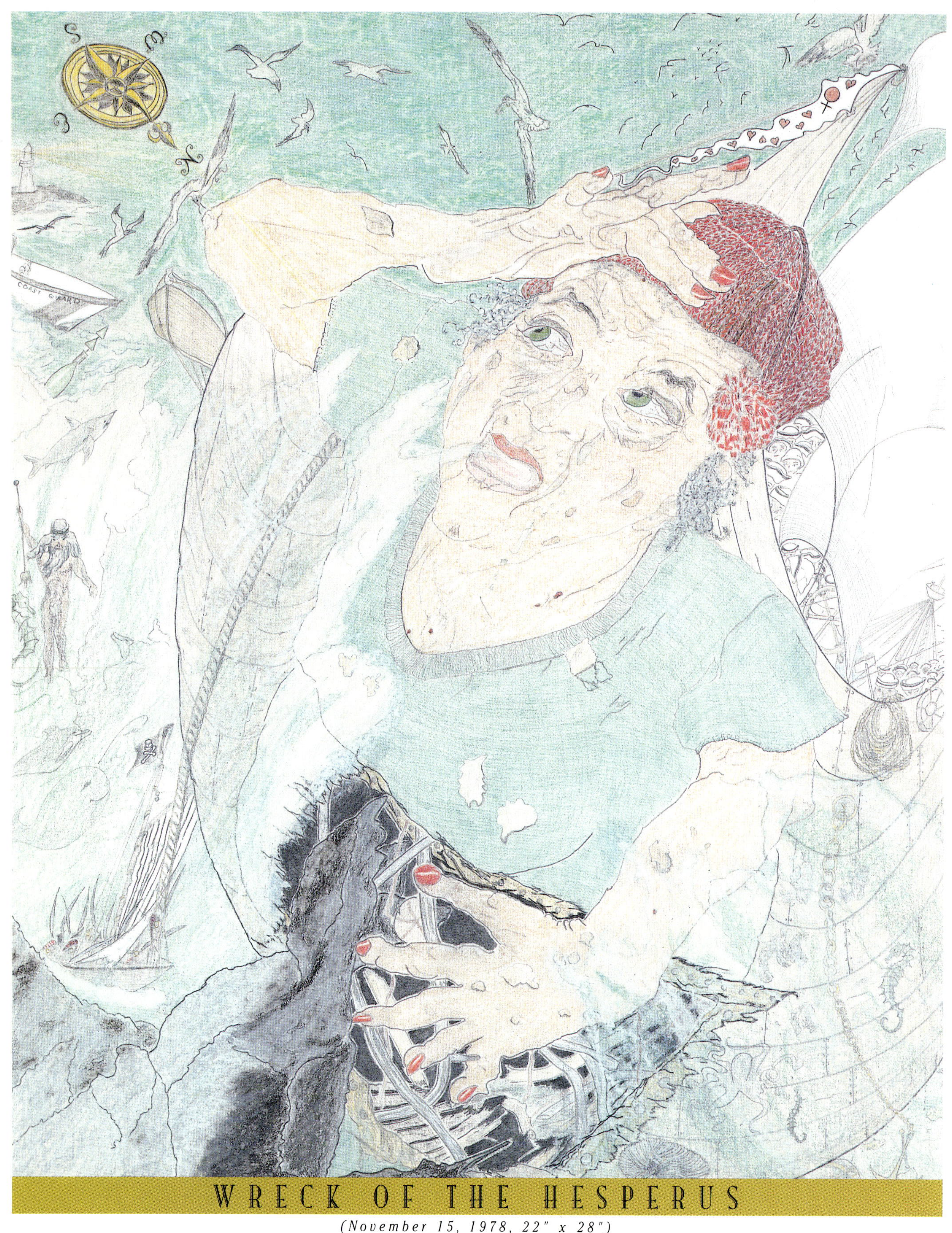

WRECK OF THE HESPERUS

(November 15, 1978, 22" x 28")

"She has run into a rock, and it's smashed this big hole in the ship because she was watching her compass closely, but the compass was upside down. We go through life doing things that we think are right, but we are clear off the beam. We are doing it right but our goal was wrong."

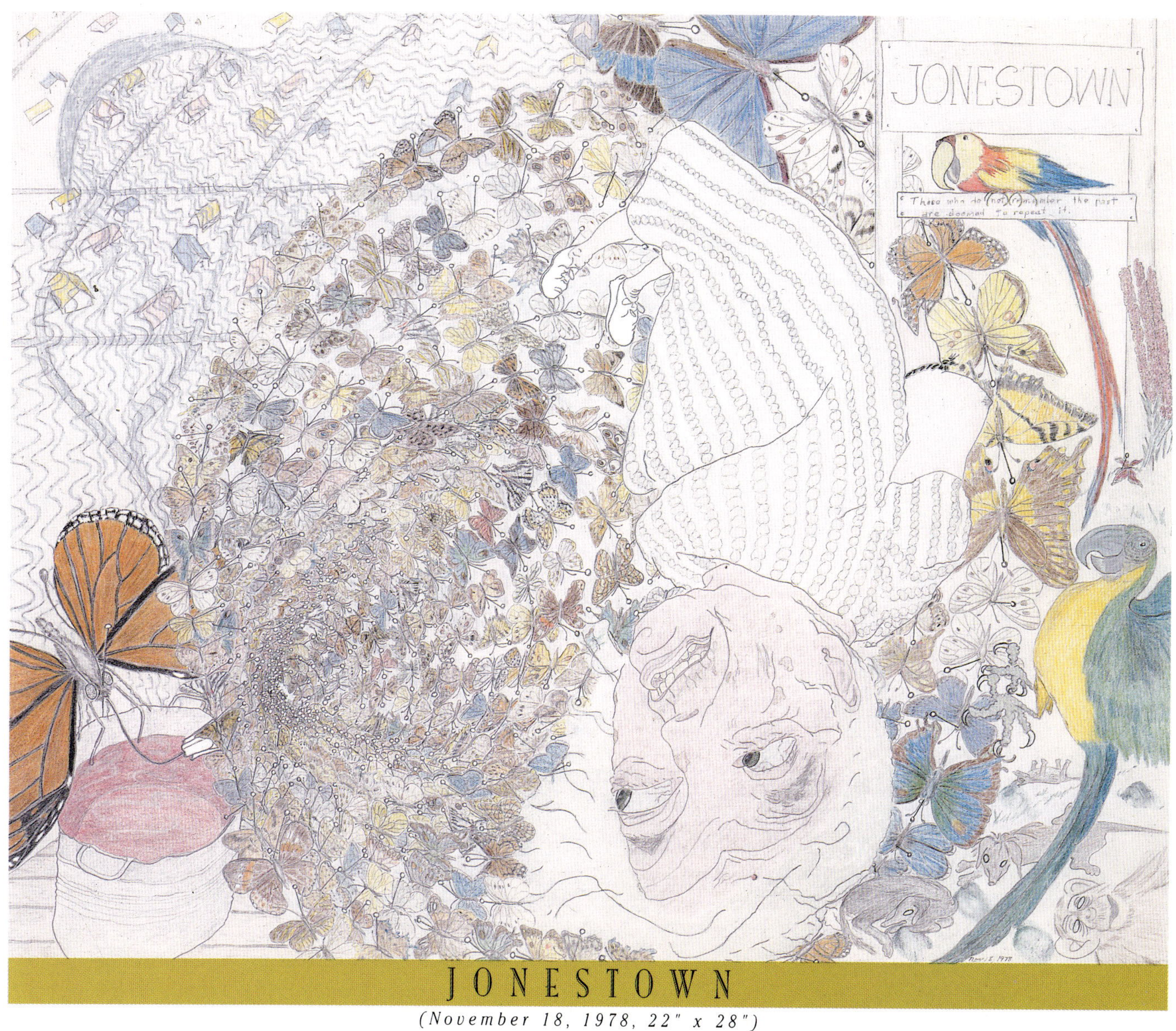

JONESTOWN
(November 18, 1978, 22" x 28")

66*The Guyana suicides, I had trouble handling it. So, I tried to draw a different butterfly for everybody. And they were dead, so I stuck these pins through them. Thinking about that particular life, I will feel better about it. They won't feel any better but I will. This figure is to show that she gets involved whether she wants to or not. She gets swirled up in that. This monarch butterfly is Jim Jones, see he's dead, too. I used a monarch because the monarch is a beautiful butterfly, but the birds don't eat it, it tastes terrible. It's not what it appears.*99

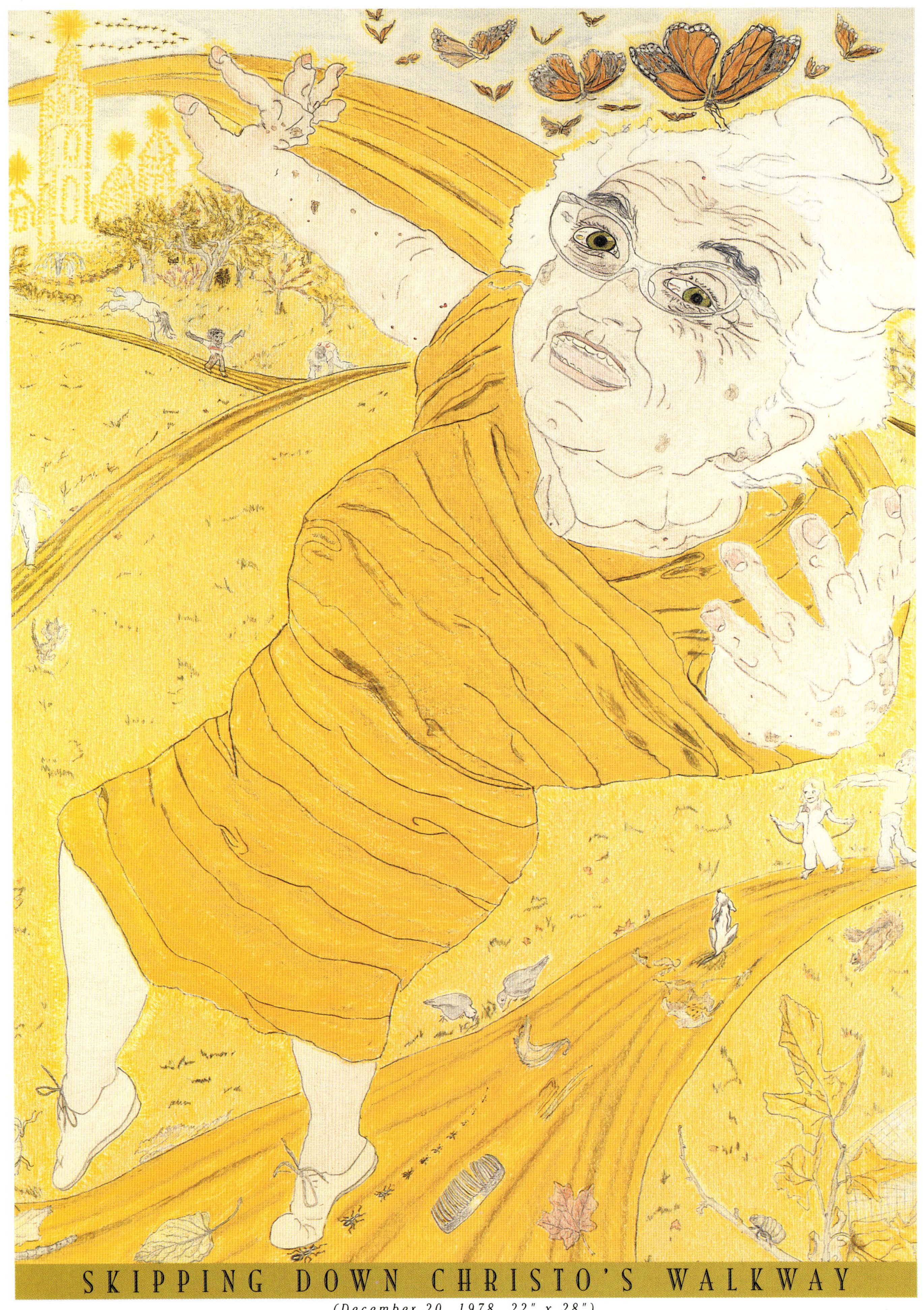

SKIPPING DOWN CHRISTO'S WALKWAY

(December 20, 1978, 22" x 28")

From the collection of the Nelson-Atkins Museum of Art, Kansas City, Missouri

54

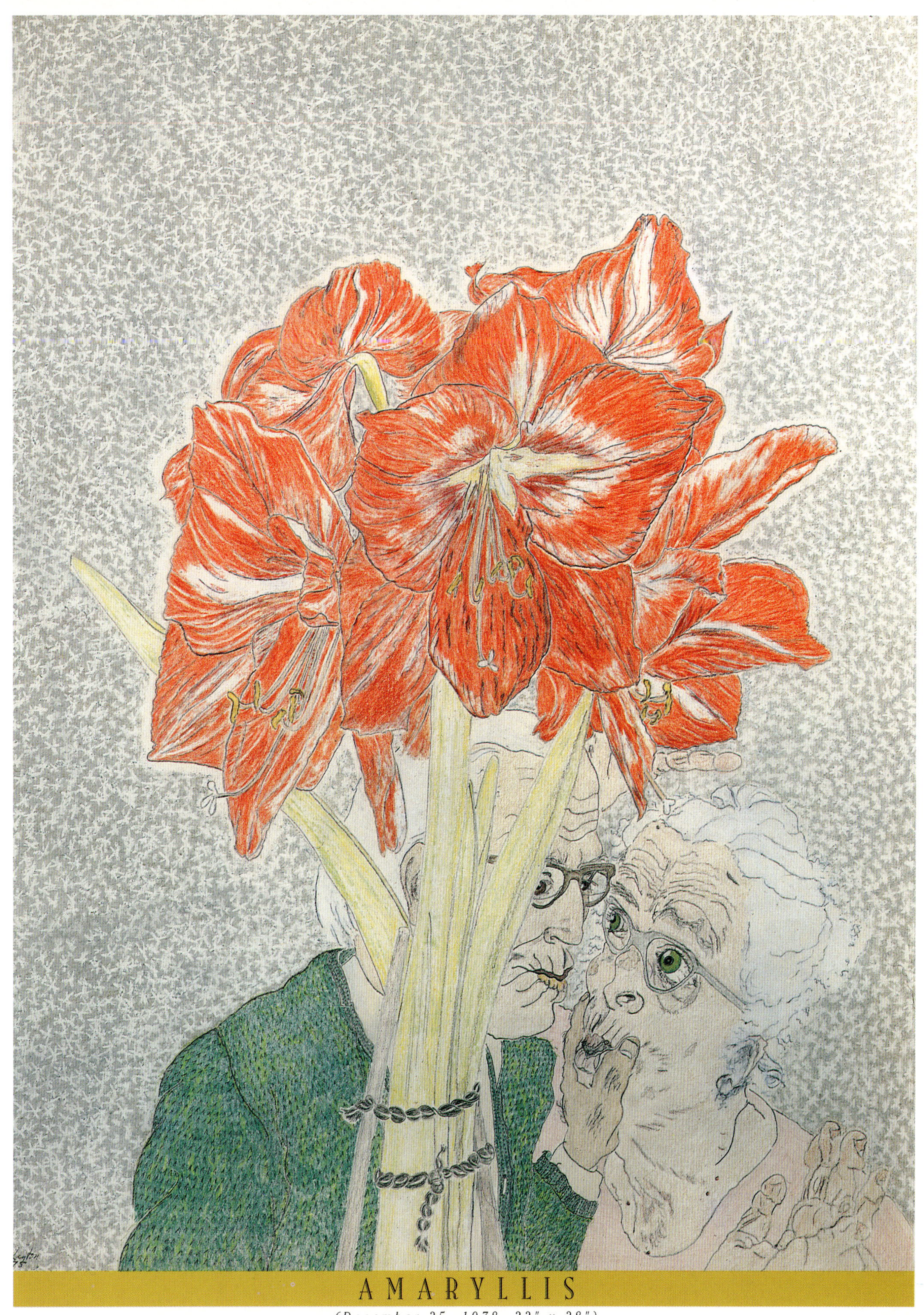

AMARYLLIS

(December 25, 1978, 22" x 28")

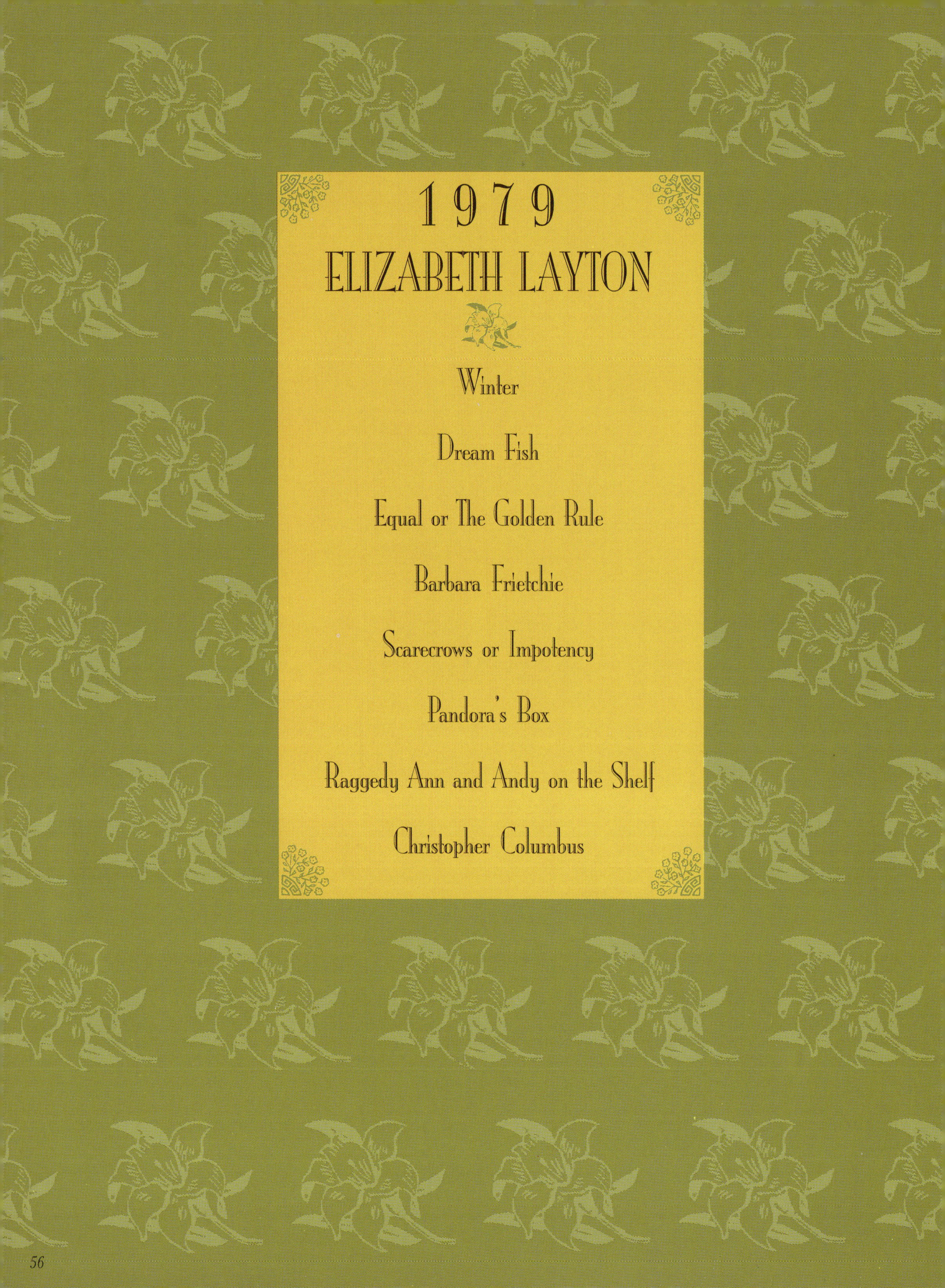

1979
ELIZABETH LAYTON

Winter

Dream Fish

Equal or The Golden Rule

Barbara Frietchie

Scarecrows or Impotency

Pandora's Box

Raggedy Ann and Andy on the Shelf

Christopher Columbus

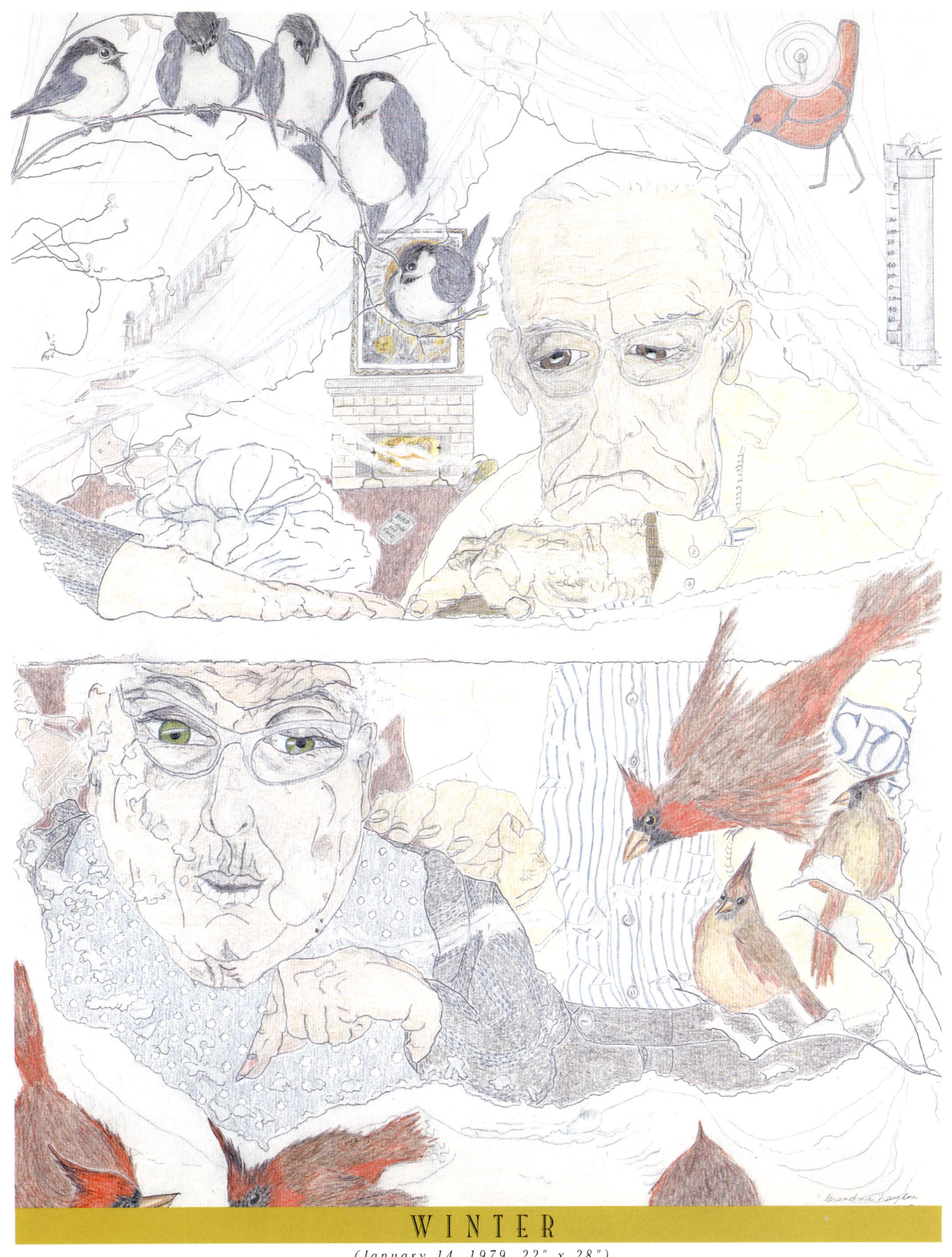

W I N T E R

(January 14, 1979, 22" x 28")

"*Glenn looks a little sad in that drawing because he doesn't like to be pinned up, but I just love it.*
*I'd be a good one to put in prison, wouldn't bother me at all.***"**

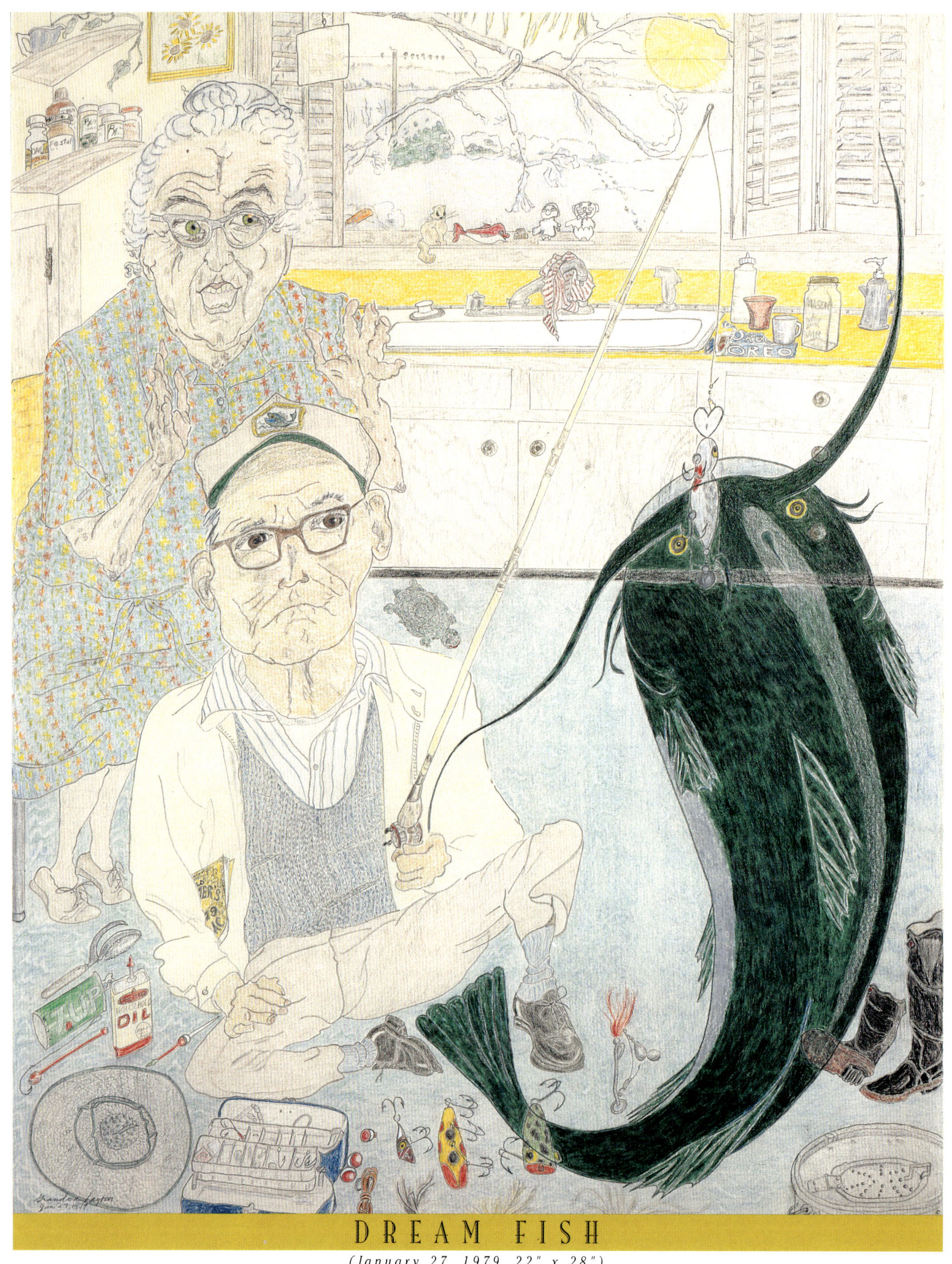

D R E A M   F I S H

(January 27, 1979, 22" x 28")

"*Do fishermen lie, or just dream?***"**

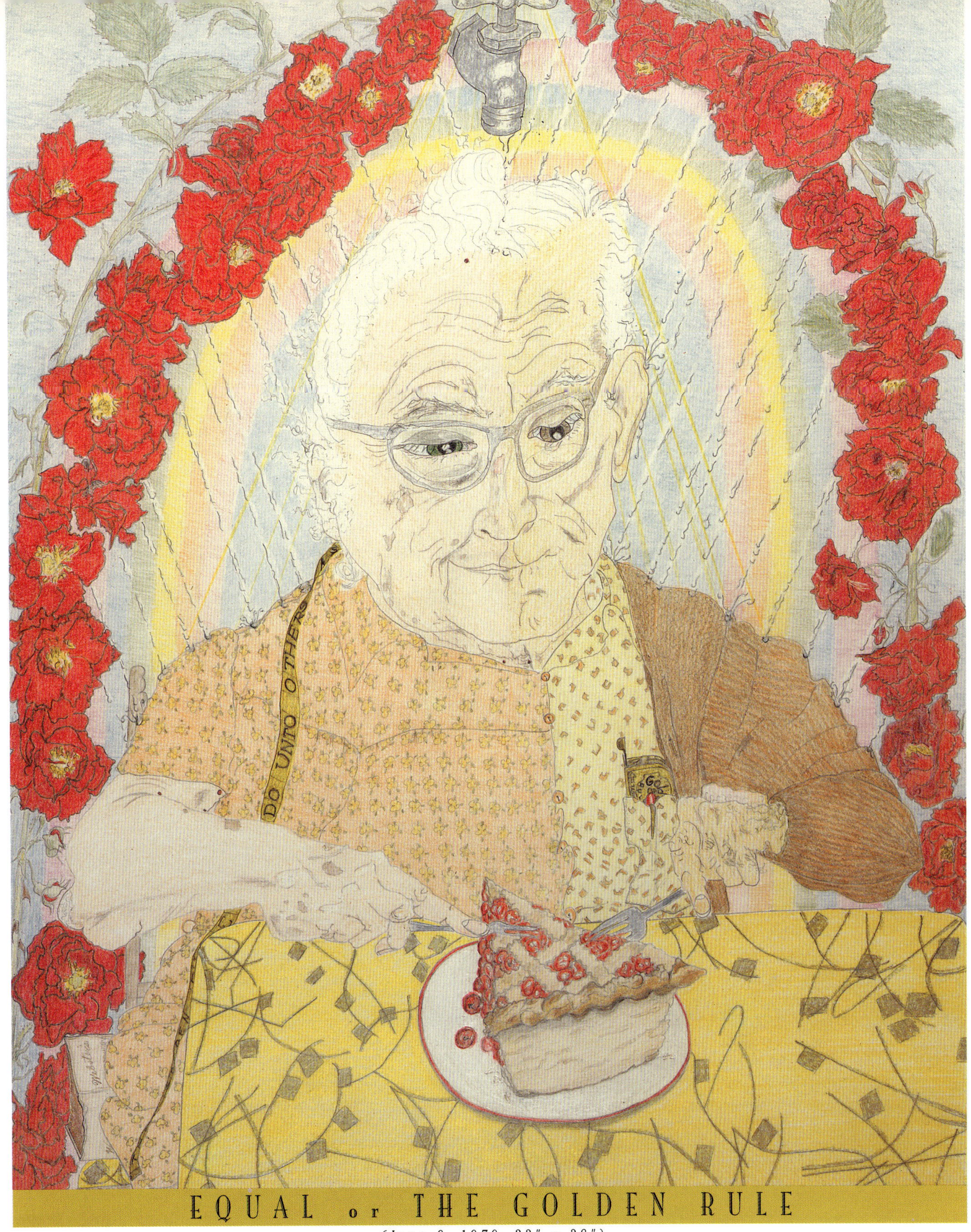

E Q U A L o r THE G O L D E N R U L E

(June 9, 1979, 22" x 28")

"*Half and half. One side is the woman, one side the man. (Or, simply, two people.) Both are eating the cherry pie. Whatever one takes in also nourishes the other. Both carry The Golden Rule — hers a sewing tape around her neck; his a carpenter's rule in his pocket. The red roses, rain, sun, snow, rainbow, are distributed by Nature impartially. The dripping faucet is minor irritations. My friend, Don Lambert, insists that she, being shorter, compensates by sitting on the Dictionary, so betters herself by becoming wiser. Grandpa Glenn says that just means she talks more. Oh, well!*"

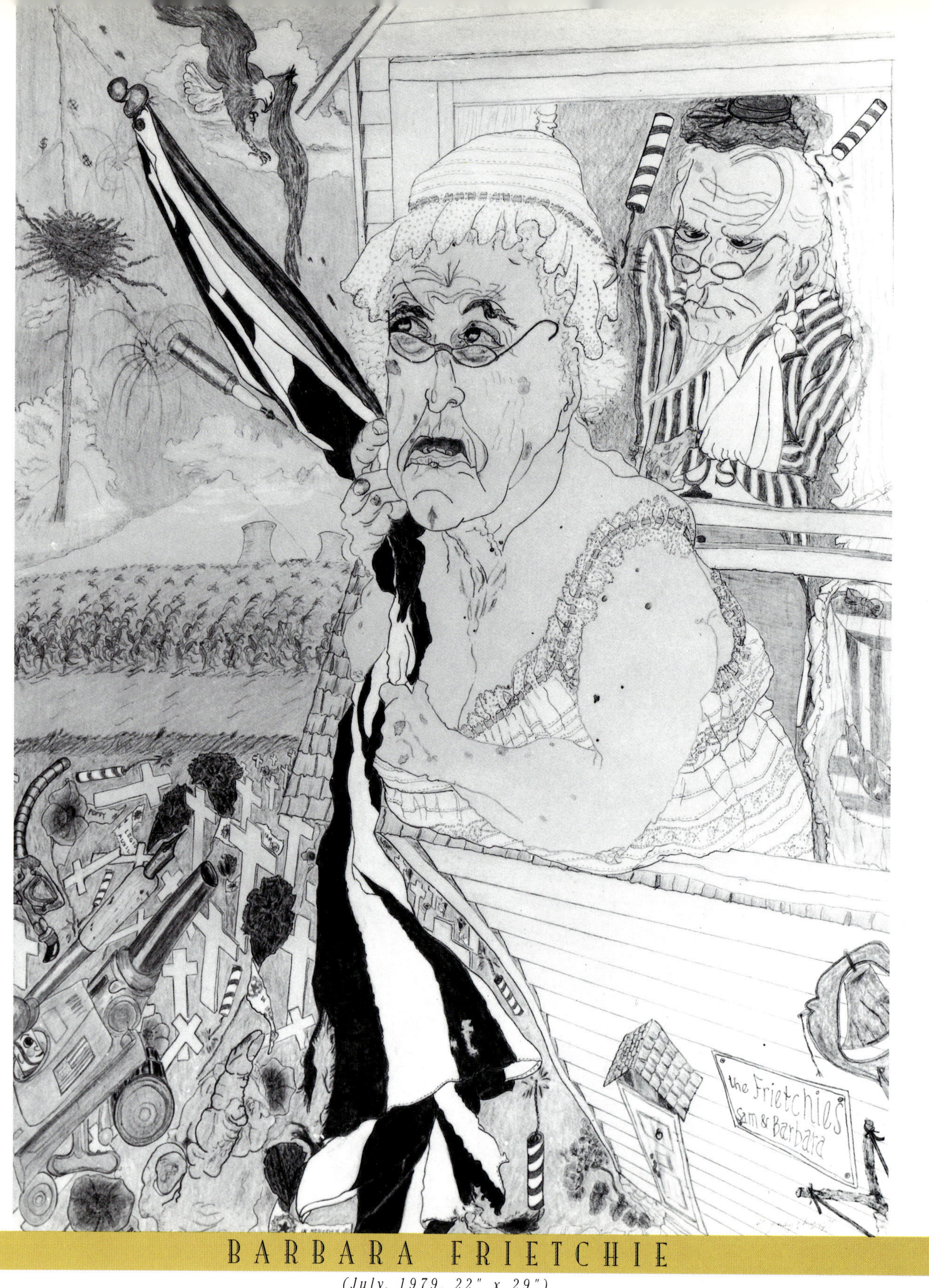

BARBARA FRIETCHIE

(July, 1979, 22" x 29")

From a Civil War incident immortalized in a poem by John Greenleaf Whittier

"*Confederate troops entering a town were ordered by General Stonewall Jackson to shoot down all American flags. Barbara rescued her flag flying from her upstairs window and shouted down this dare to the passing troops. 'Shoot if you must this old gray head, but spare my country's flag,' she said. Today's enemies—nuclear war, gas wars, an over eager military playing its games, an unprincipled media, and guilt—have replaced the Confederacy.*"

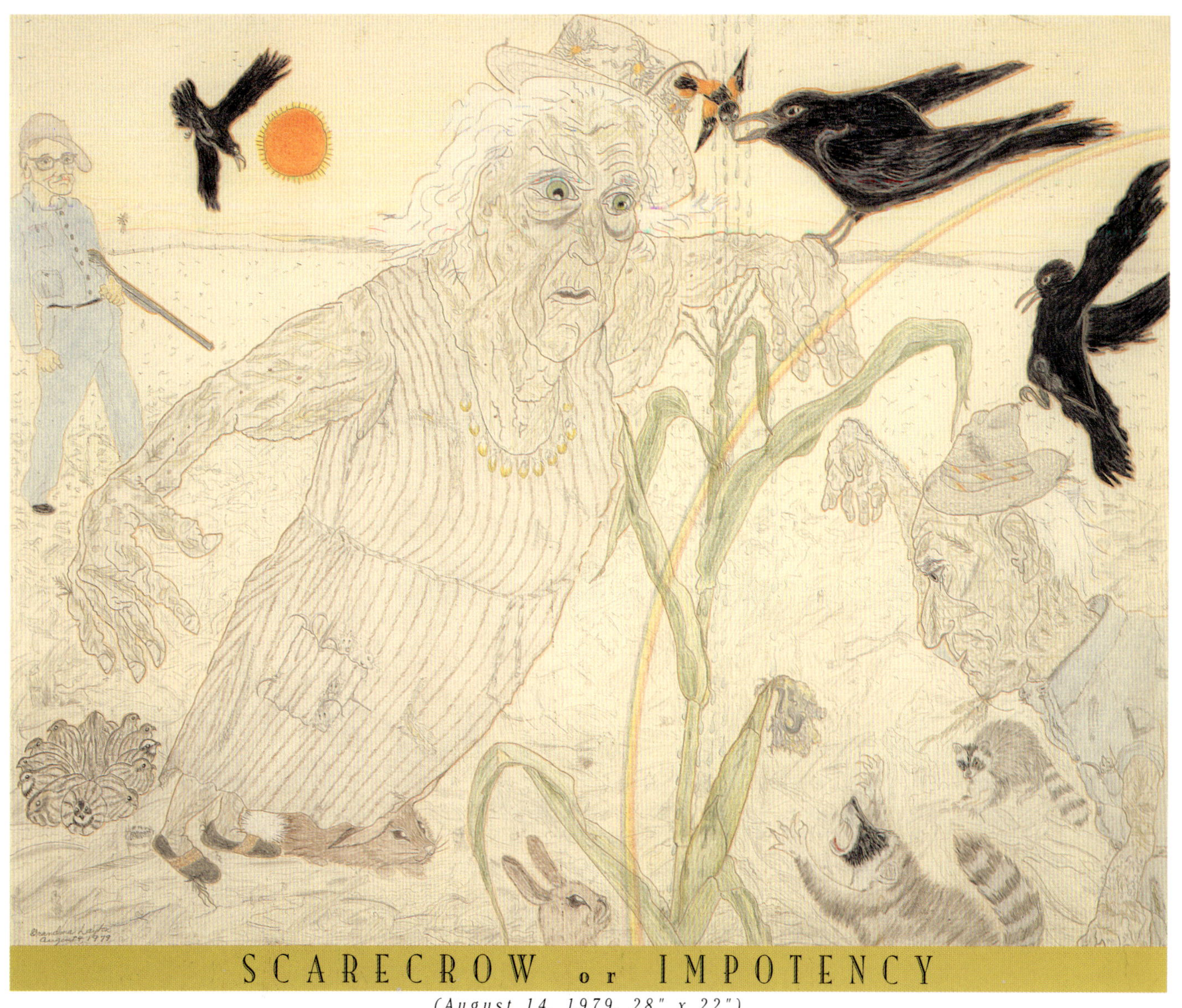

SCARECROW or IMPOTENCY

(August 14, 1979, 28" x 22")

Collection of the Metropolitan Museum of Art, New York, New York.

"'Work for the night is coming.' An old man and woman painstakingly guard the tiny spark of life. I see the hunter as someone on the way to help, a doctor, nurse, social worker, one of our many old age advocates."

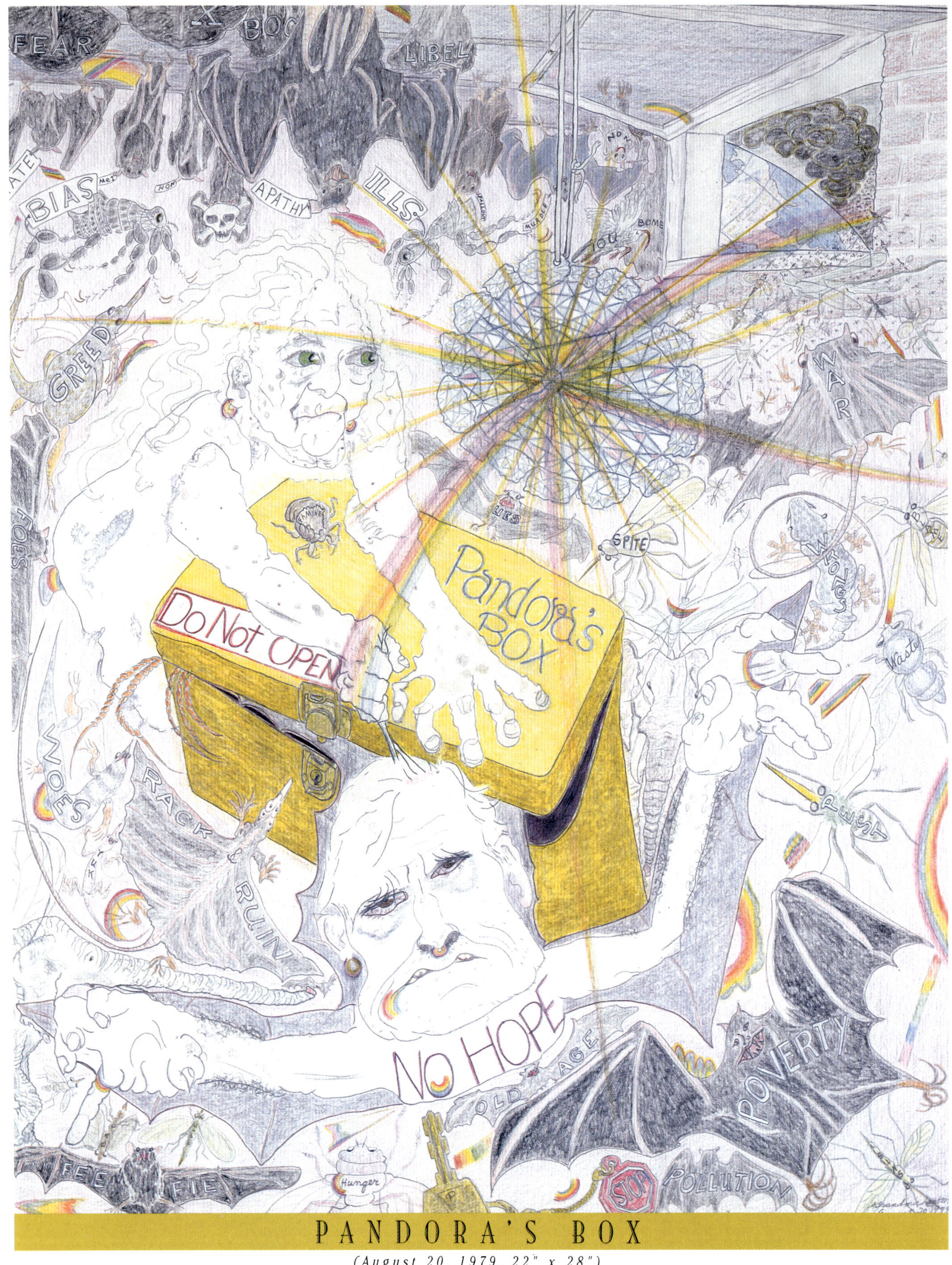

P A N D O R A ' S   B O X

(August 20, 1979, 22" x 28")

66 *Pandora is hanging onto no hope for all of her life, she's got hold of his hair, she is trying to keep him in the box because she has already let all of these other ills out. You got to have some hope, otherwise we all give up and die. One tiny ray of sun that comes through the window and hits that hope diamond and make these millions of rainbows.* 99

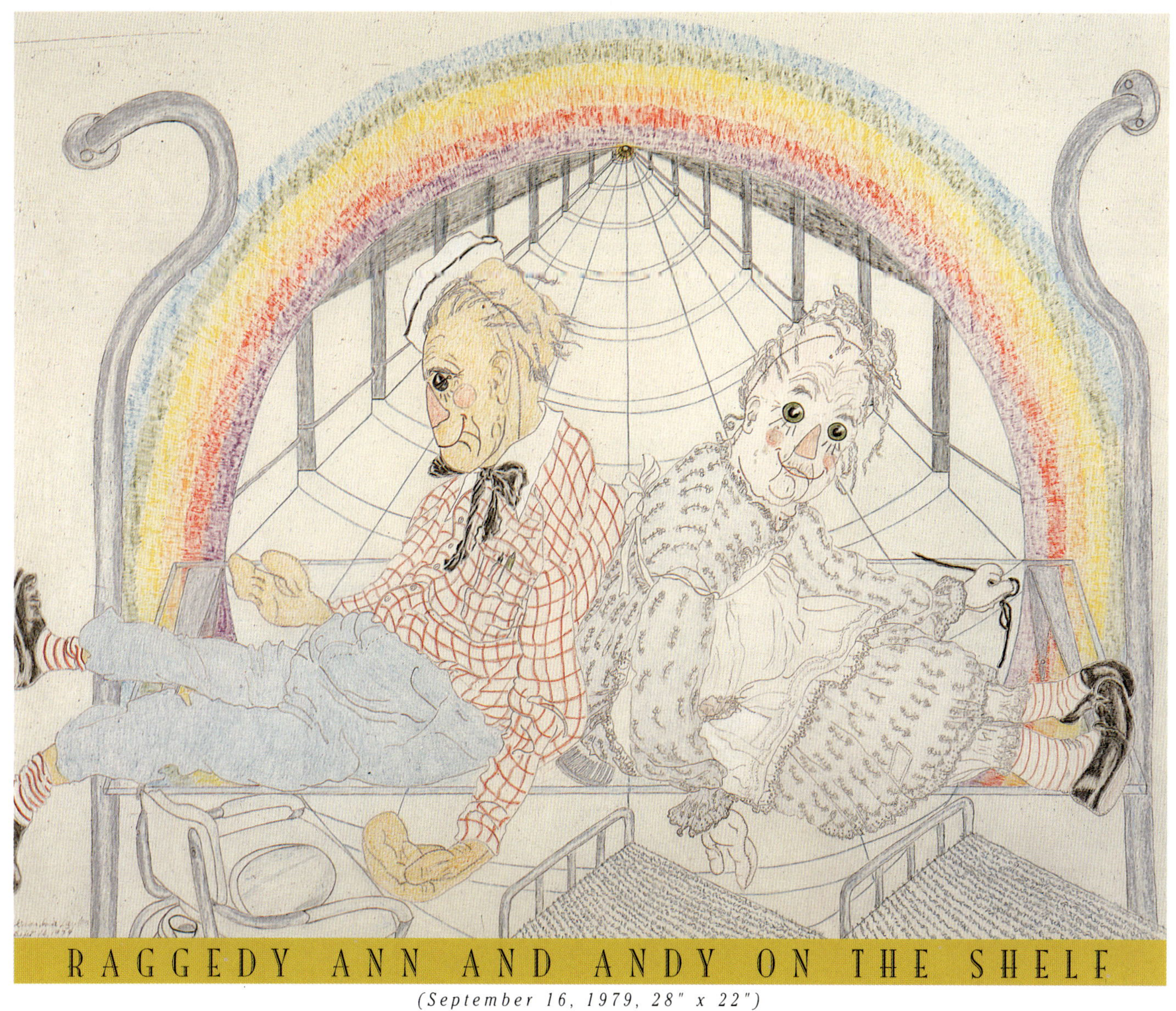

RAGGEDY ANN AND ANDY ON THE SHELF

(September 16, 1979, 28" x 22")

"*The shelf is made out of glass and it's in front of a glass window. You know in nursing homes and institutions, or hospitals there is no privacy.*"

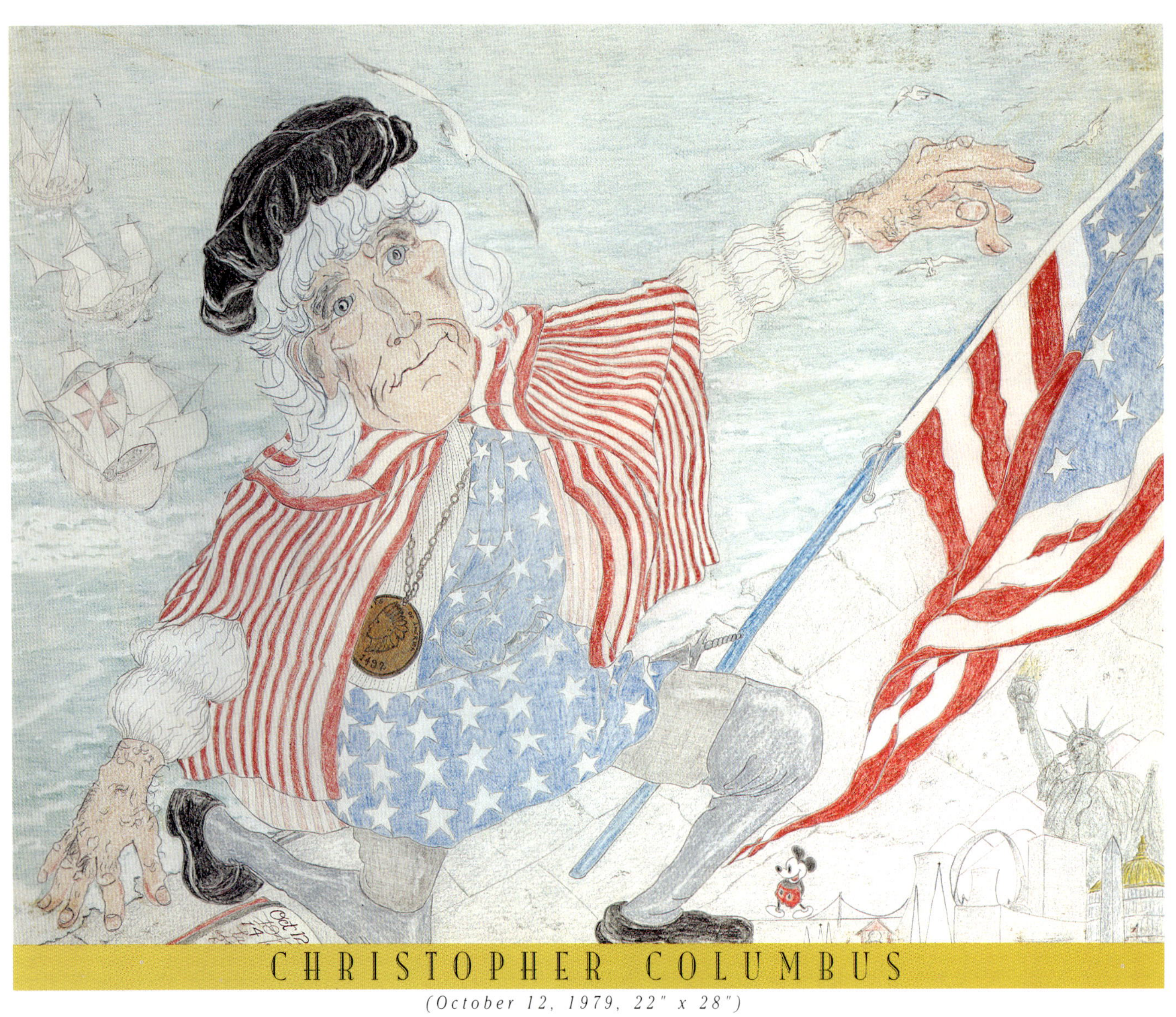

CHRISTOPHER COLUMBUS

(October 12, 1979, 22" x 28")

"Here's Glenn, landing on a concrete America, being greeted by Mickey Mouse."

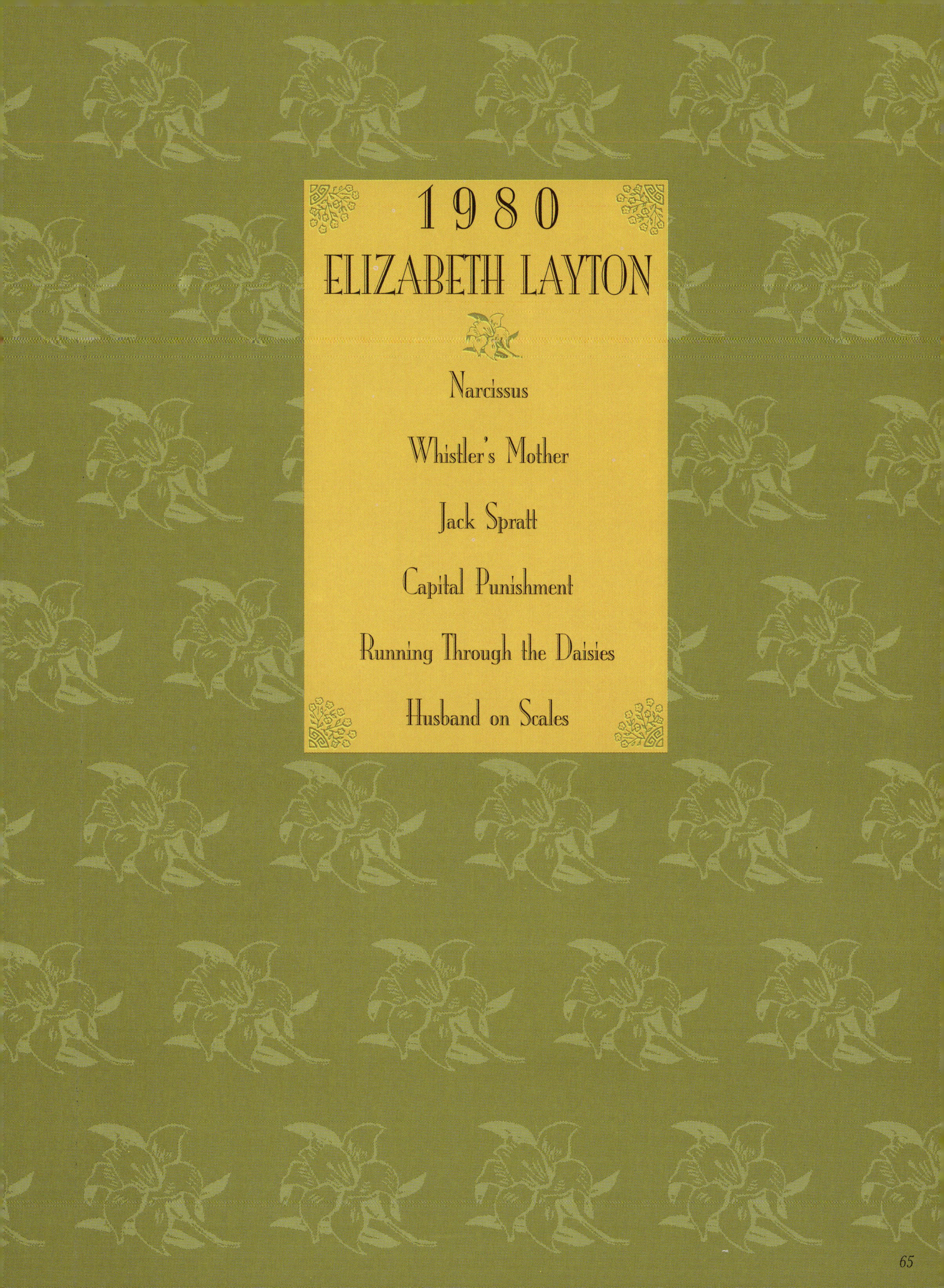

1980
ELIZABETH LAYTON

Narcissus

Whistler's Mother

Jack Spratt

Capital Punishment

Running Through the Daisies

Husband on Scales

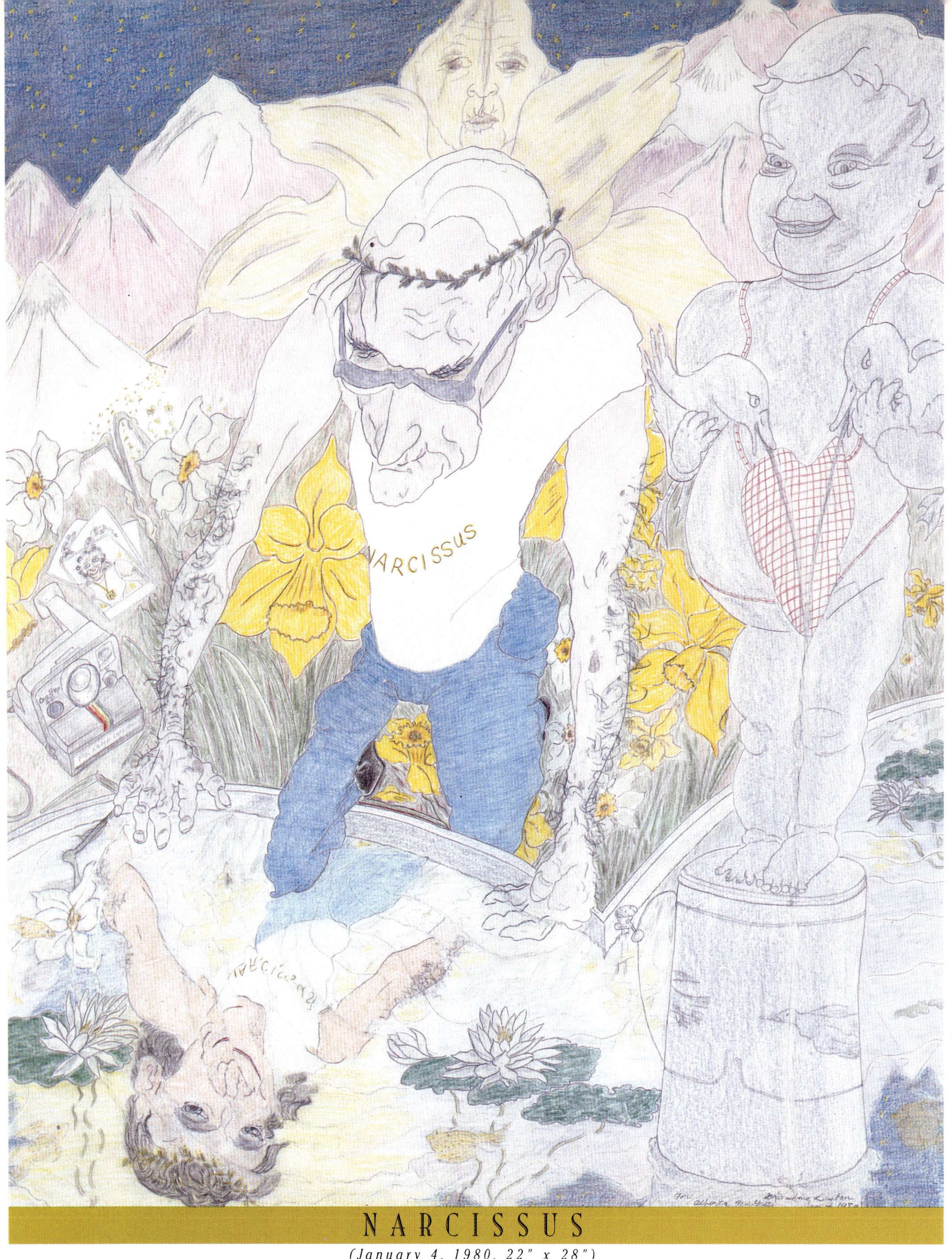

NARCISSUS

(January 4, 1980, 22" x 28")

"*I call it Narcissus. It's off that old myth. The water that he is looking into is kind of a fountain of youth. People now days, they worship youth a lot. But the idea is that he sits there by the water looking at himself until he turns into a Narcissus. But the idea I've tried to bring out is that he has grown old there, but he still sees himself as young and beautiful. In the myth, Echo is the one who died of love of Narcissus, because he couldn't return her love. So this is her, the flower with the face on it. I didn't know how to draw a sound.*"

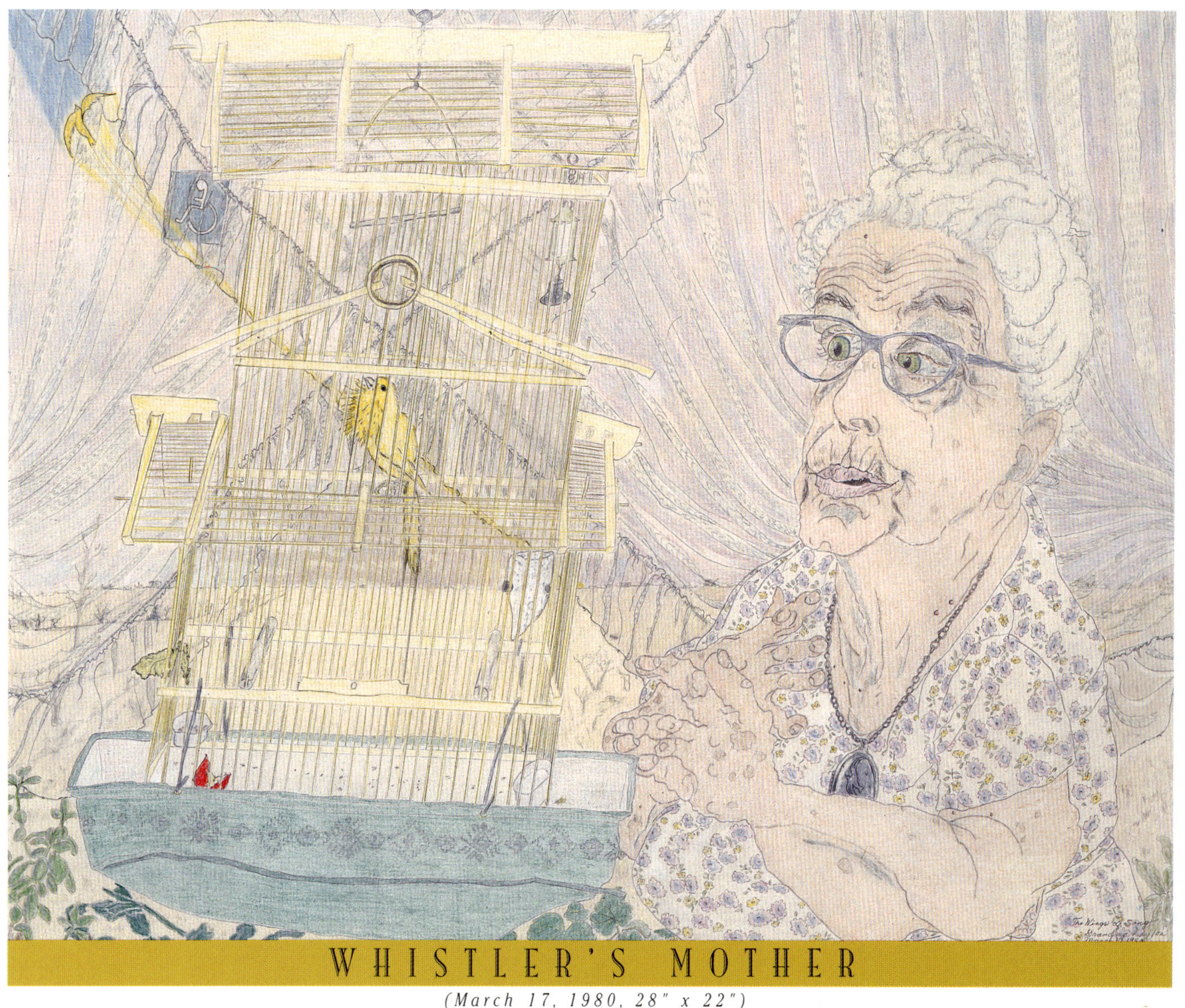

WHISTLER'S MOTHER

(March 17, 1980, 28" x 22")

> **"**The idea was that your body's a cage but your spirit is free. People who are paralyzed, they draw with their mouth or their head, they do miraculous things. Maybe you're old, maybe you can't get your thoughts out, just living is a handicap because you are caged in this particular body whether you like it or not. You just as well should learn to like it.**"**

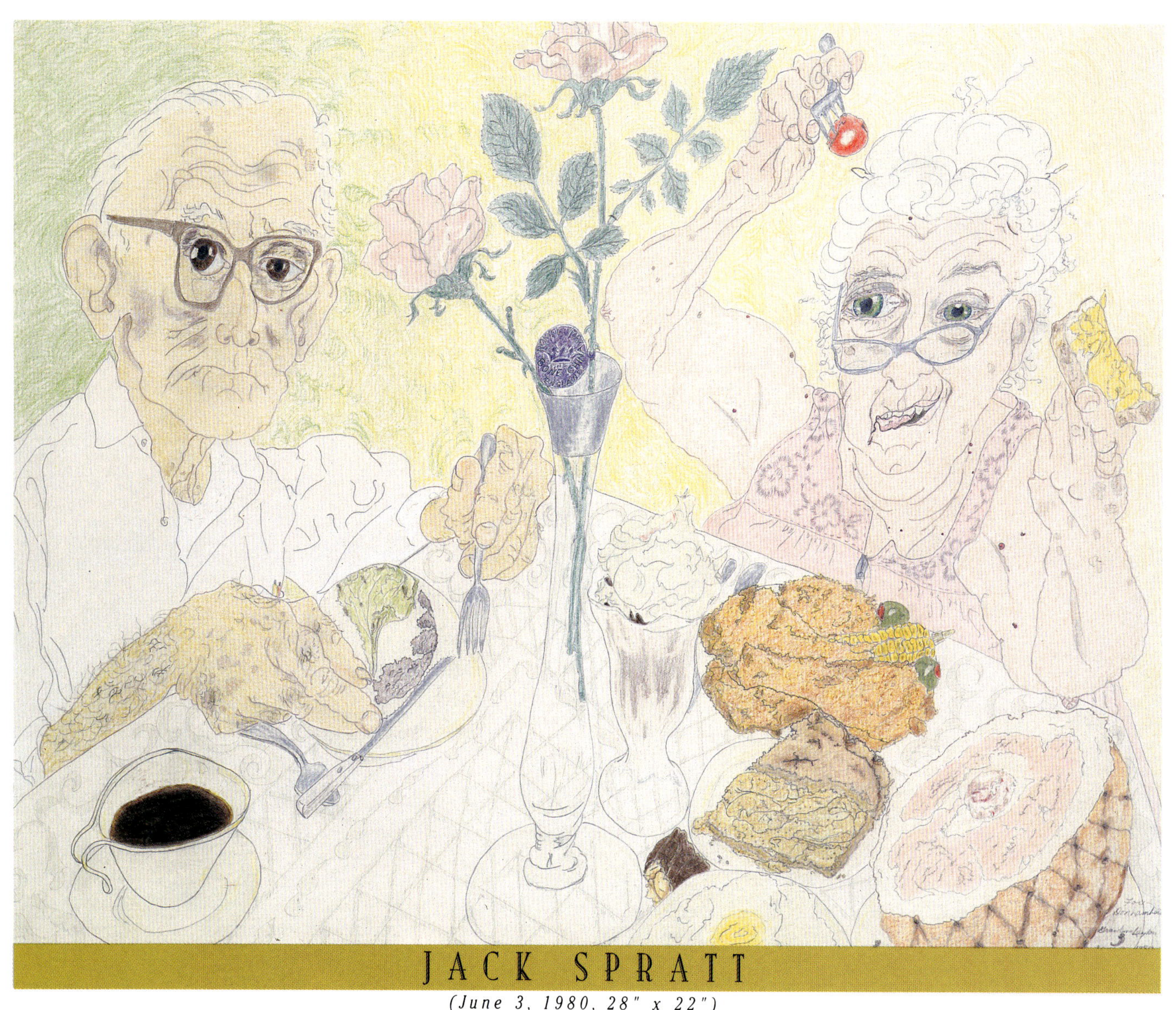

JACK SPRATT

(June 3, 1980, 28" x 22")

Jack Spratt could eat no fat
His wife could eat no lean
And so betwixt them both, you see,
They licked the platter clean.

– Mother Goose

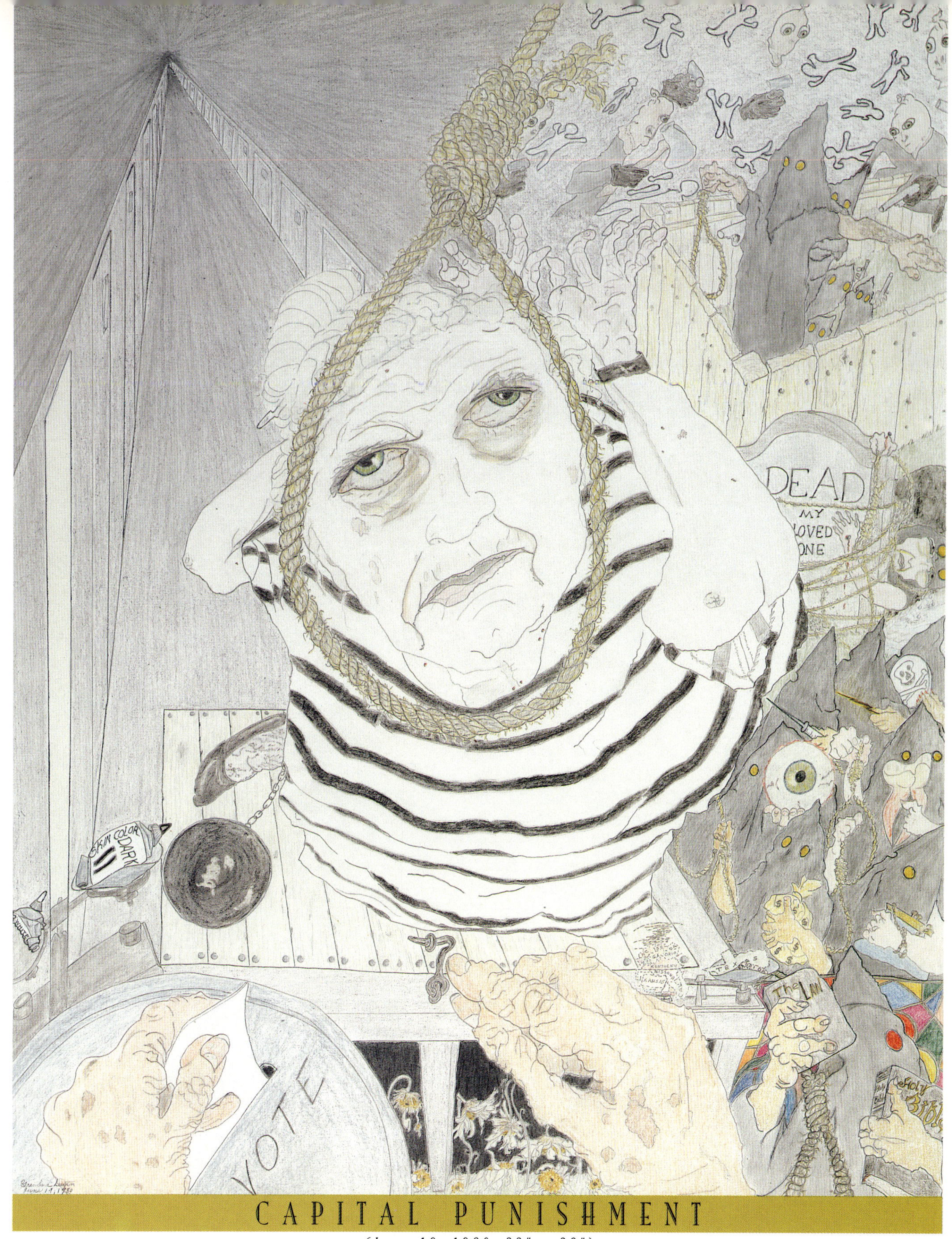

C A P I T A L   P U N I S H M E N T

(June 19, 1980, 22" x 28")

❝*She grovels for her life, to end or not to end at the whim of Society and its vote. The bottomless pit, lined by daisies with little broken necks, is in the wait — at the end of a long Death Row. The two scales are unbalanced. There are more executions in four states than all the rest. White skin in not as expendable. In the background are chalk outlines with guns and hatchets running amuck in spite of any prospective punishments.*❞

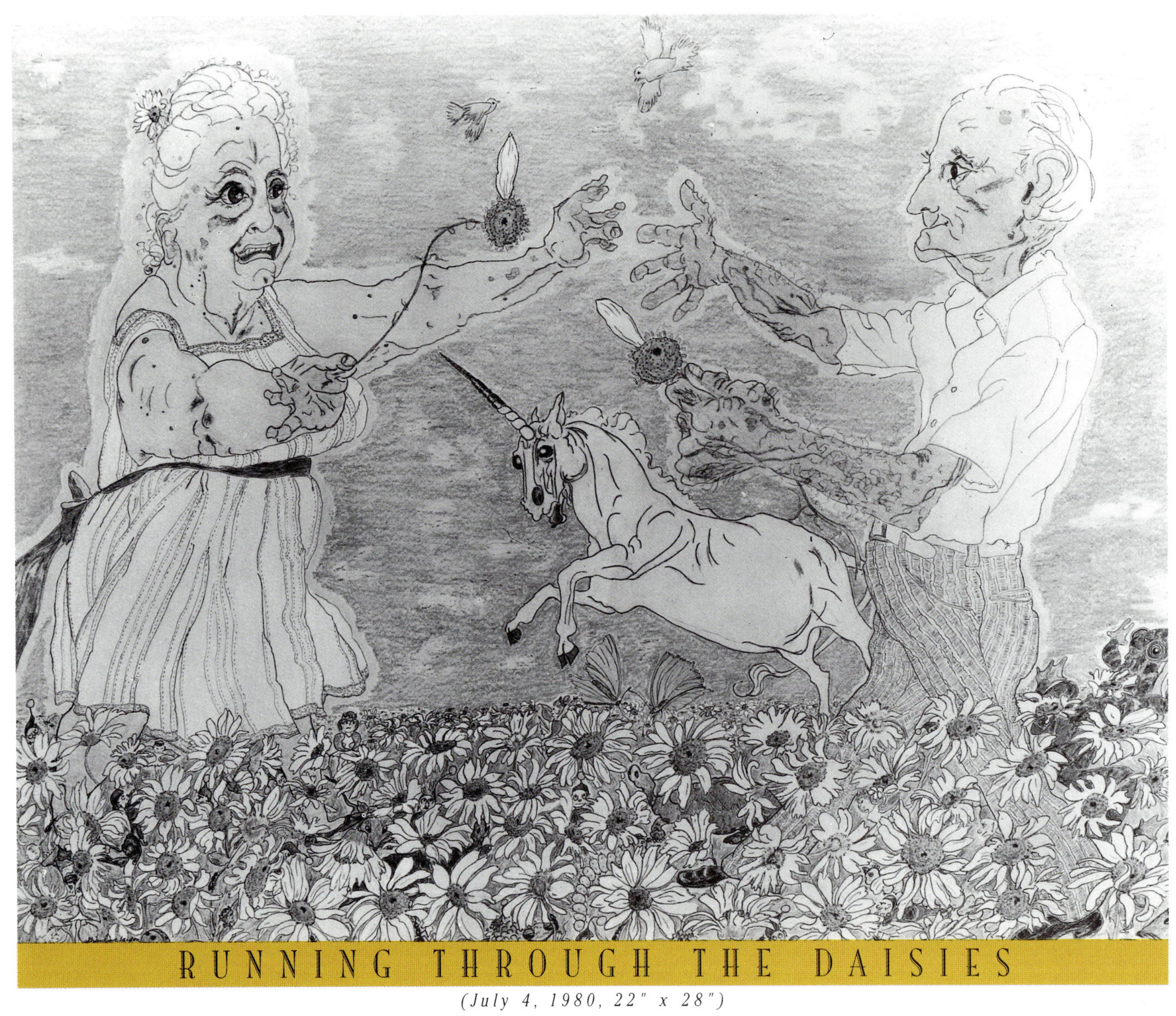

R U N N I N G   T H R O U G H   T H E   D A I S I E S

(July 4, 1980, 22" x 28")

"I'd always thought old people saw each other as still young. I meant to draw young bodies over these two. (Don't ask me how.) But I discovered when I got this far, that this is the way we see and love each other, just as we are."

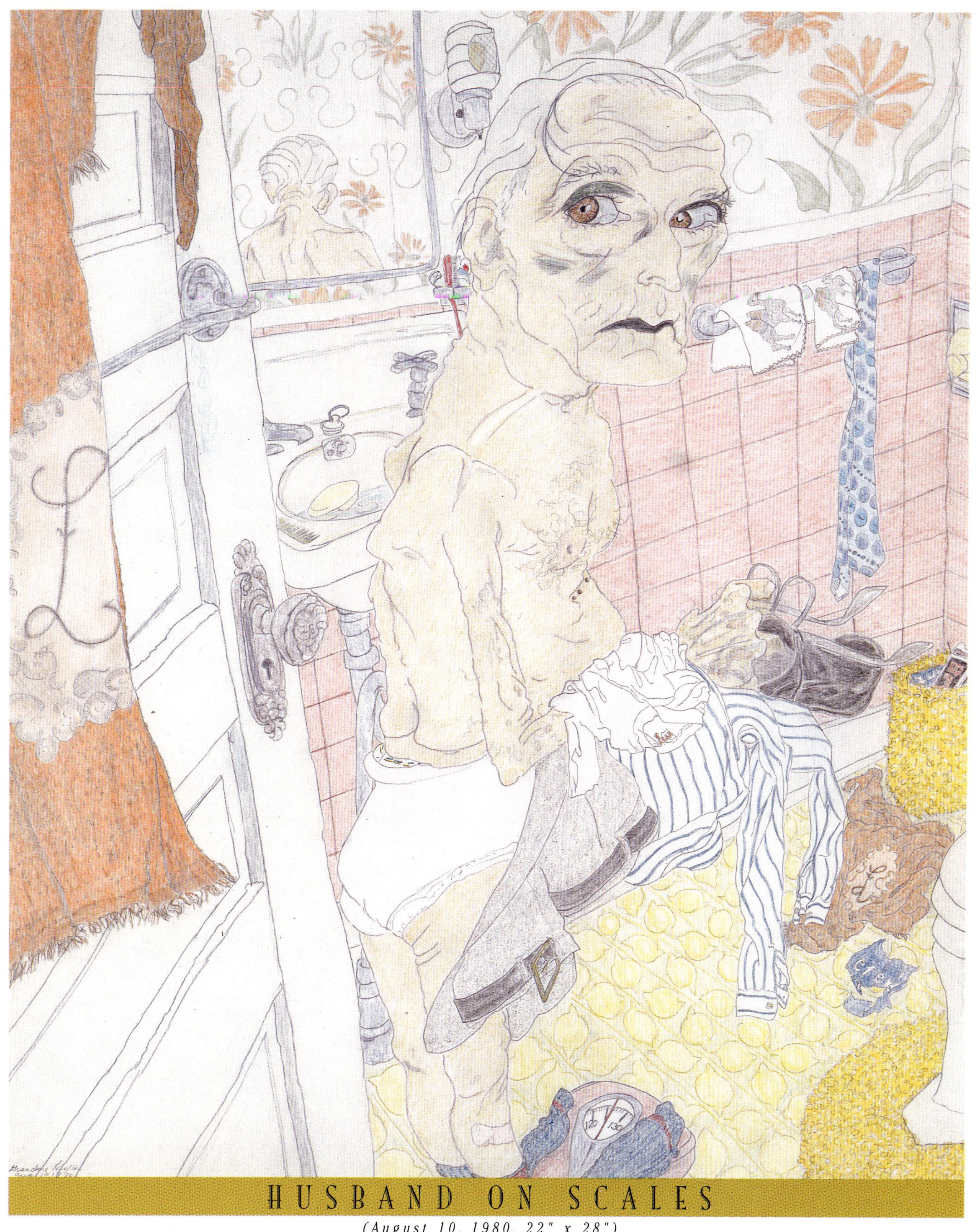

"My husband Glenn was just home from the hospital, struggling mightily to gain pounds,
even an ounce. I barged in on this scene. Glenn is game to pose for me however I need. He may balk at first.
'I can't stand it. You want me to be a bunny rabbit? NO bunny rabbit.' But he always comes through."

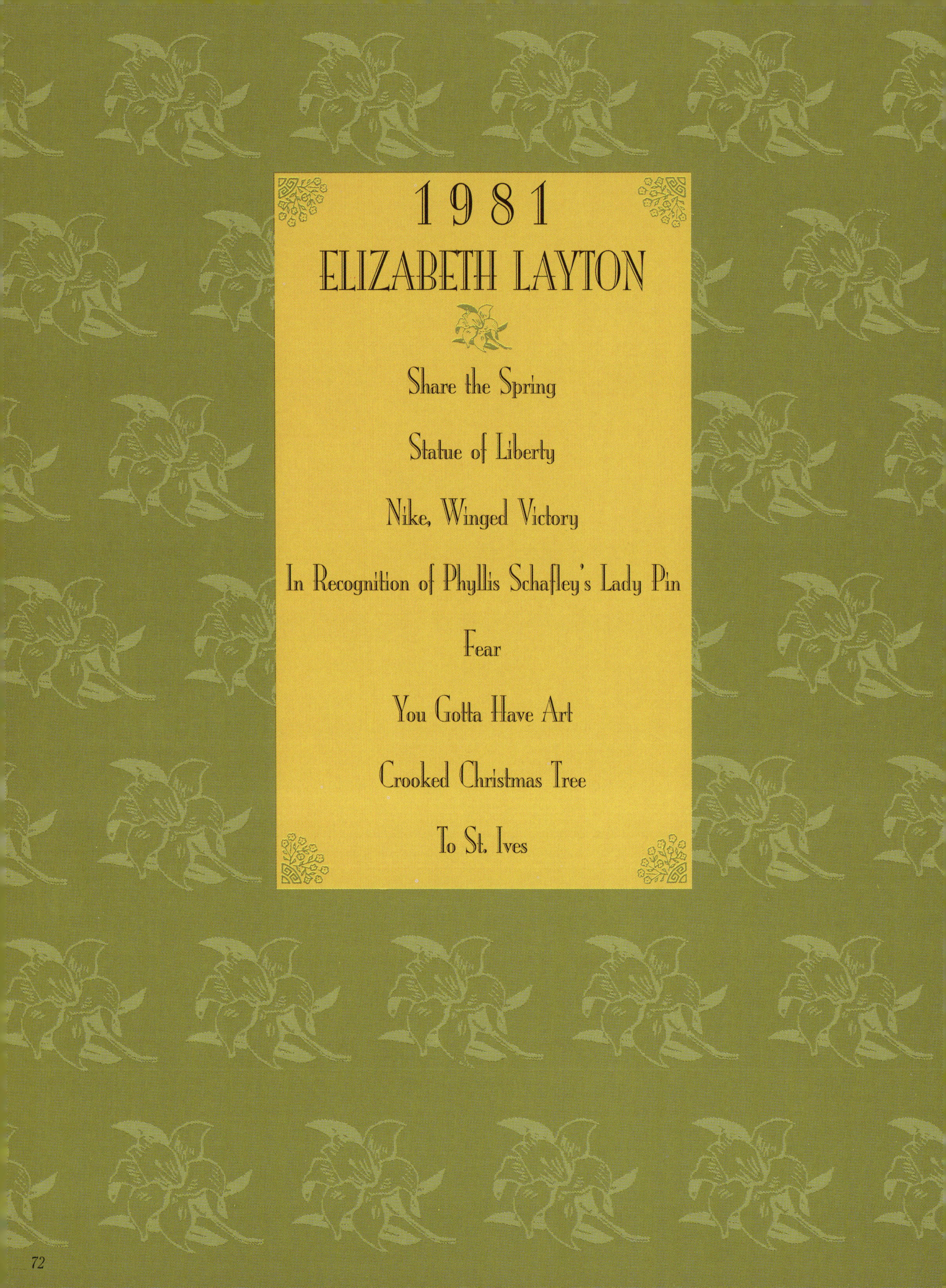

1 9 8 1
ELIZABETH LAYTON

Share the Spring

Statue of Liberty

Nike, Winged Victory

In Recognition of Phyllis Schafley's Lady Pin

Fear

You Gotta Have Art

Crooked Christmas Tree

To St. Ives

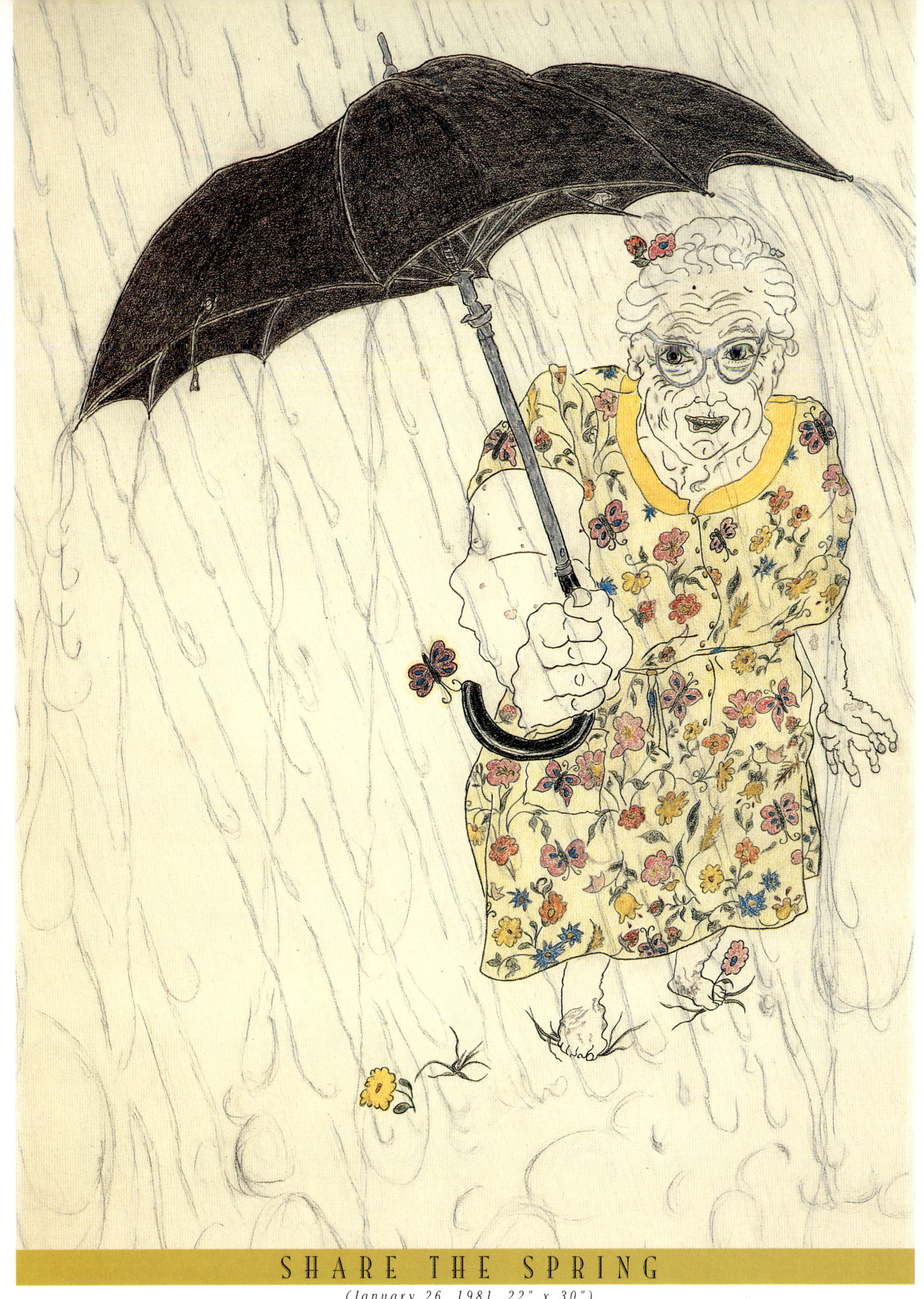

SHARE THE SPRING

(January 26, 1981, 22" x 30")

From the collection of the Lawrence Art Center, Lawrence, Kansas

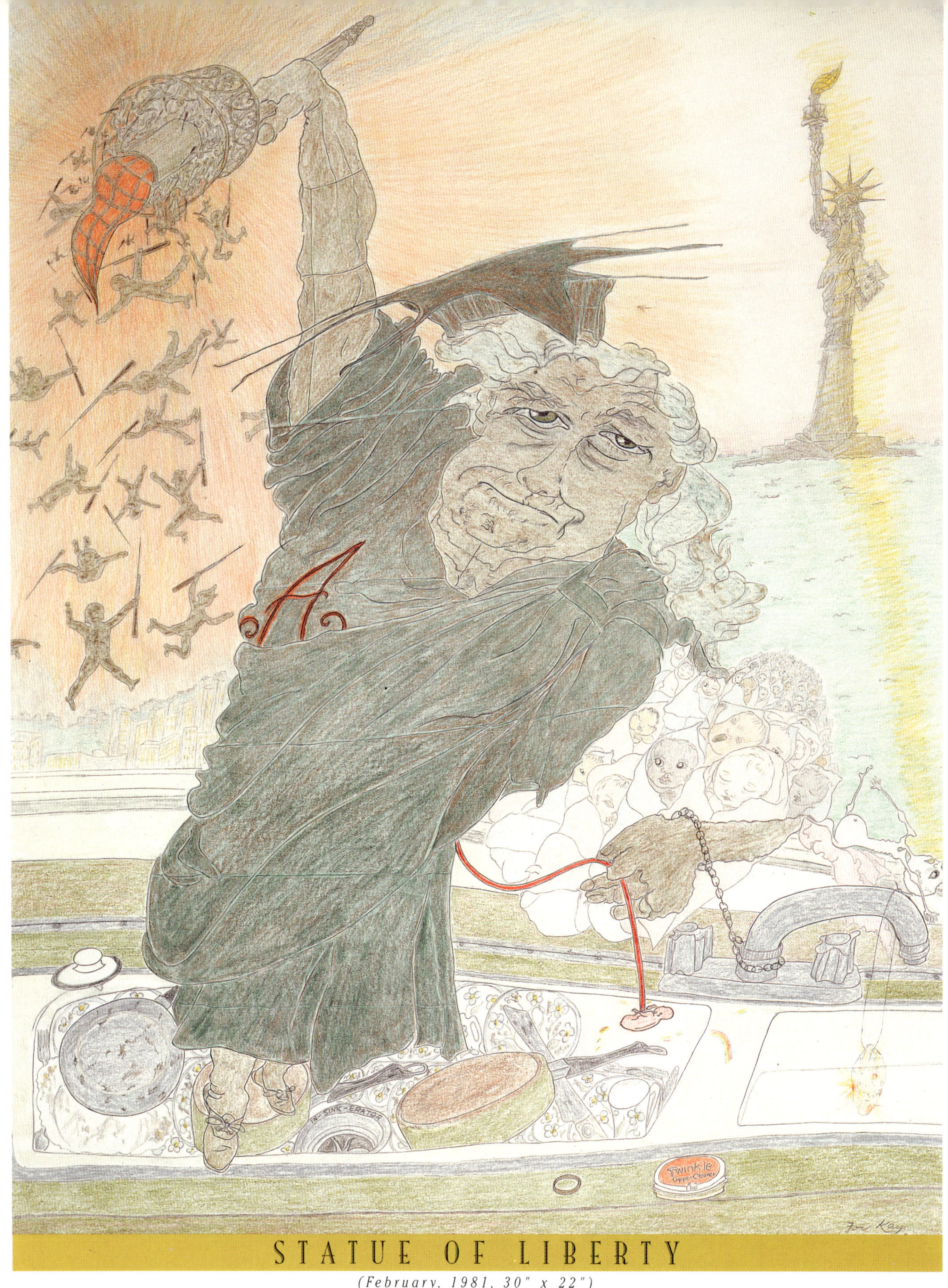

STATUE OF LIBERTY

(February, 1981, 30" x 22")

"*She is tired from reading and fostering children to be used as cannon fodder. Her responsibilities exhaust her but she does the best she can. She stands on her copper base (copper-bottomed pans) in a double sink (double standard.) The Scarlet Letter "A" brands her. The blame and burden are hers. Individual woman? Our Nation?*"

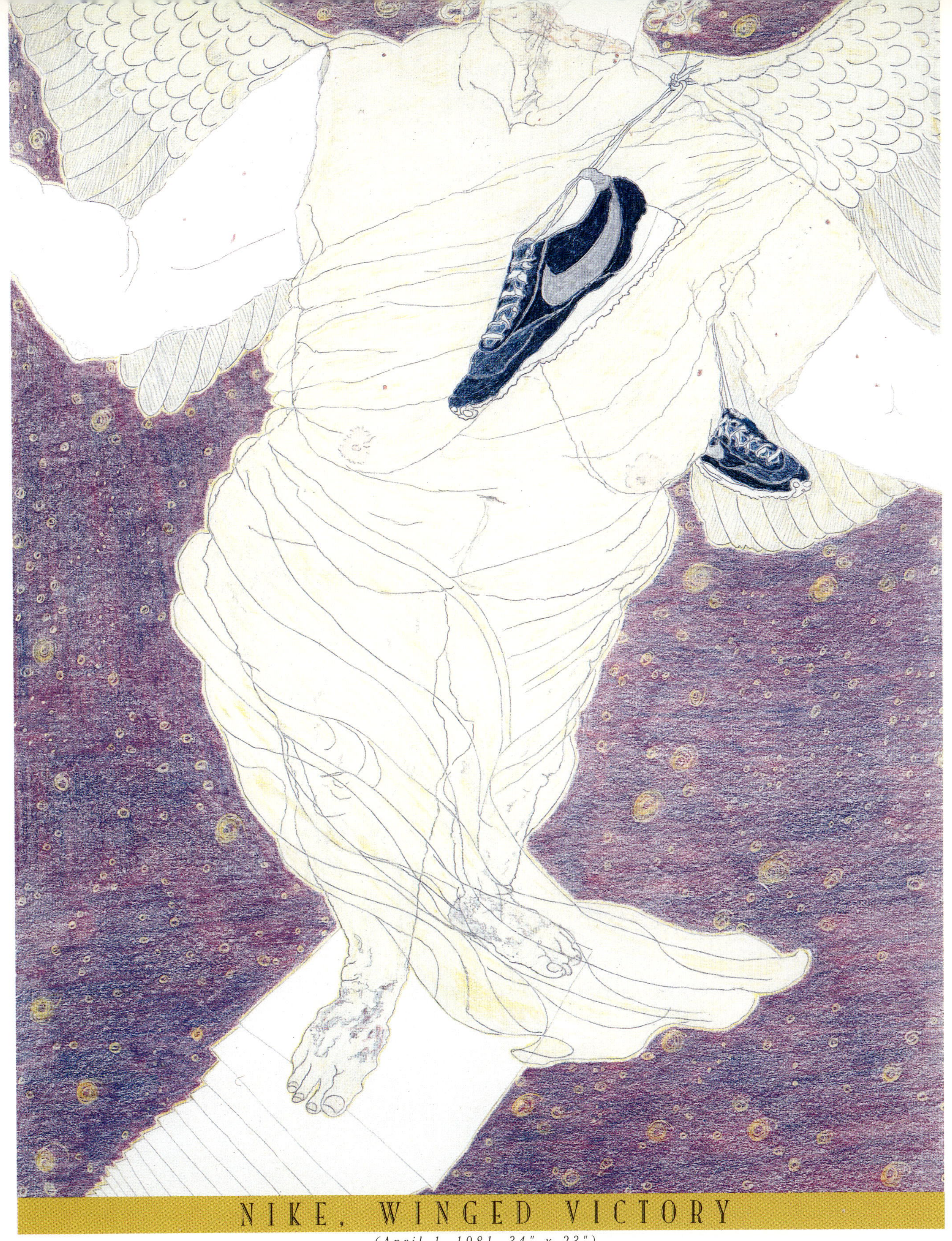

NIKE, WINGED VICTORY

(April 1, 1981, 34" x 23")

Collection of the National Museum of Women in the Arts, Washington, D.C.

"She has struggled and toiled up a lifetime of steps. Now she is where she wants to be, has taken off her running shoes, and is ready to fly. Scars, where the arms and head of the statue were broken off, now are only hallmarks of the new and everlasting growth."

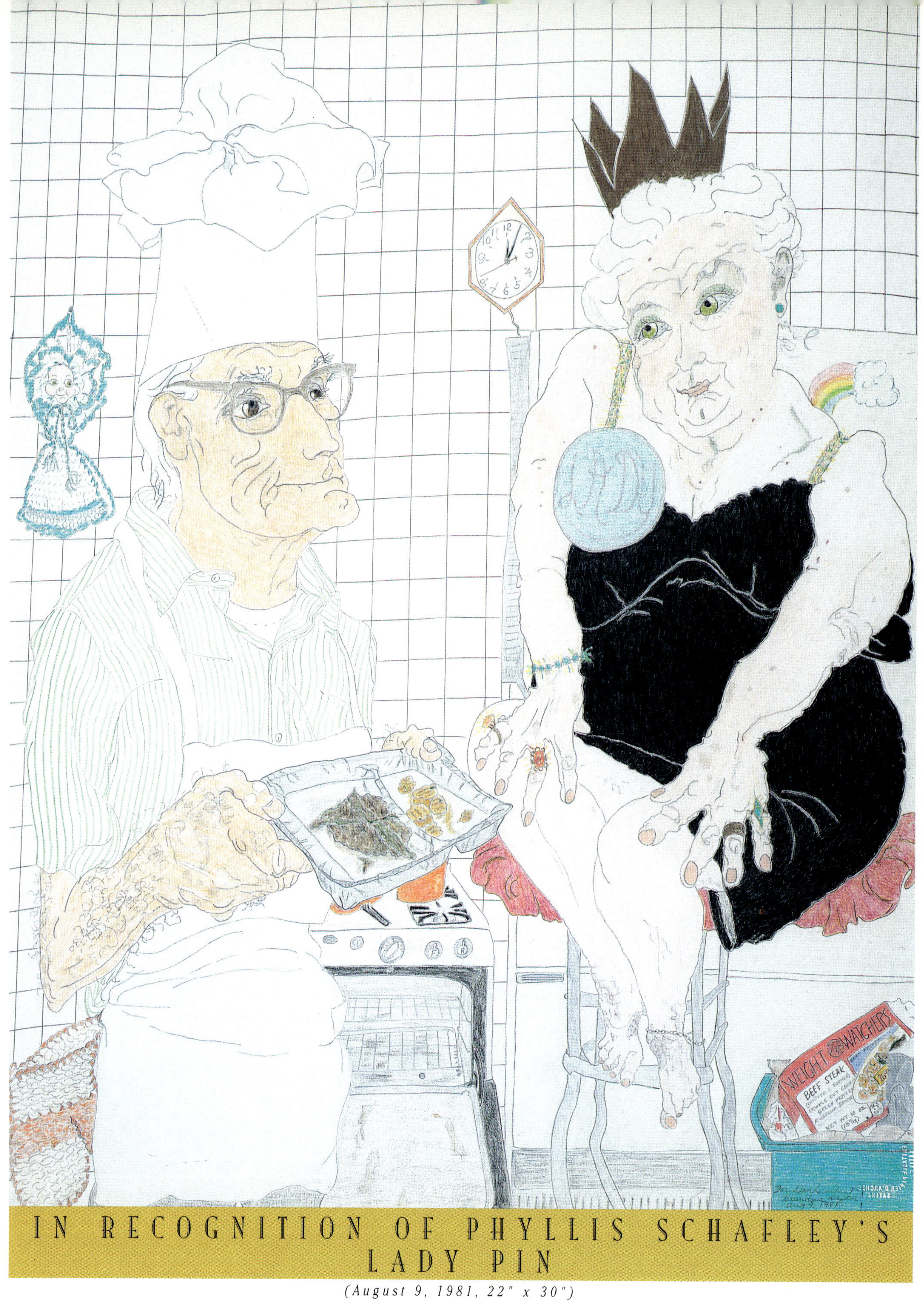

IN RECOGNITION OF PHYLLIS SCHAFLEY'S LADY PIN

(August 9, 1981, 22" x 30")

"*Shades of the Victorian ERA.***"**

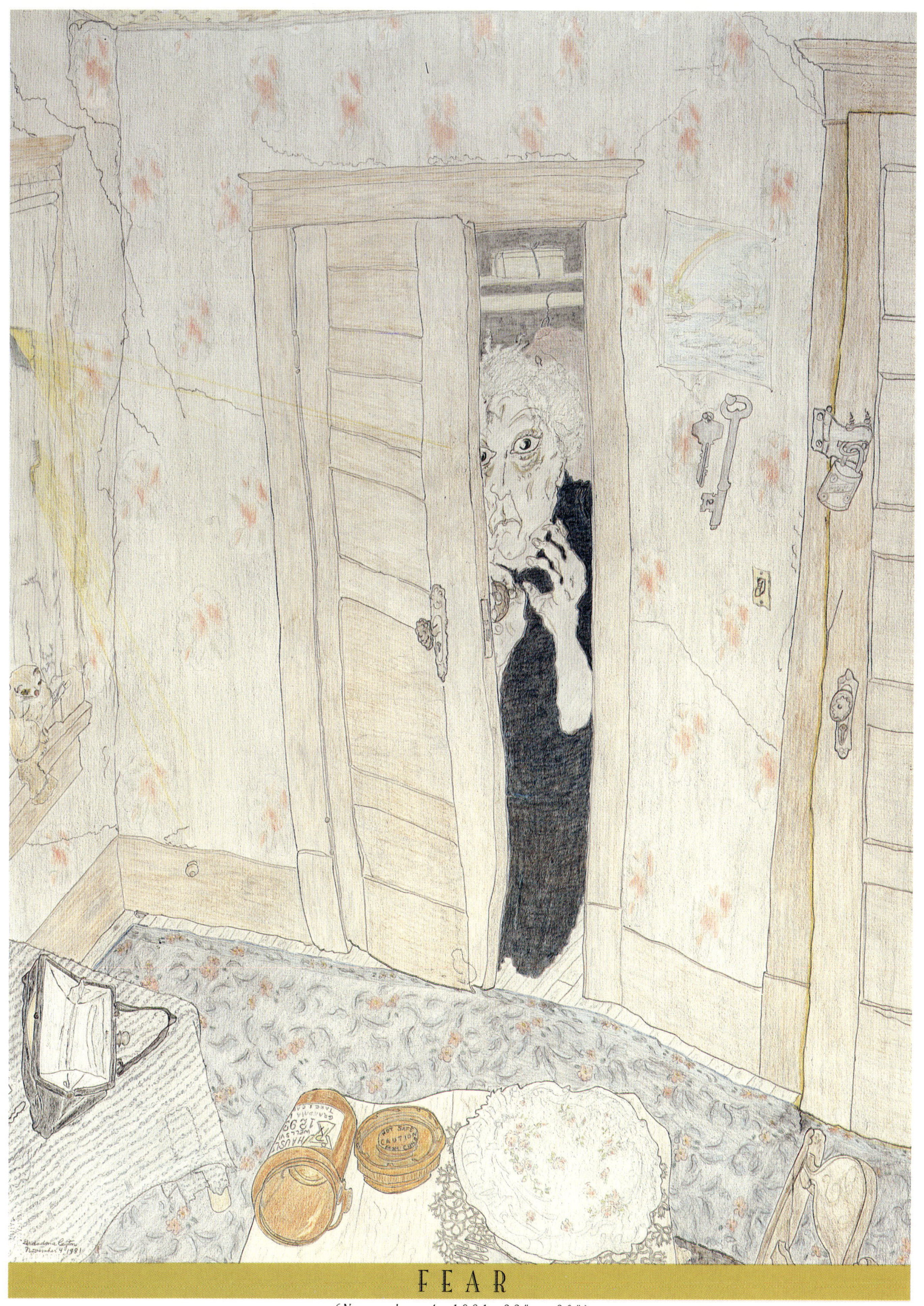

F E A R

(November 4, 1981, 22" x 30")

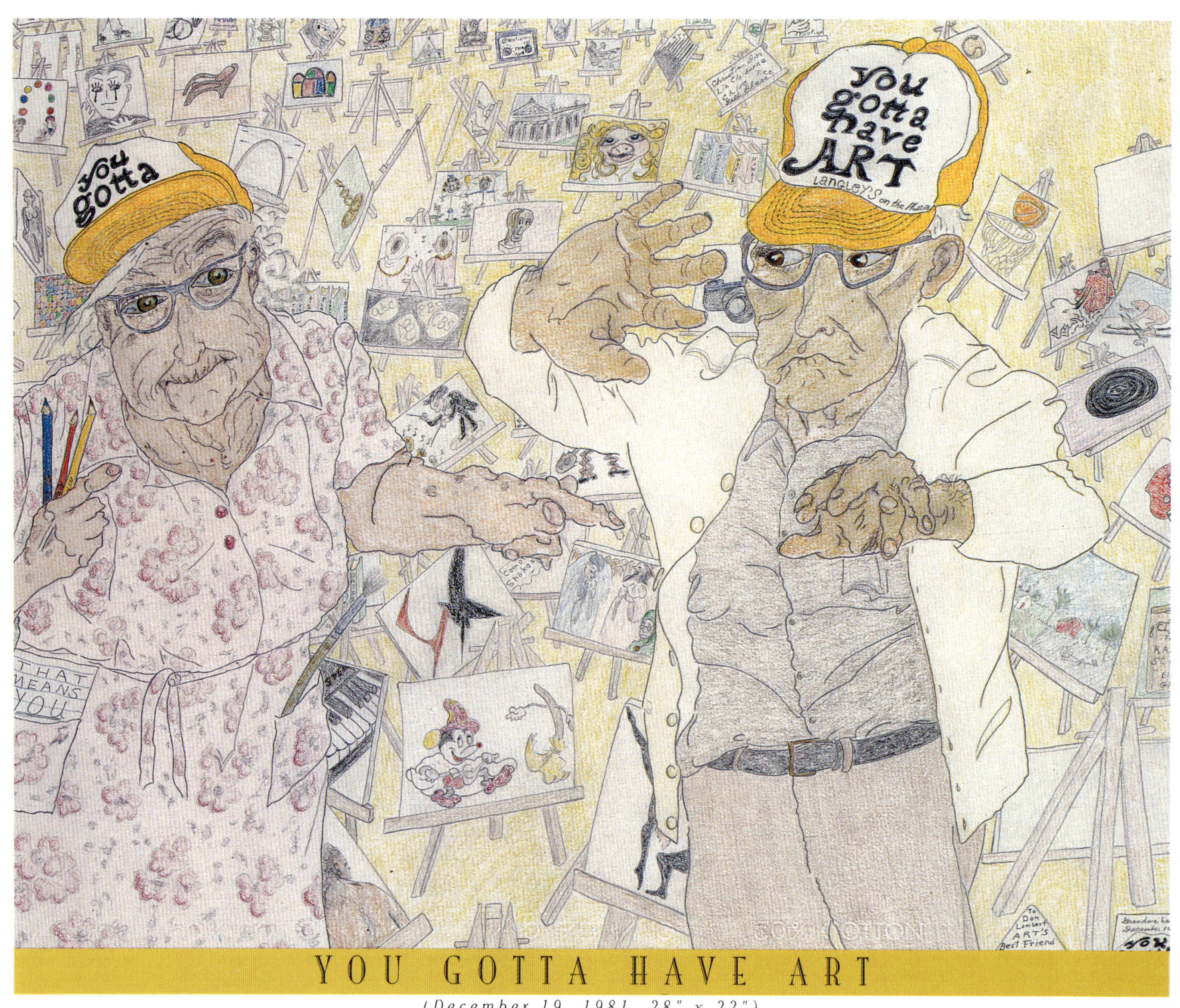

YOU GOTTA HAVE ART

(December 19, 1981, 28" x 22")

Don Lambert brought us these caps to spread our message. Art does so much for me I want everybody to try it. If you get tired of my ranting, do like Glenn does — duck. My sister Carolyn kept coaxing me to try Art, like her husband Henry Francis Misselwitz, had persuaded her to paint out in Burlingame, California. Daughter Kay even brought me the Art assignments to do — a child's movie screen in a shoebox, nursery rhymes to illustrate. Big sisters and Little daughters sometimes know best. So, timidly, I ventured out to the World of Art and enrolled in Basic Drawing and discovered CONTOUR!

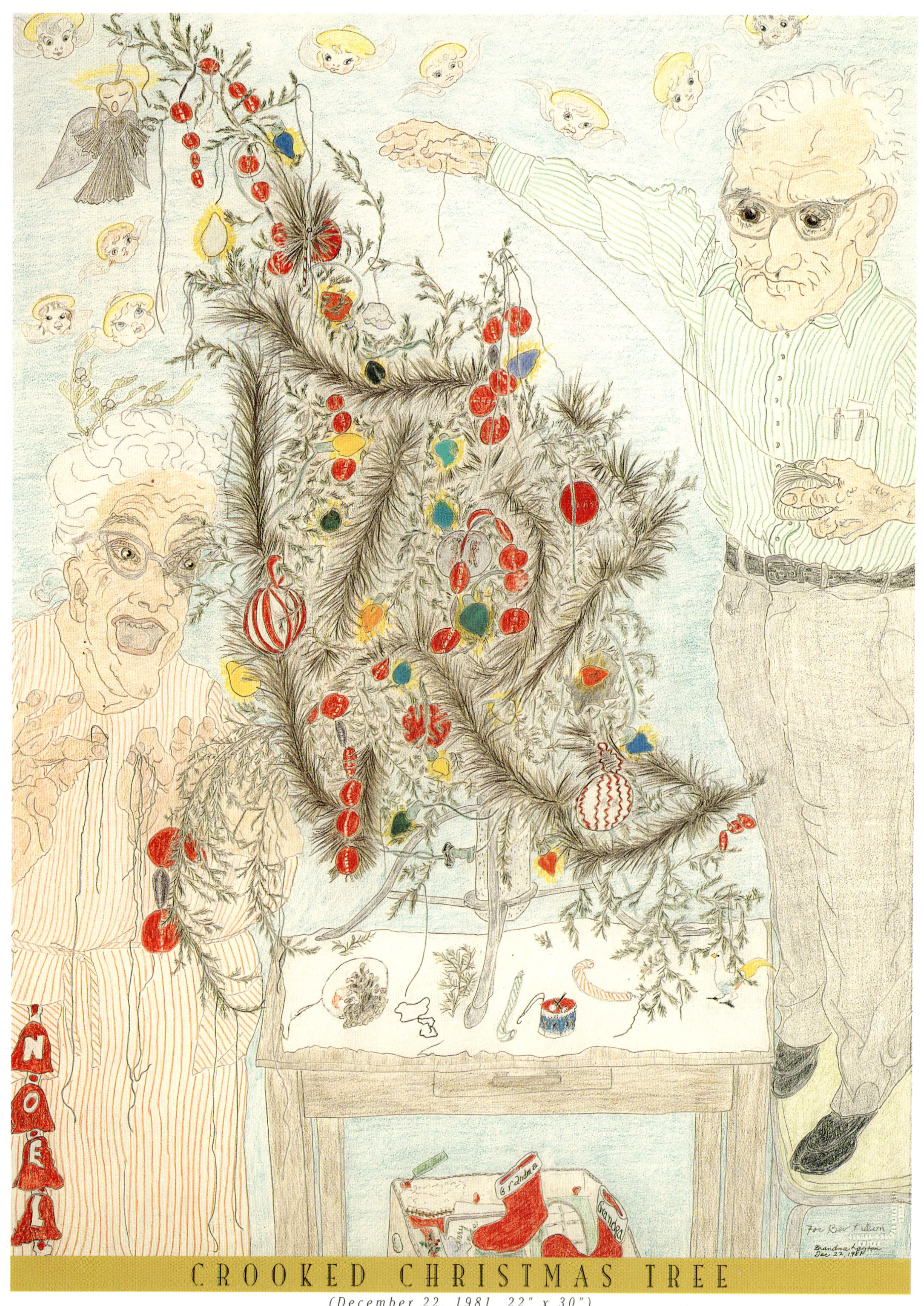

C R O O K E D   C H R I S T M A S   T R E E

(December 22, 1981, 22" x 30")

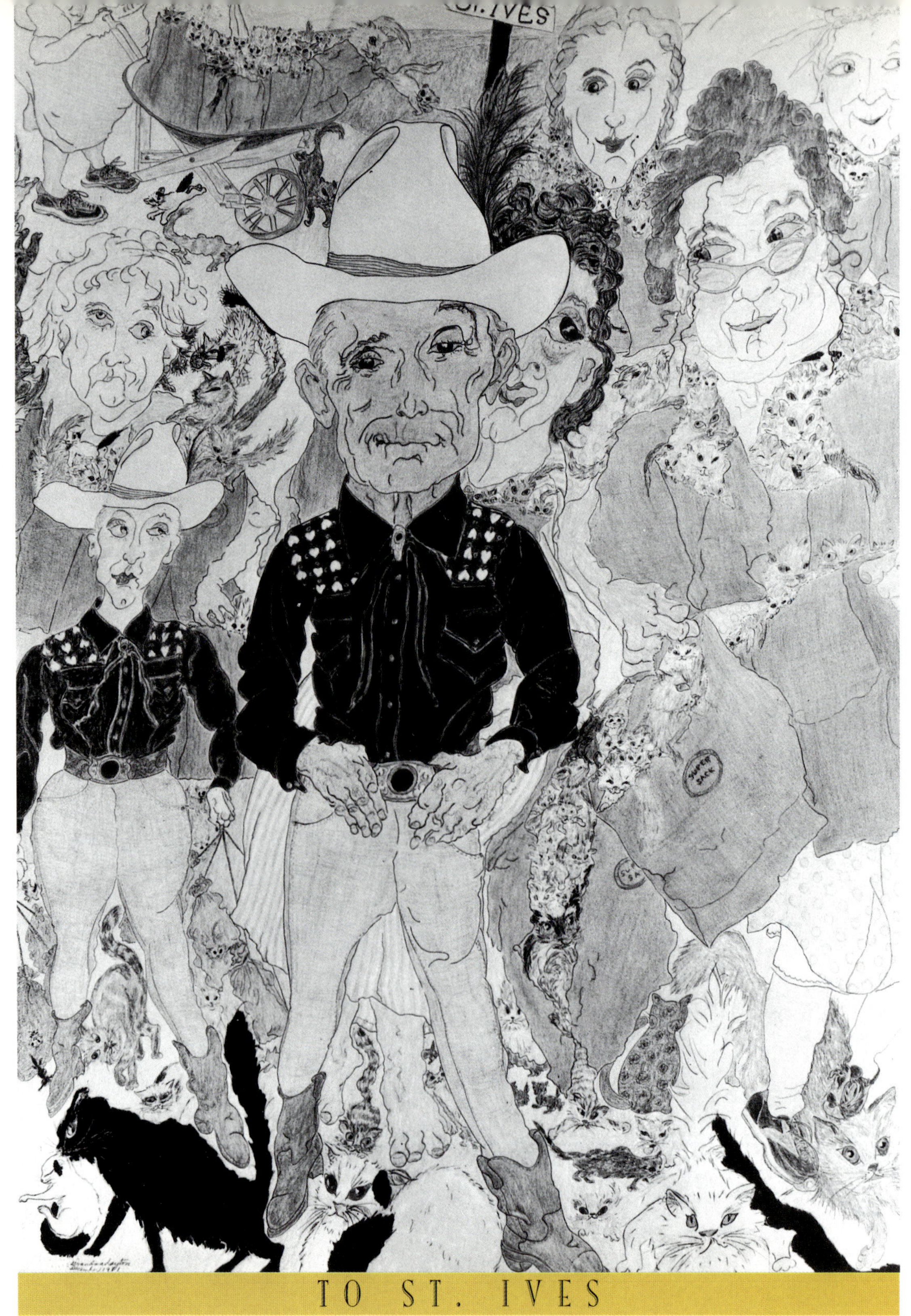

TO ST. IVES

(December, 1981, 22" x 30")

"As I was going to St. Ives

I met a man with seven wives.

Each wife had seven sacks.

Each sack had seven cats.

Each cat had seven kits.

How many were going to St. Ives?"

"At times a husband might expect seven wives all rolled into one."

1982

ELIZABETH LAYTON

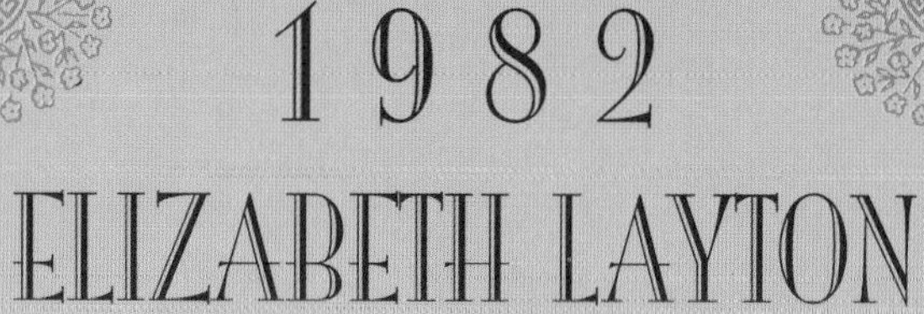

Indian Wrestling

Pink Bubbles

Le Danse D'Les Demoiselles

Mother's Day

Cinderella

Mixed Flowers

Buttons

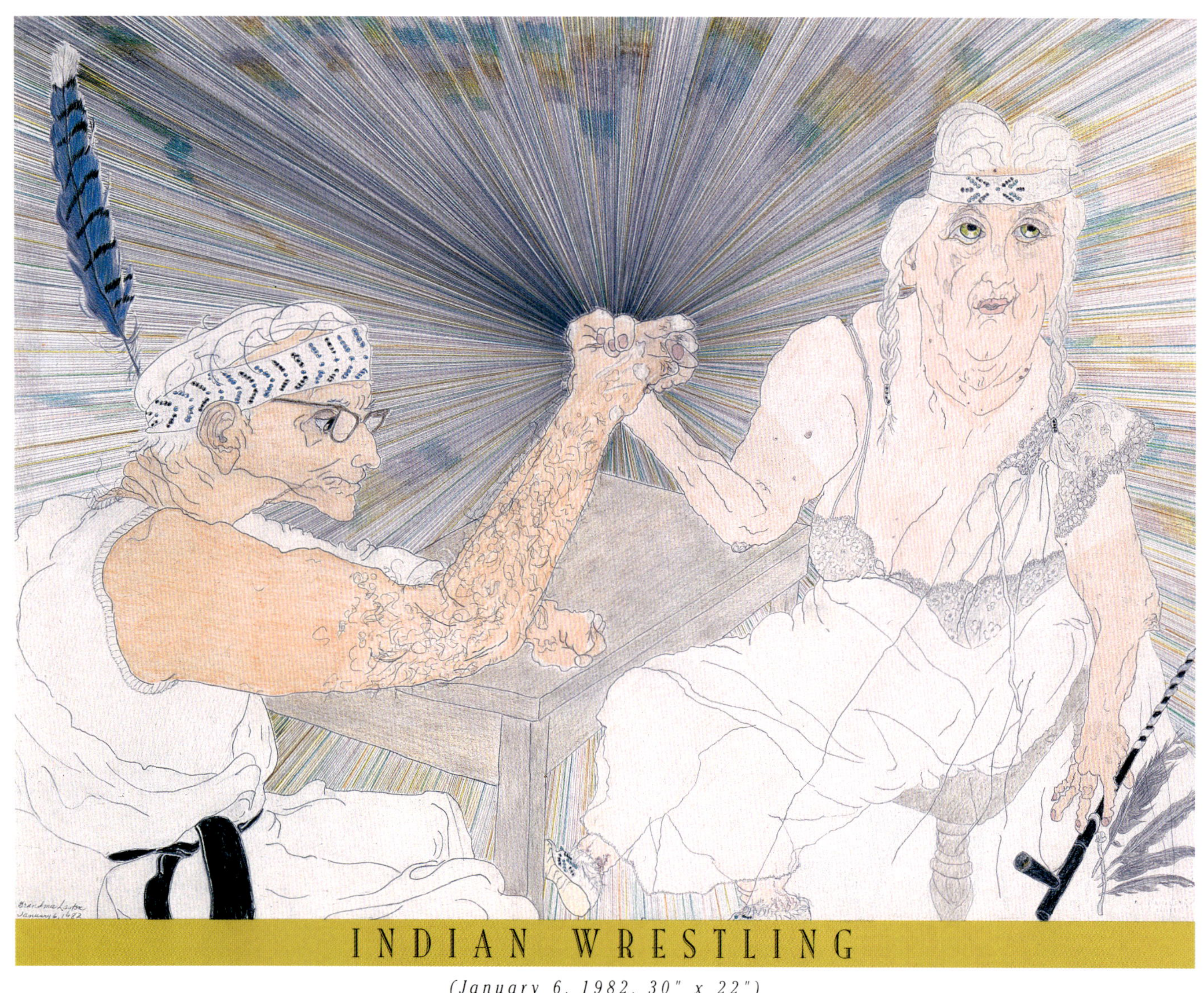

(*January 6, 1982, 30" x 22"*)

"*This Indian Brave and Maiden are at an eternal counterbalance. Though very different, all are equal.*"

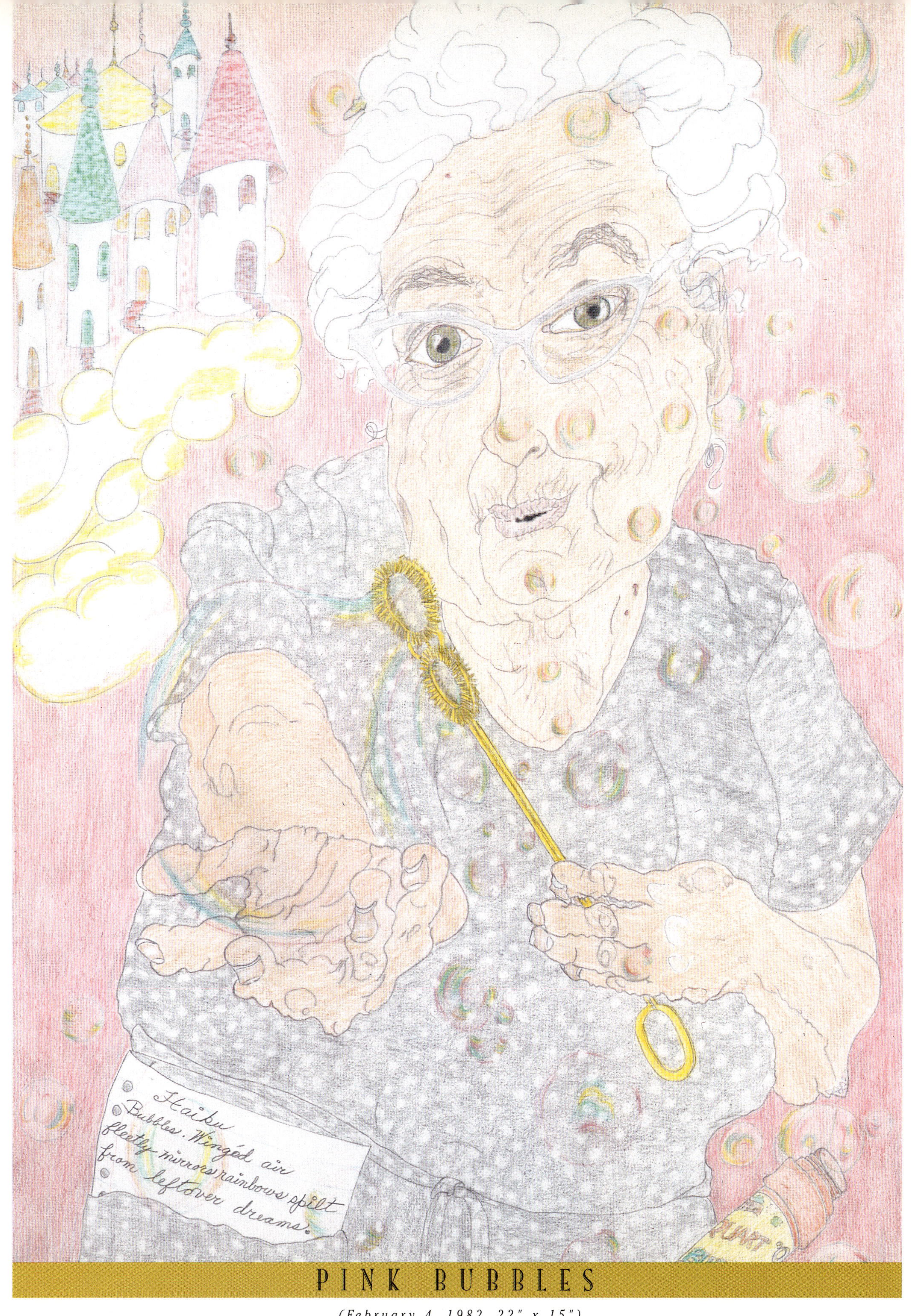

P I N K   B U B B L E S

(February 4, 1982, 22" x 15")

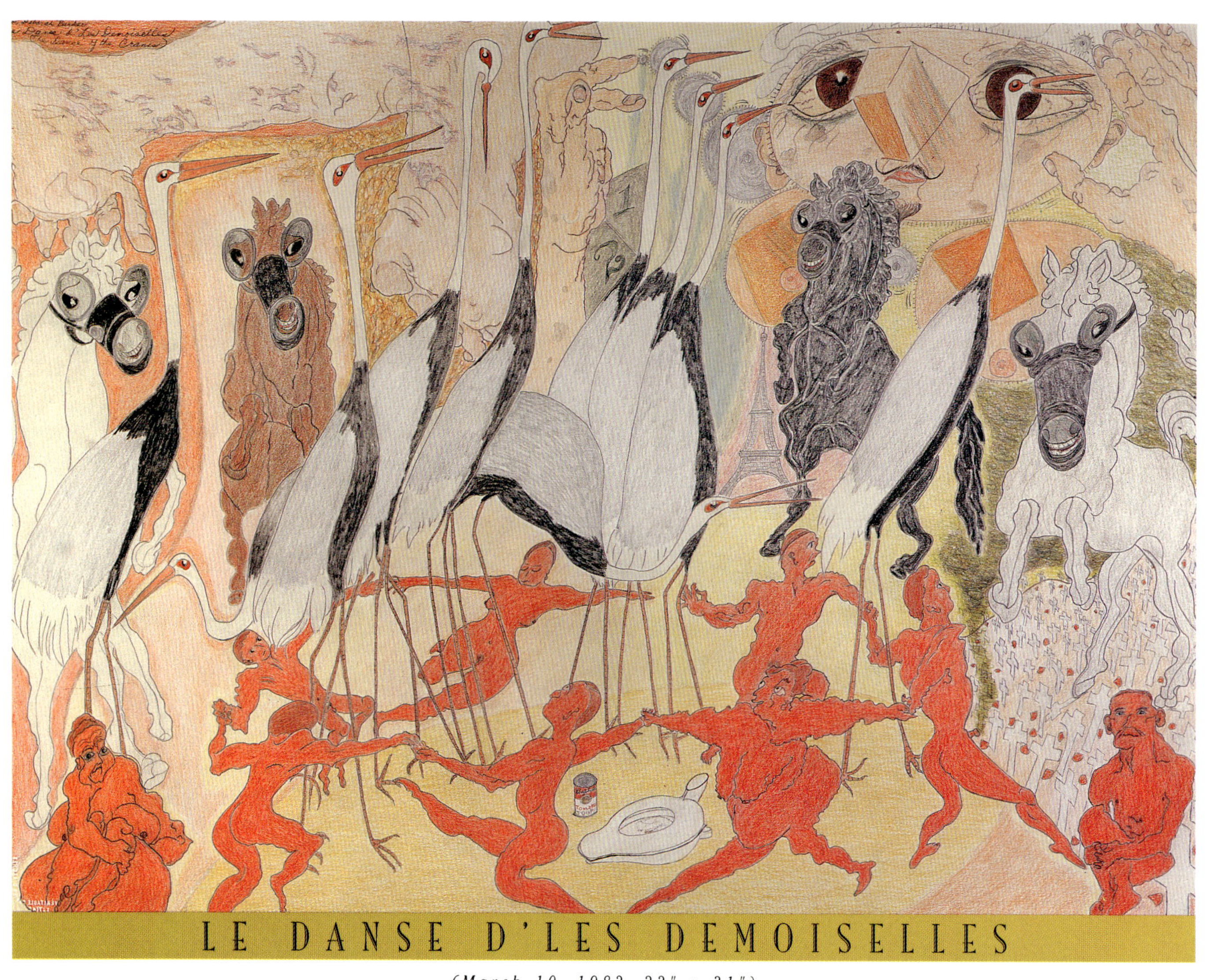

LE DANSE D'LES DEMOISELLES

(March 10, 1982, 22" x 31")

(Based on an adult education course in modern art history which the artist took.
Instructor: Deborah Barker, to whom the artist gave the drawing)

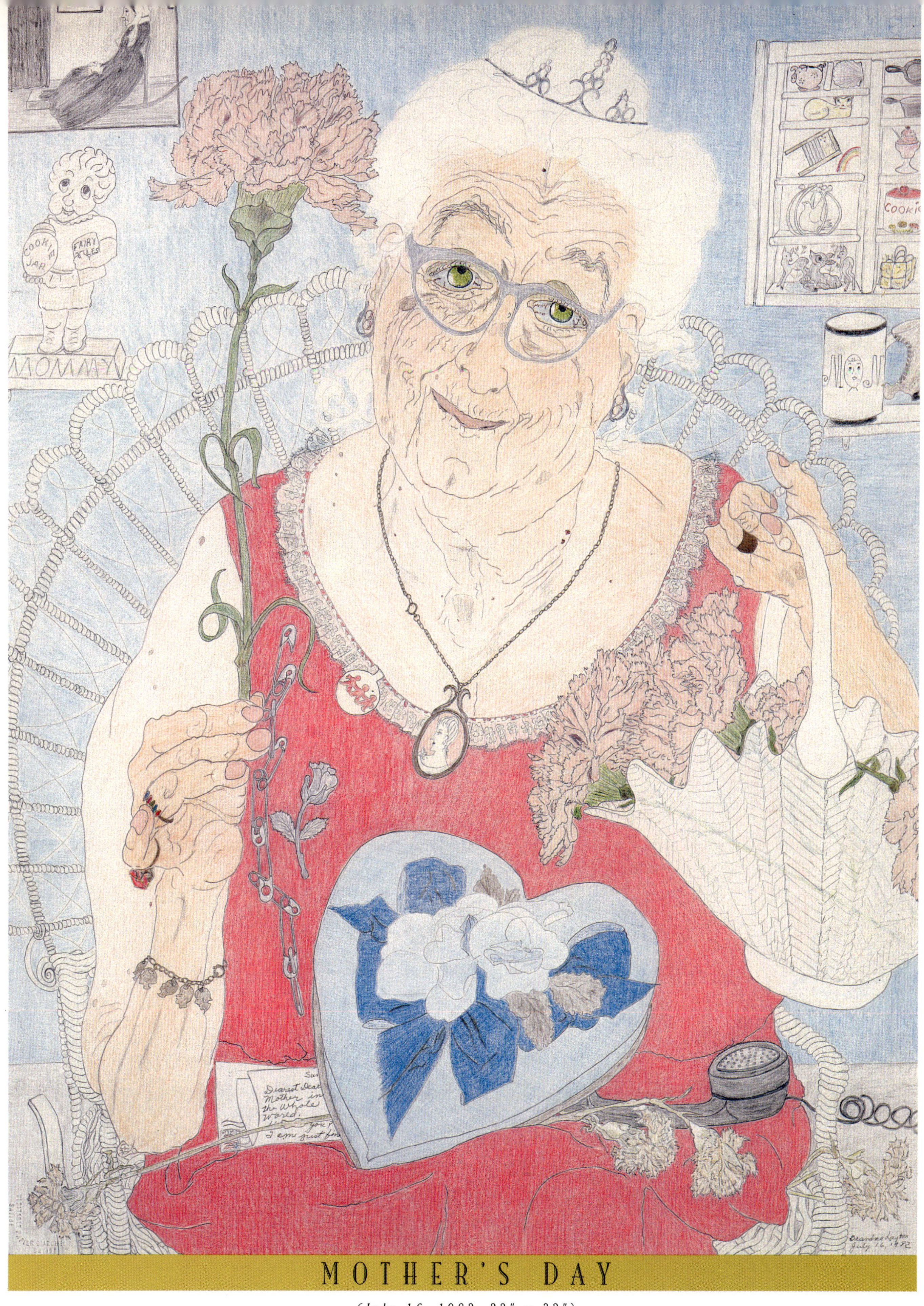

M O T H E R ' S   D A Y

(July 16, 1982, 22" x 32")

"*Here sits the Matriarch on her throne, taking, taking, yet demanding more. I call this my sick cow look.***"**

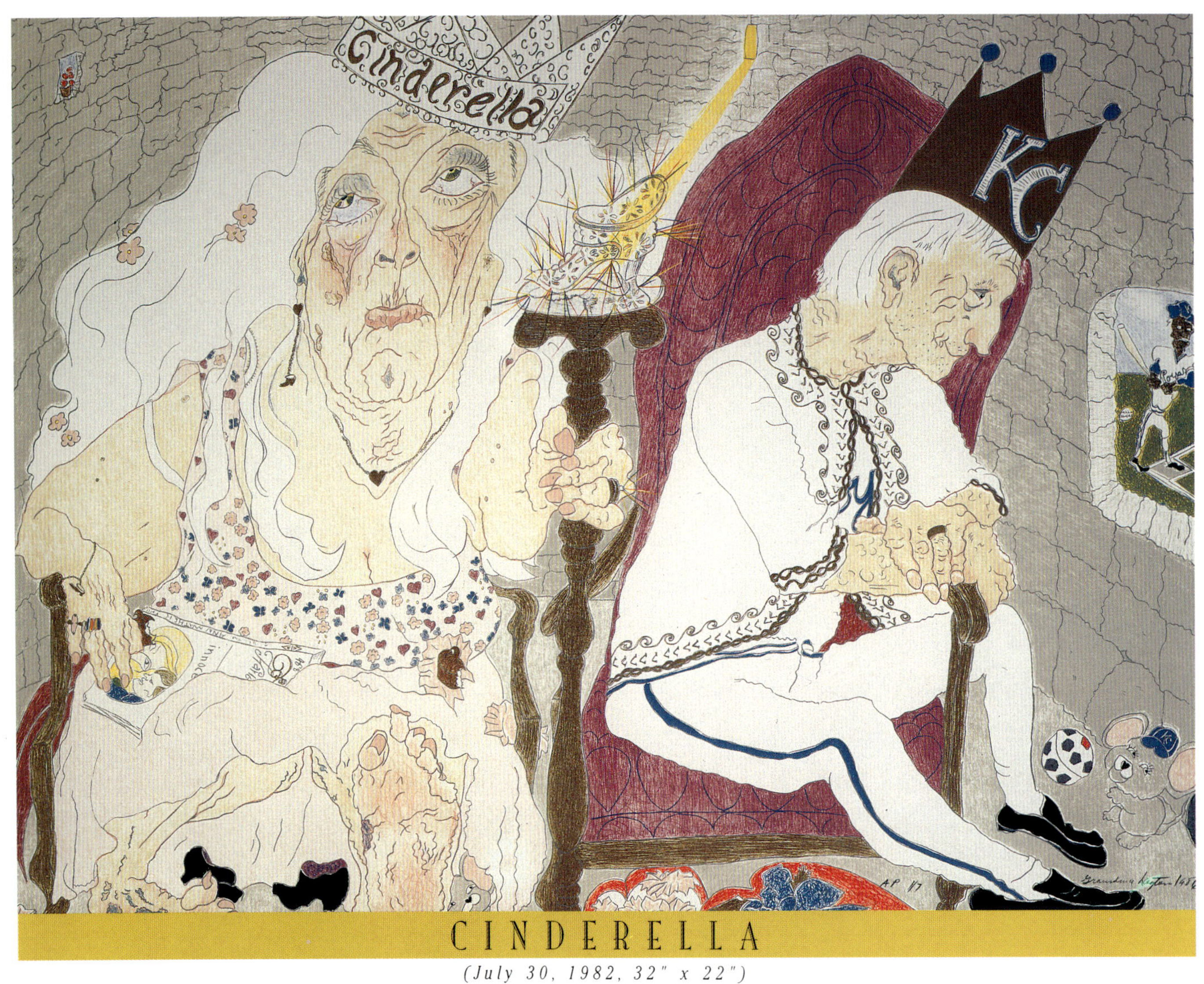

C I N D E R E L L A

(July 30, 1982, 32" x 22")

"*Fairy tales end. 'Cinderella and her prince get married and live happily ever after.' Not necessarily so.
He sits there, glued to the television set. She pouts, feeling neglected. She consoles herself with
chocolates, romance novels, and the thought that she is a pretty little thing whose
tiny pink foot slips easily into the treasured glass slipper.*"

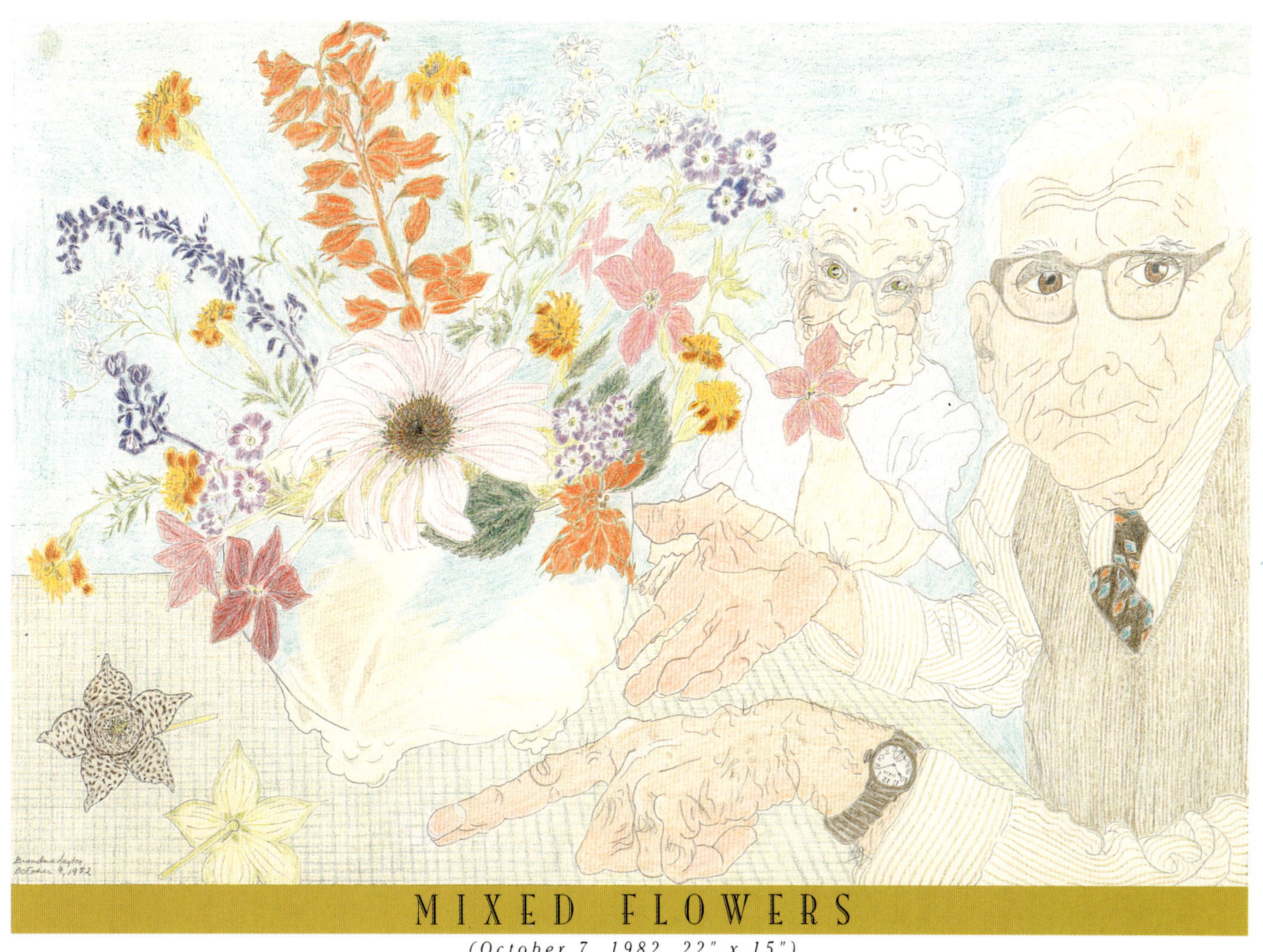

MIXED FLOWERS

(October 7, 1982, 22" x 15")

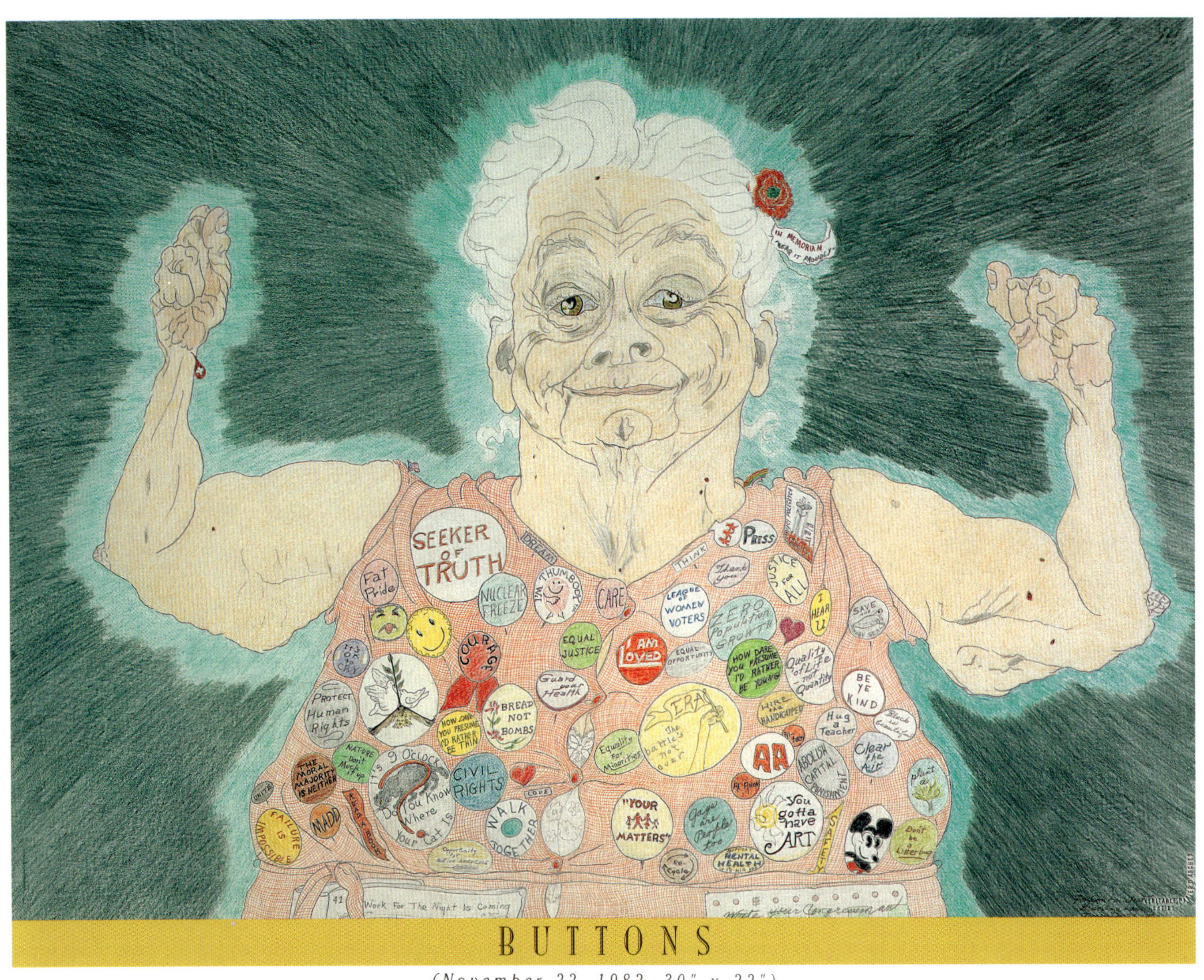

B U T T O N S

(November 22, 1982, 30" x 22")

"*Her strength is in her principles.***"**

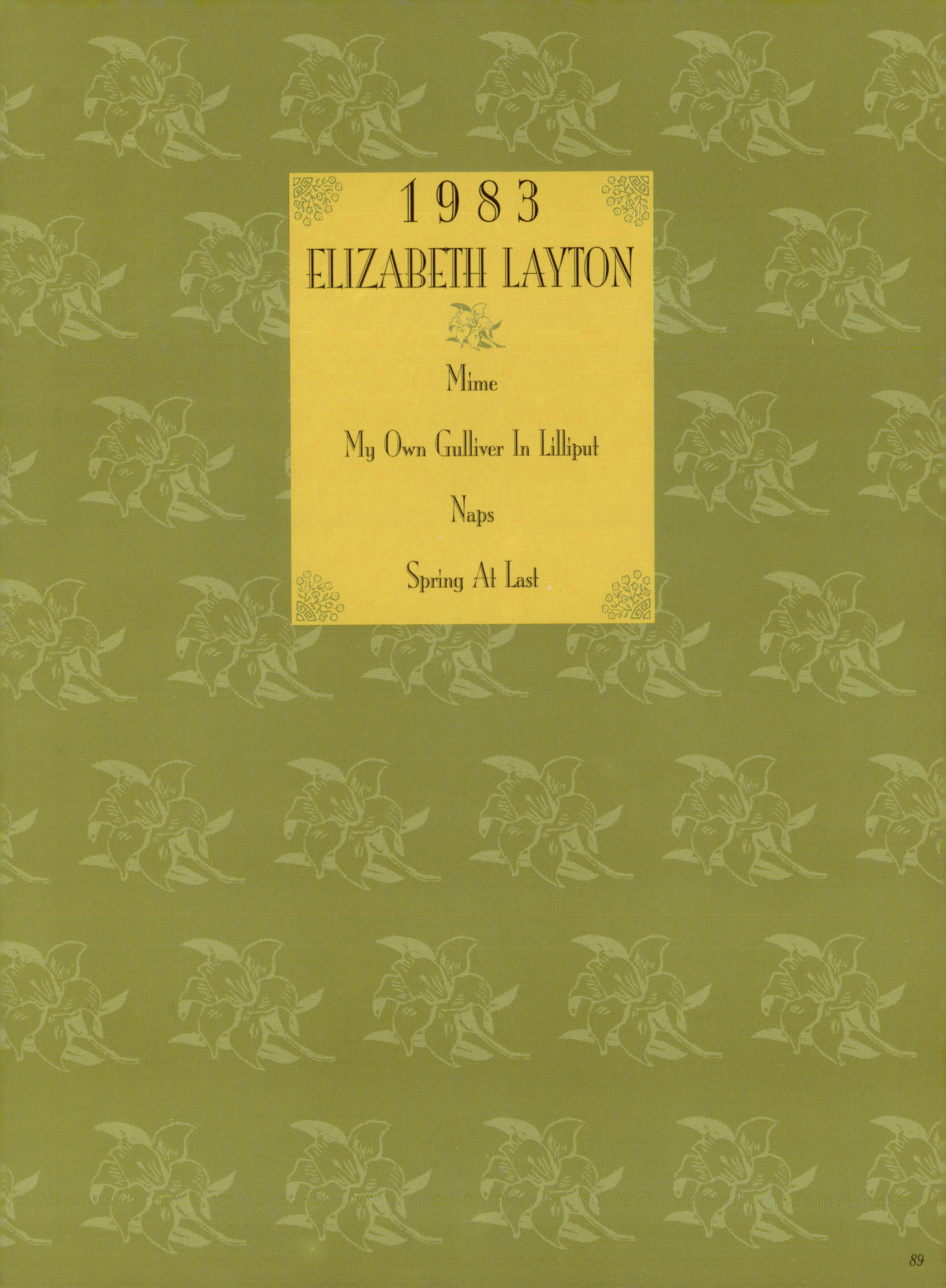

1983

ELIZABETH LAYTON

Mime

My Own Gulliver In Lilliput

Naps

Spring At Last

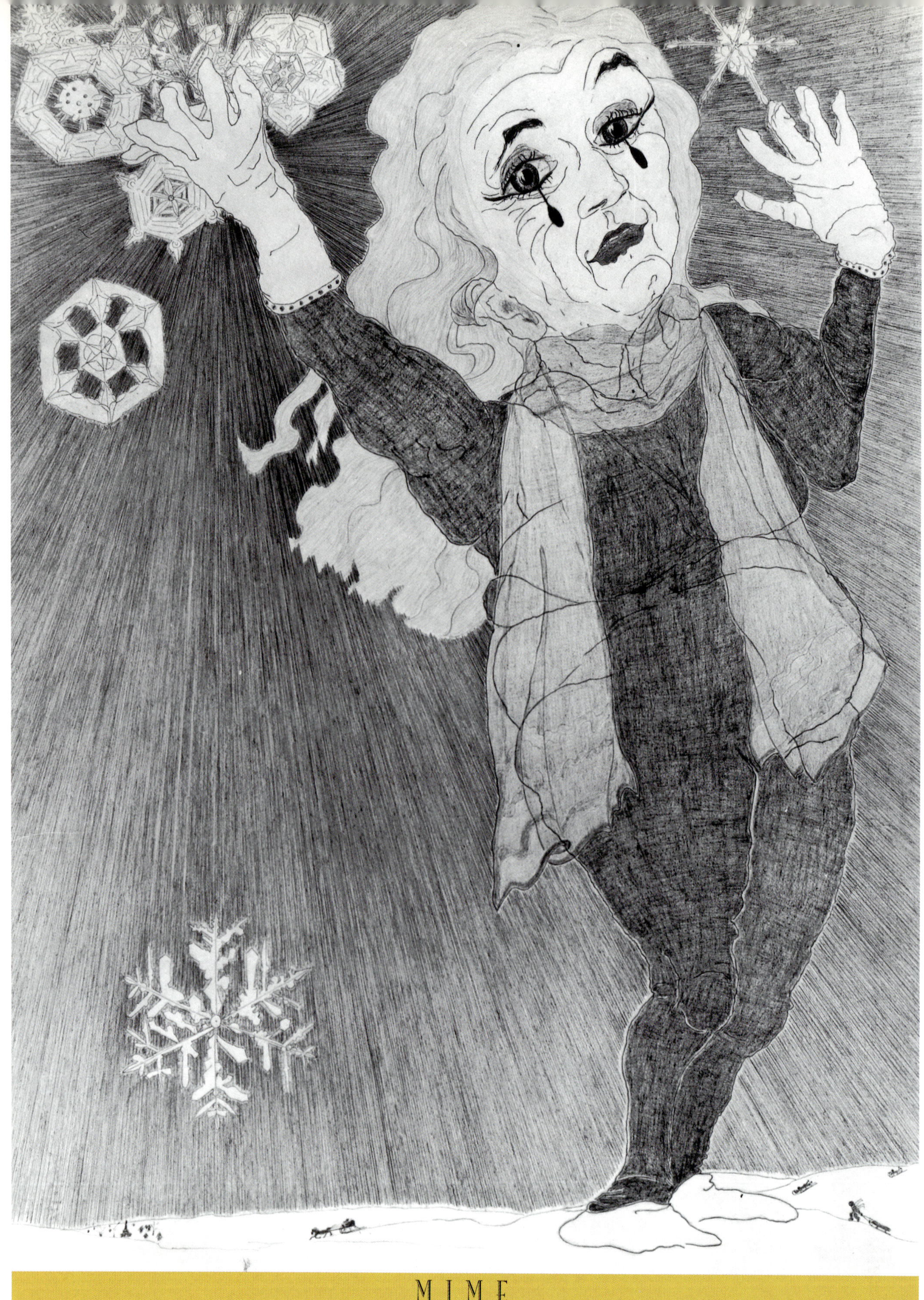

M I M E

(January 24, 1983, 22" x 30")

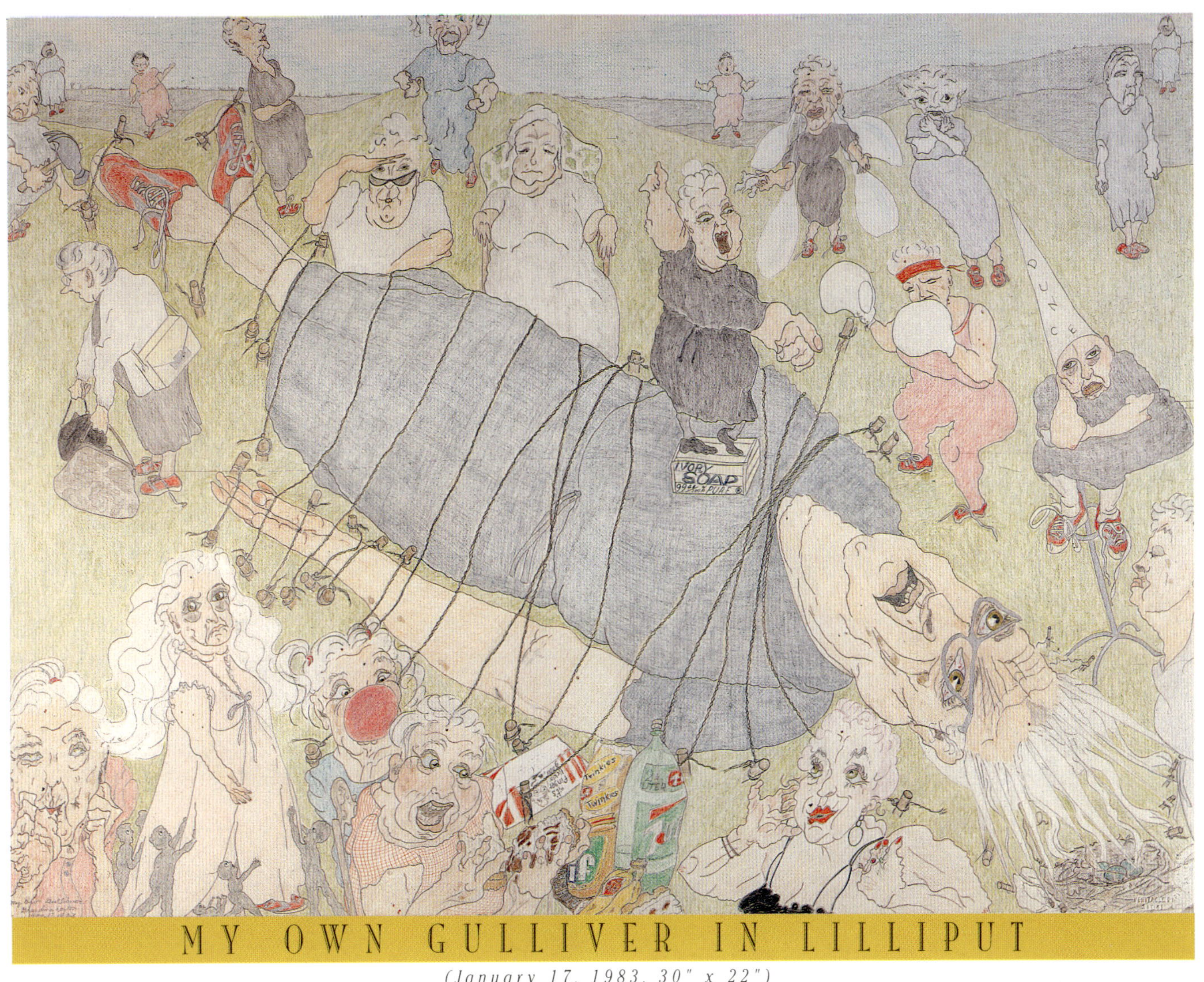

MY OWN GULLIVER IN LILLIPUT

(January 17, 1983, 30" x 22")

66 *Oh, me! What she couldn't do if so many characteristics didn't hold her down. Sexuality, gluttony, her childish ways, motherhood, her infantile habits, greed. She's stuck up, has temper tantrums, is self-righteous, lazy and sheds crocodile tears. She's timid, quarrelsome and full of hate. From her soapbox her conscience (or her mother) berails [sic] and blames her. She's idiotic and does stupid things. She looks down her nose at herself, a poor self-image.* 99

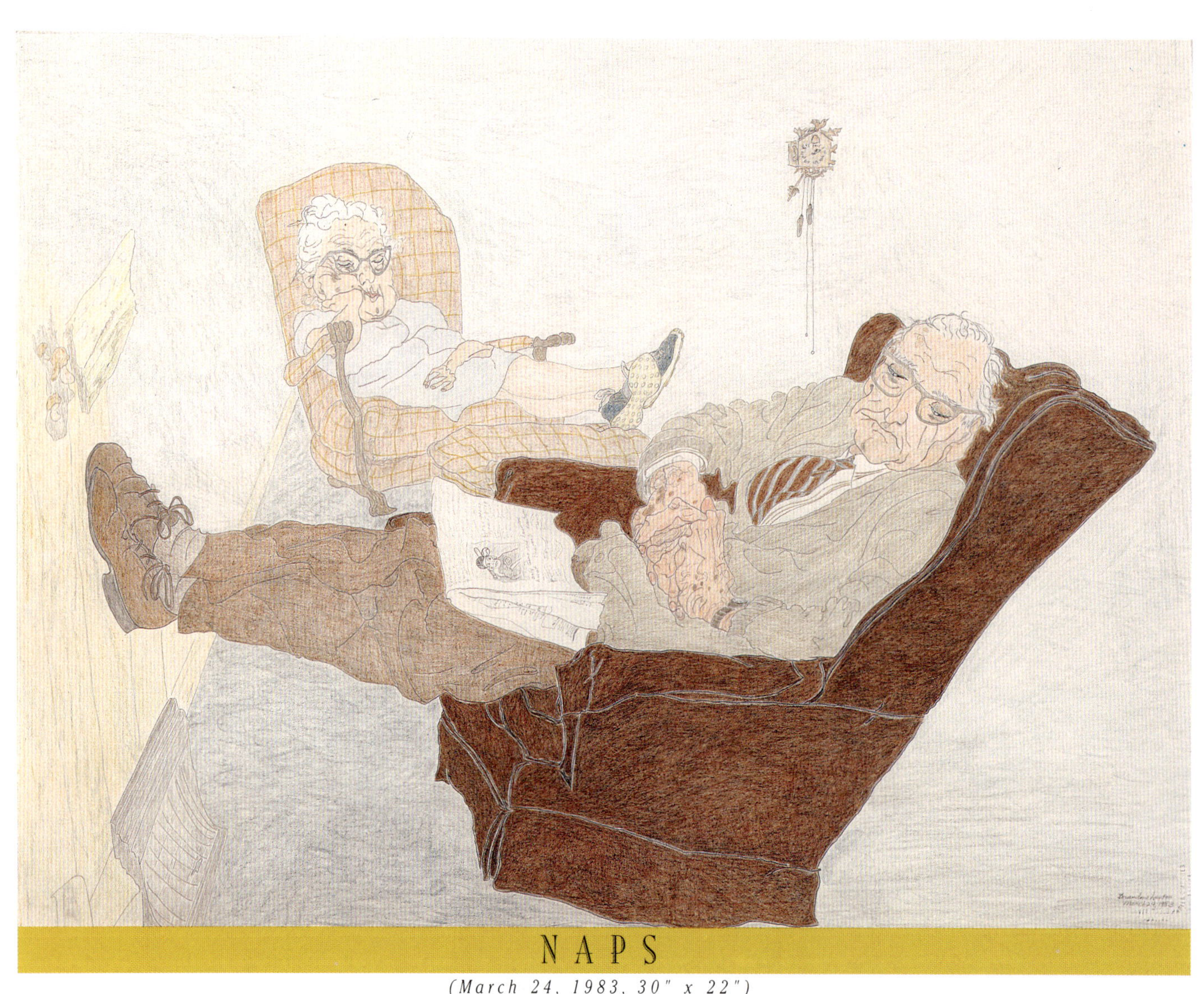

N A P S

(March 24, 1983, 30" x 22")

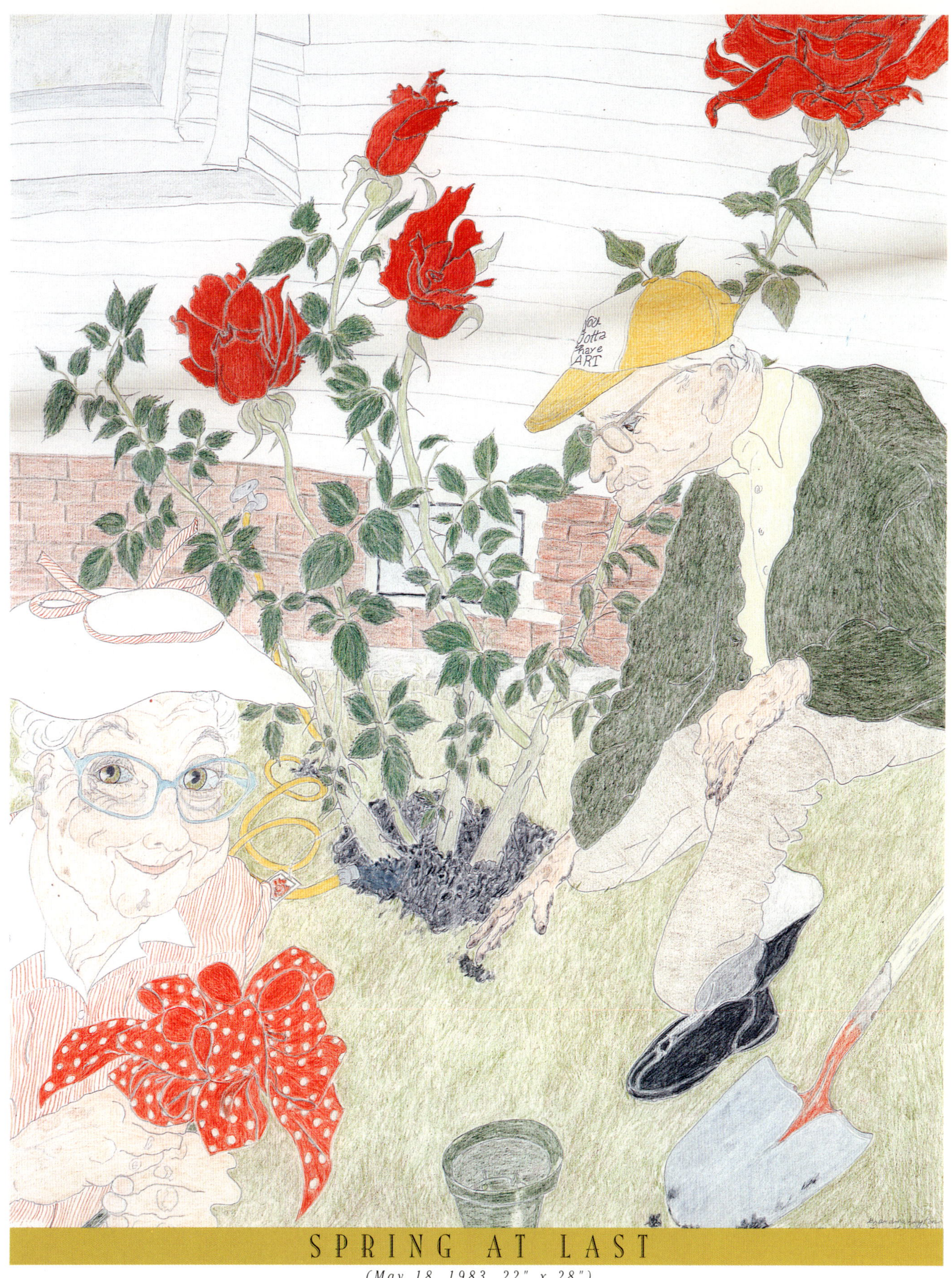

SPRING AT LAST

(May 18, 1983, 22" x 28")

"*The red rosebush, a gift, came all abloom this way. We just set it to the ground. To be very truthful, a grandson dug the hole. He just doesn't show in the picture.*"

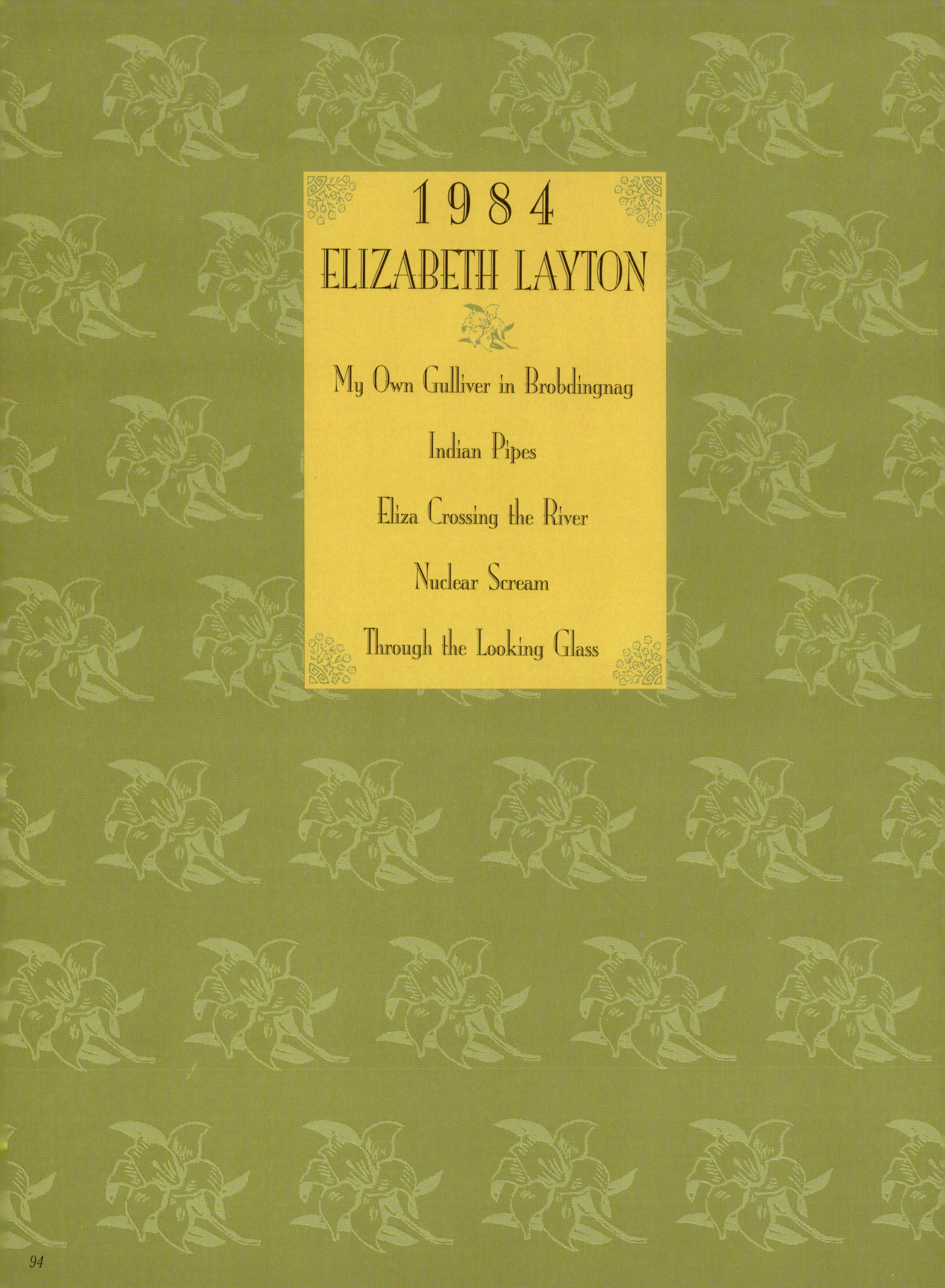

1 9 8 4

ELIZABETH LAYTON

My Own Gulliver in Brobdingnag

Indian Pipes

Eliza Crossing the River

Nuclear Scream

Through the Looking Glass

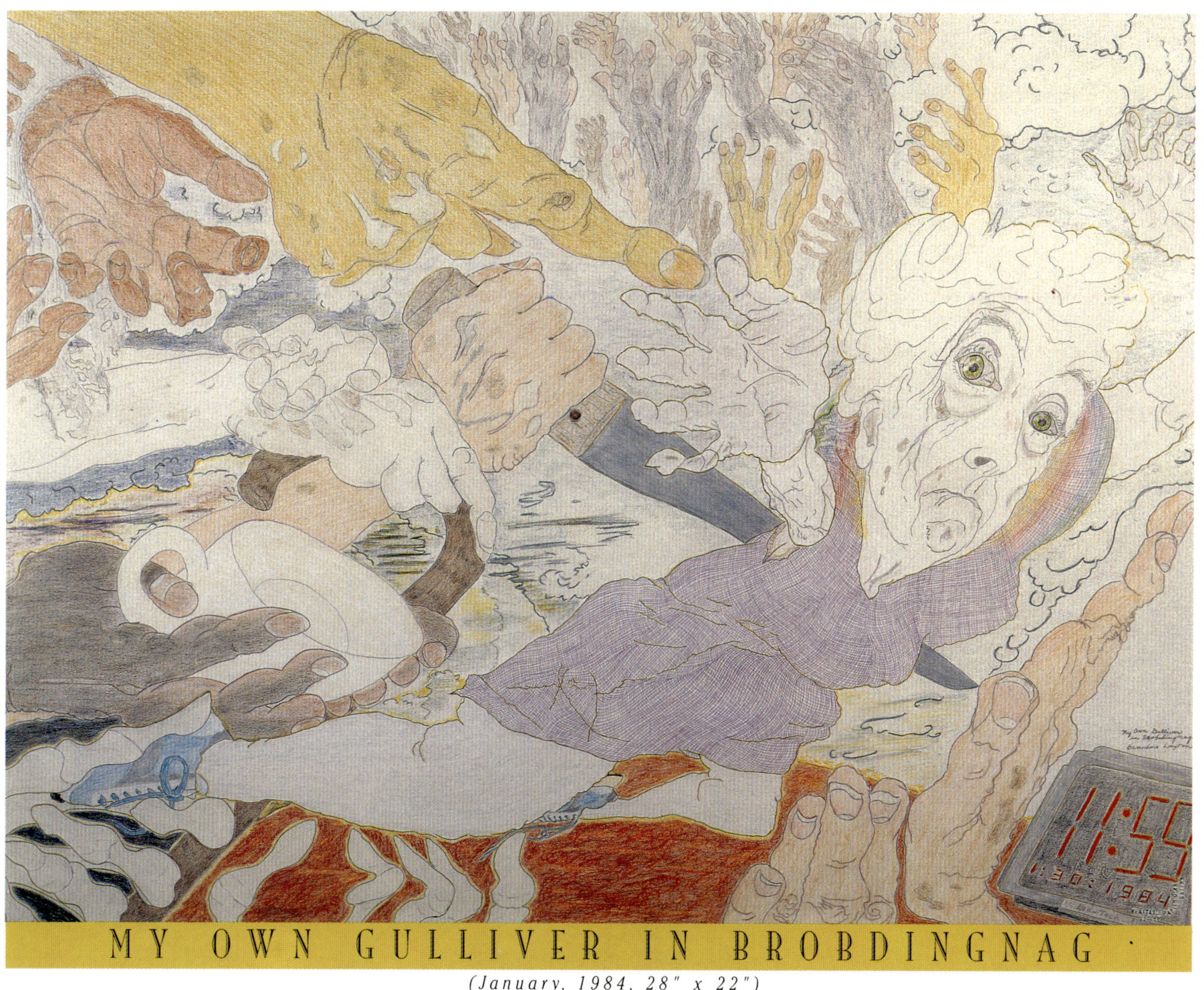

MY OWN GULLIVER IN BROBDINGNAG ·

(January, 1984, 28" x 22")

❝ *These are things that overwhelm her, still she does the best she can. She has one foot in the grave.*
Hunger, infirmities and poverty nag. Guilt points to blame and shame. Irretractable pain slashes her.
The pitiful plights of others haunt her. Isolation and loneliness wrack her. **❞**

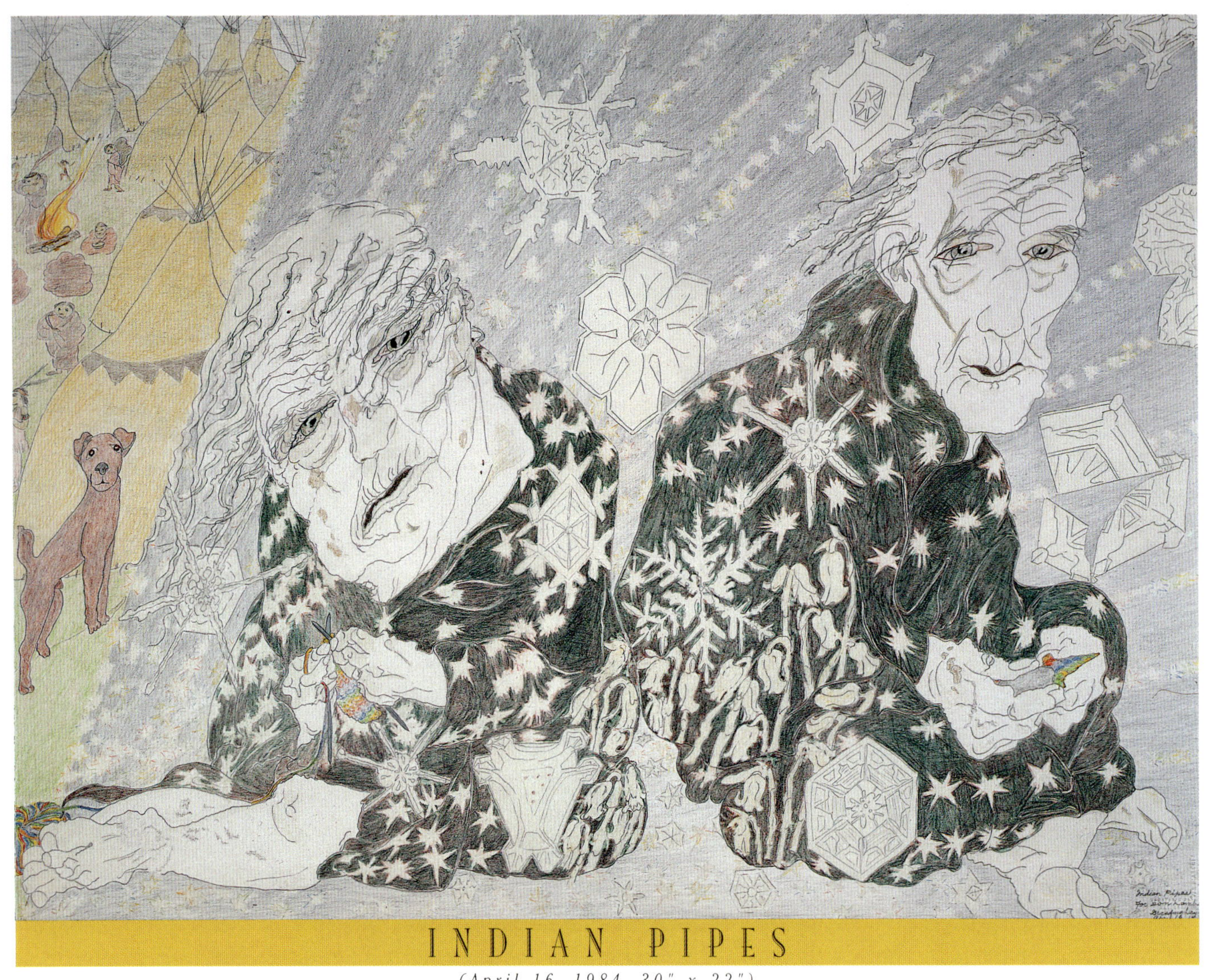

I N D I A N   P I P E S

(April 16, 1984, 30" x 22")

"*It is told that an old Indian, as his time to die drew near, went out, or was put out,*
from the teepees to the mercy of the elements.

Society tends to overlook the productivity that can continue until a person's death.
At the same time, it is the responsibility of the old people to be as productive as they can in whatever ways,
for as long as they can. Even a smile in thanks.

The rainbowed colors, to me, mean hope. Hope and wisdom go hand-in-hand.

Death zeroes in on the old people. Not something black and ugly but a silvery crystal softness.

The title, Indian Pipes, comes from that clutter of herbs (center foreground) which feed on dead
or decaying matter. Each pipe is a ghostlike, waxy-white, leafless plant. Each stem bears
one bell-shaped flower. The plant looks like the stem and bowl of a clay pipe. They are helpful in that they
are nature's way of cleaning up dead or decaying organic matter."

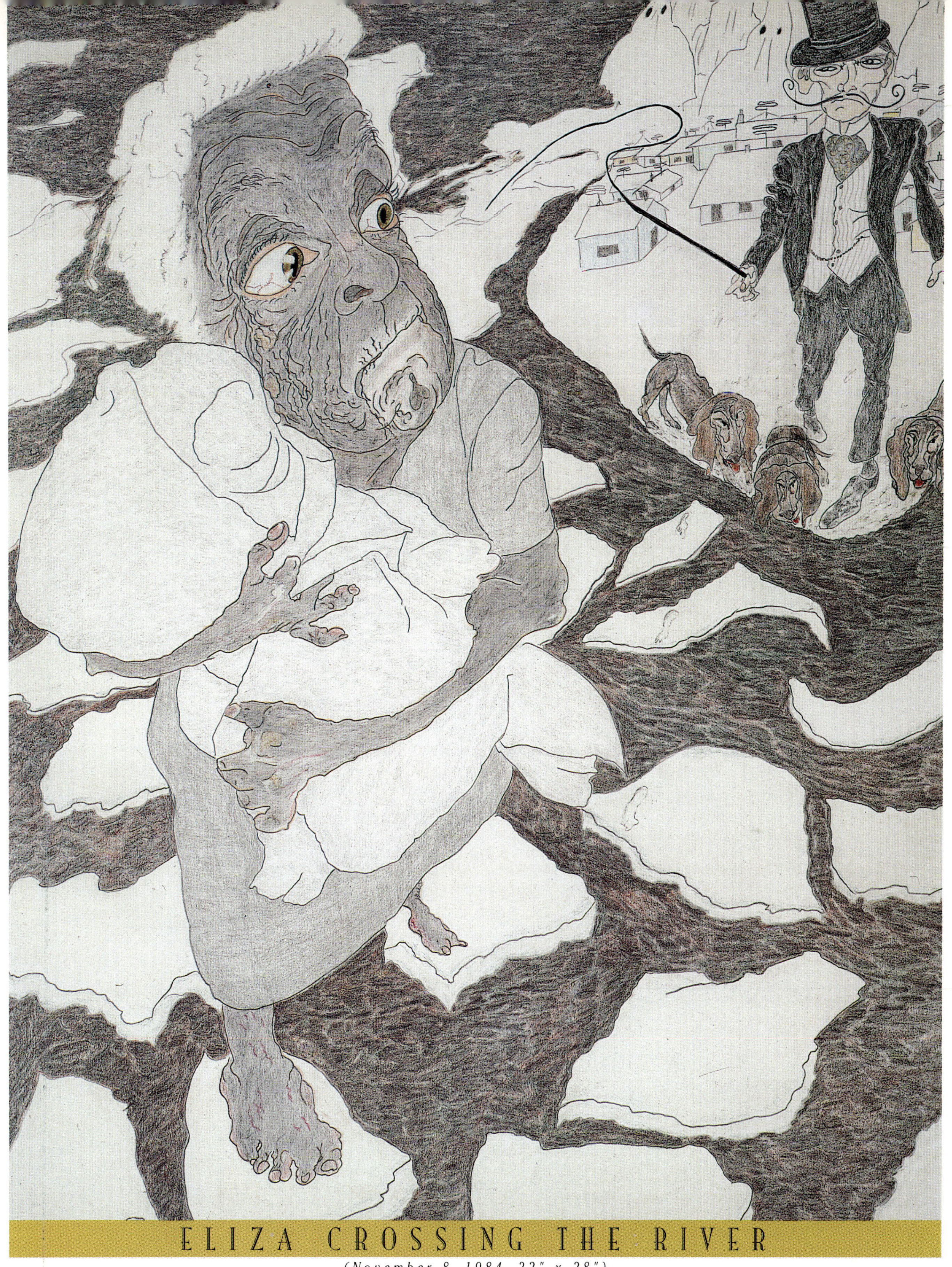

ELIZA CROSSING THE RIVER

(November 8, 1984, 22" x 28")

"*Eliza grips her child and risks their lives to escape the slave trader who has just bought the boy to sell him down the river. Eliza leaps the turbid current of the Ohio river and crosses by jumping from one ice cake to another. The trader stands on the bank afraid to follow. The houses are modern day, surburban homes, pastel colors, TV antennas, shades drawn. Unwelcoming places.*"

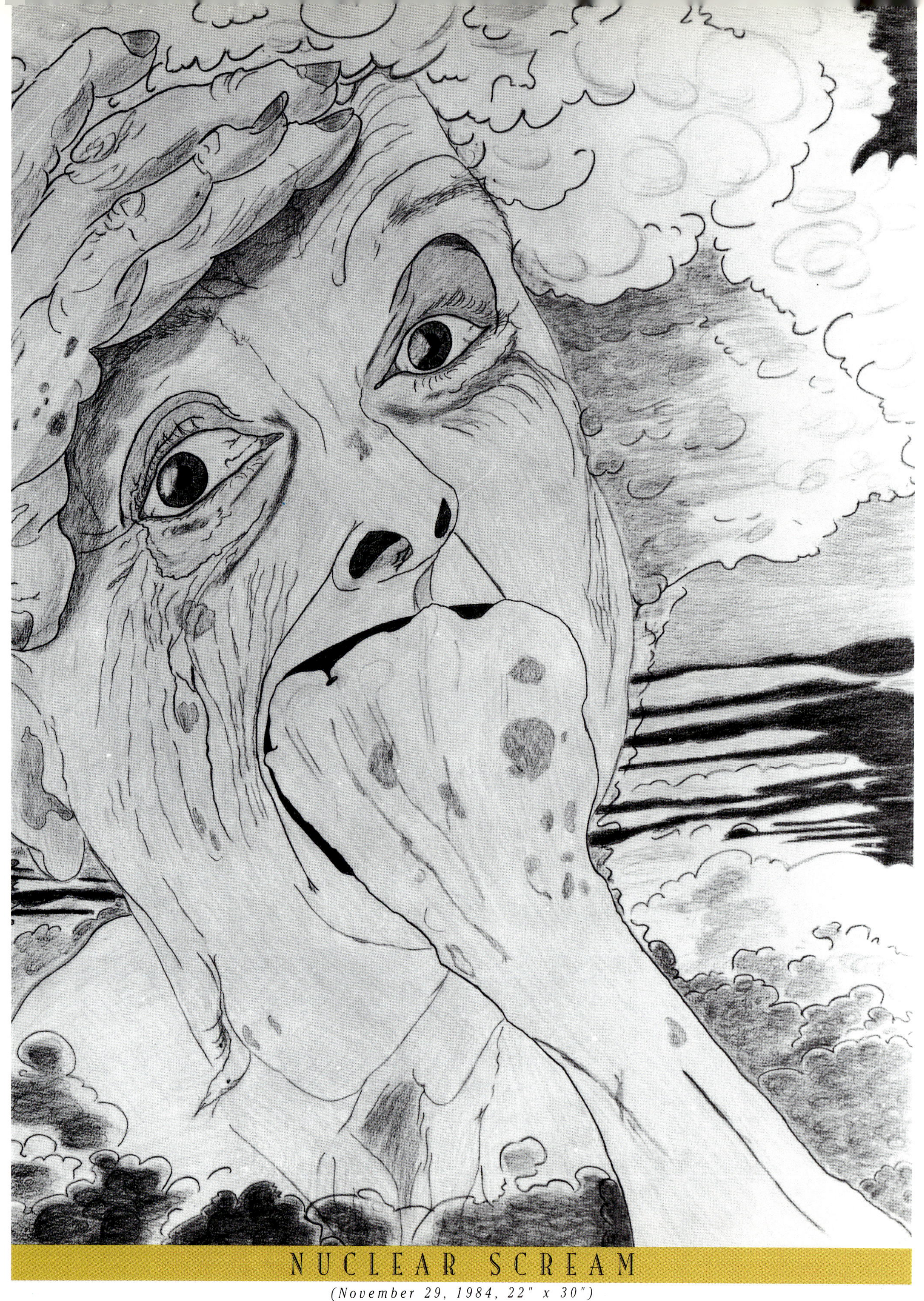

(November 29, 1984, 22" x 30")

" *Enough said.* "

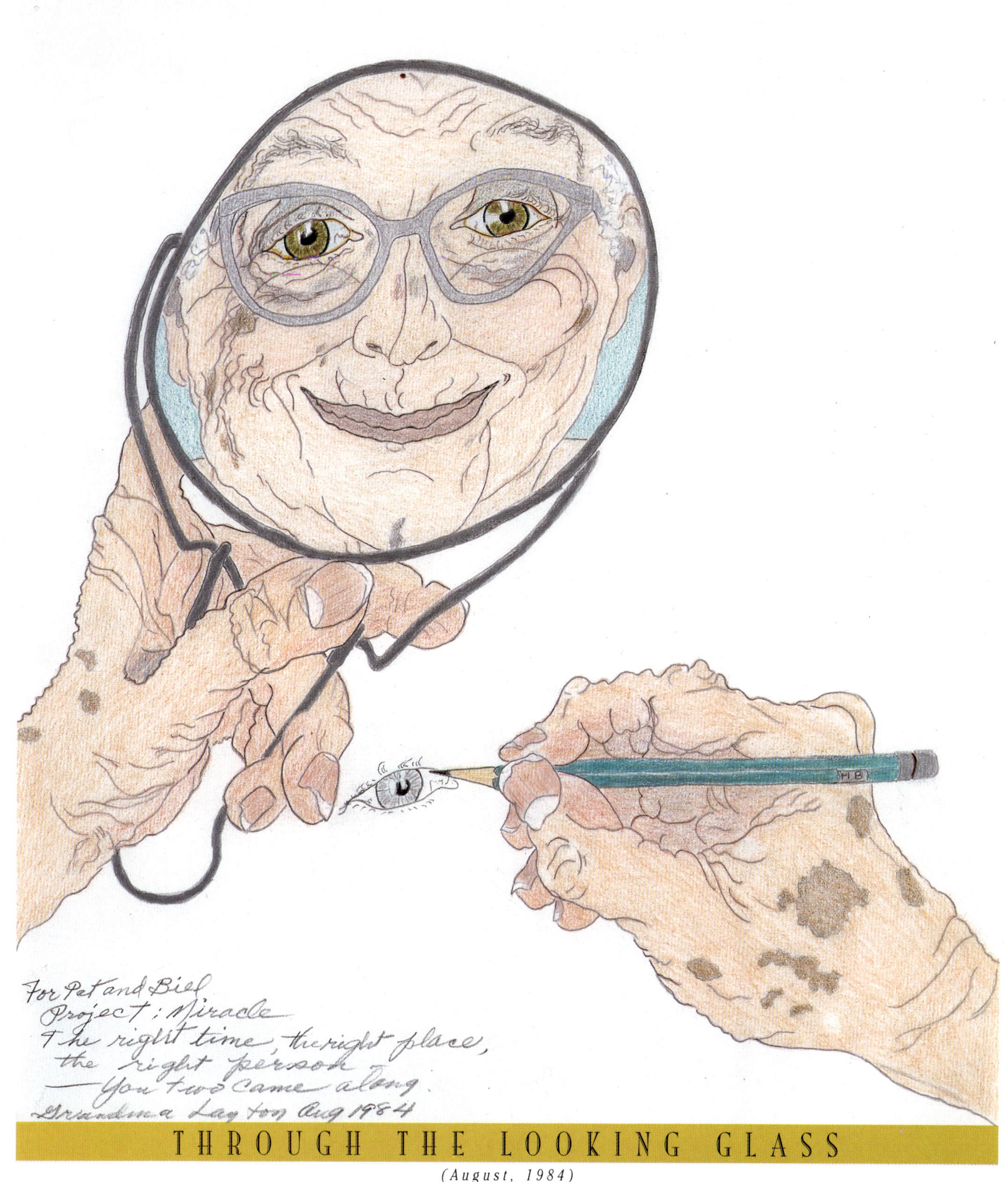

THROUGH THE LOOKING GLASS

(August, 1984)

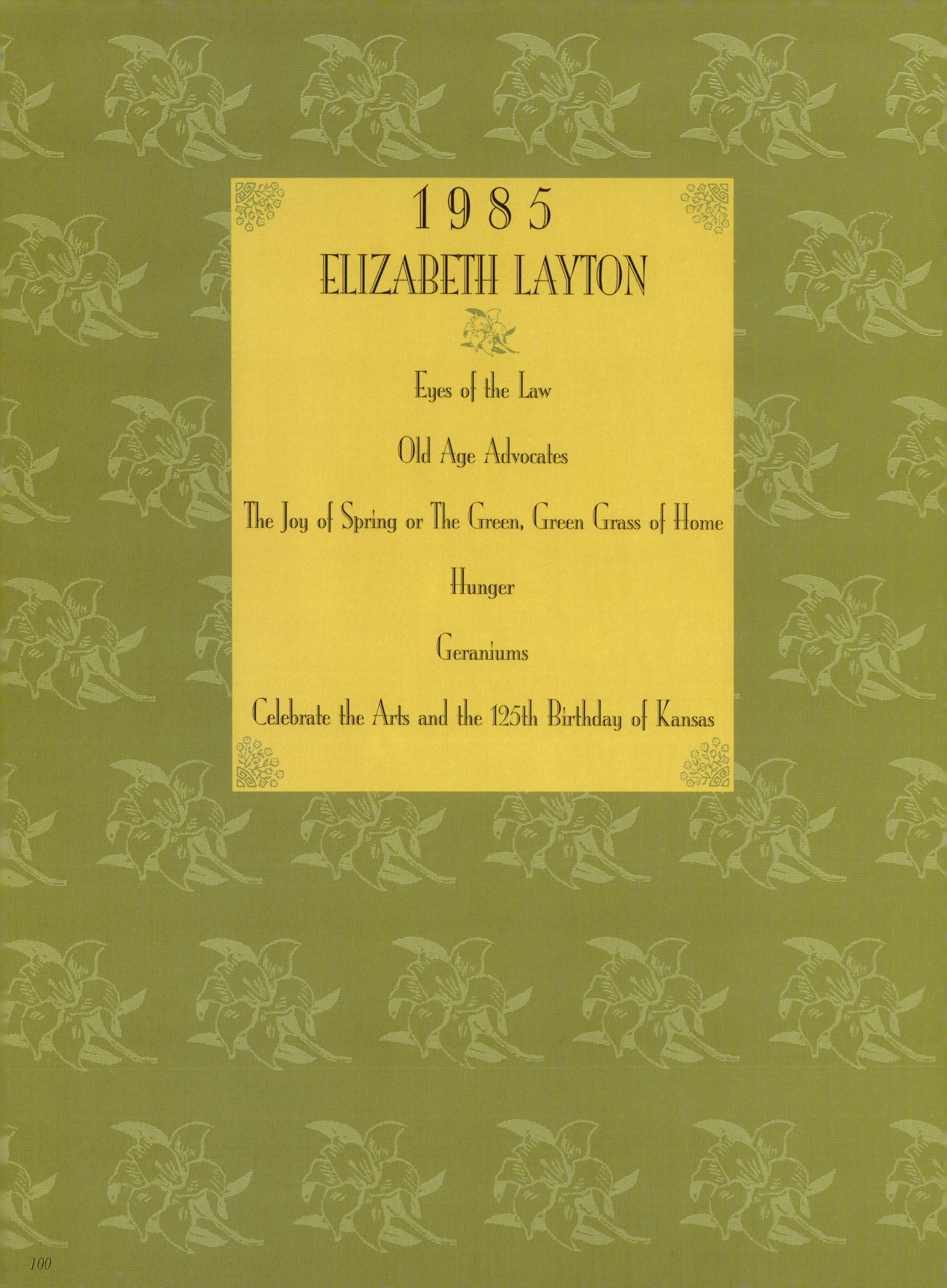

1 9 8 5
ELIZABETH LAYTON

Eyes of the Law

Old Age Advocates

The Joy of Spring or The Green, Green Grass of Home

Hunger

Geraniums

Celebrate the Arts and the 125th Birthday of Kansas

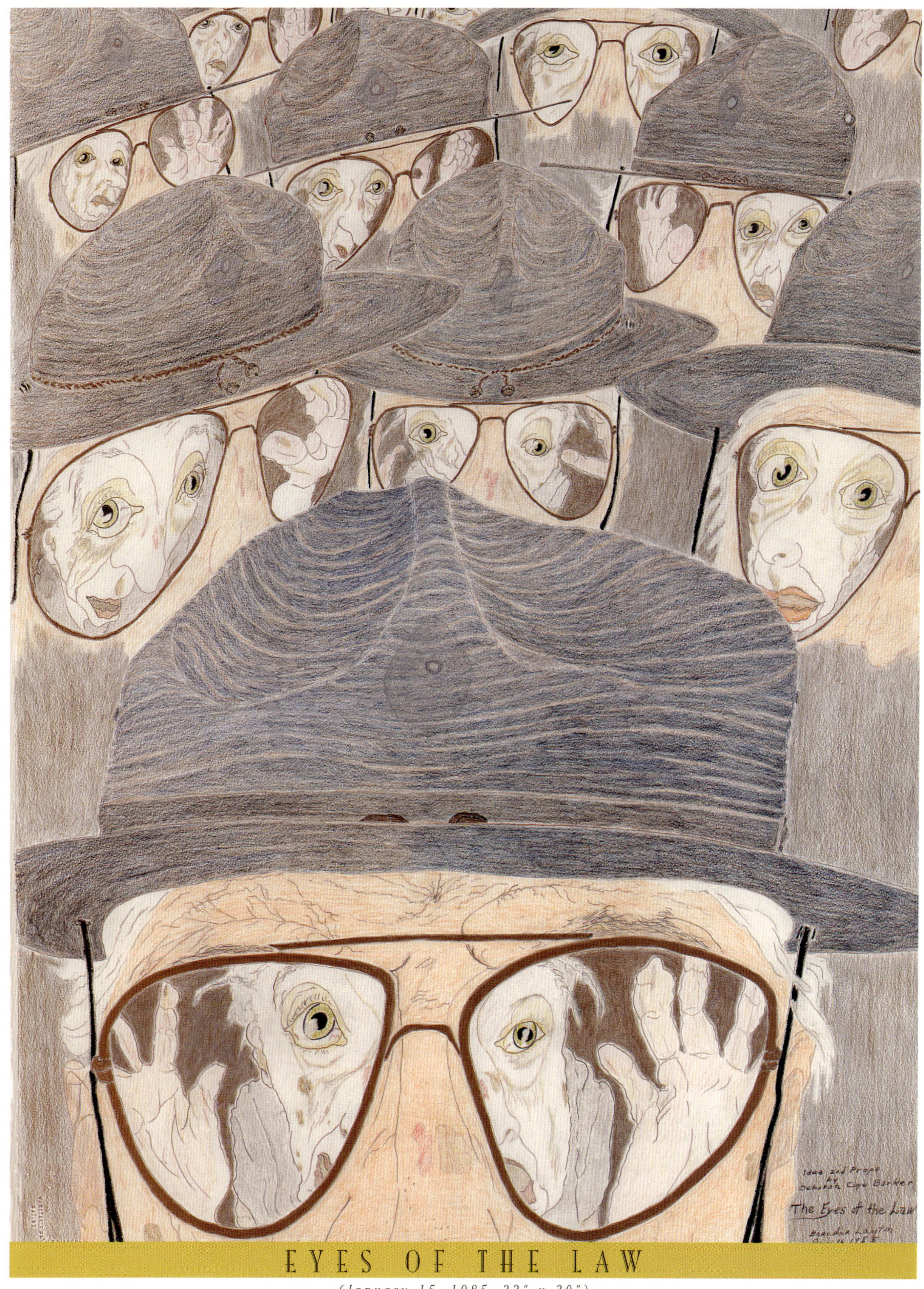

EYES OF THE LAW

(January 15, 1985, 22" x 30")

From the collection of the Spencer Museum of Art, University of Kansas, Lawrence, Kansas.

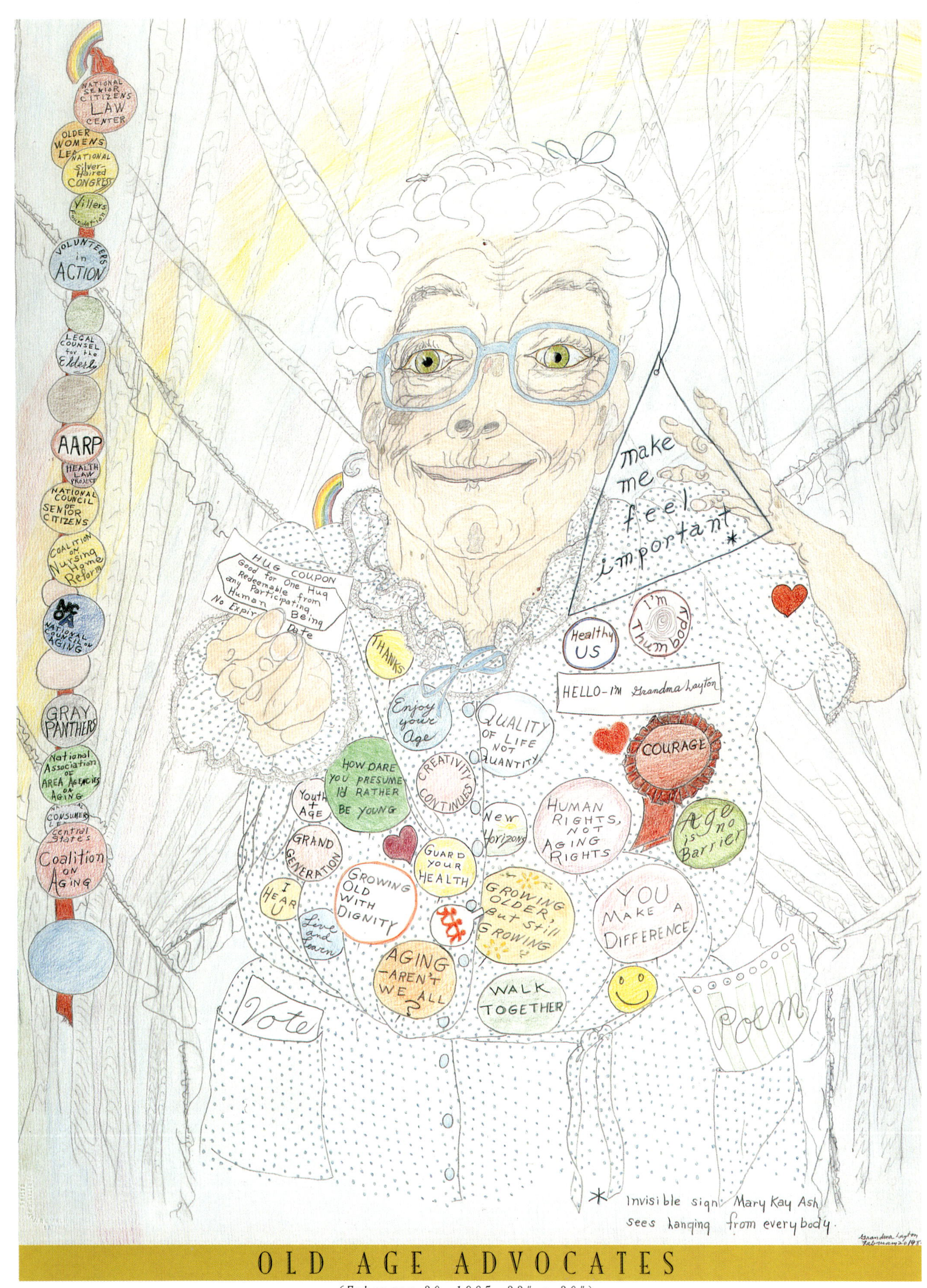

OLD AGE ADVOCATES

(February 20, 1985, 22" x 30")

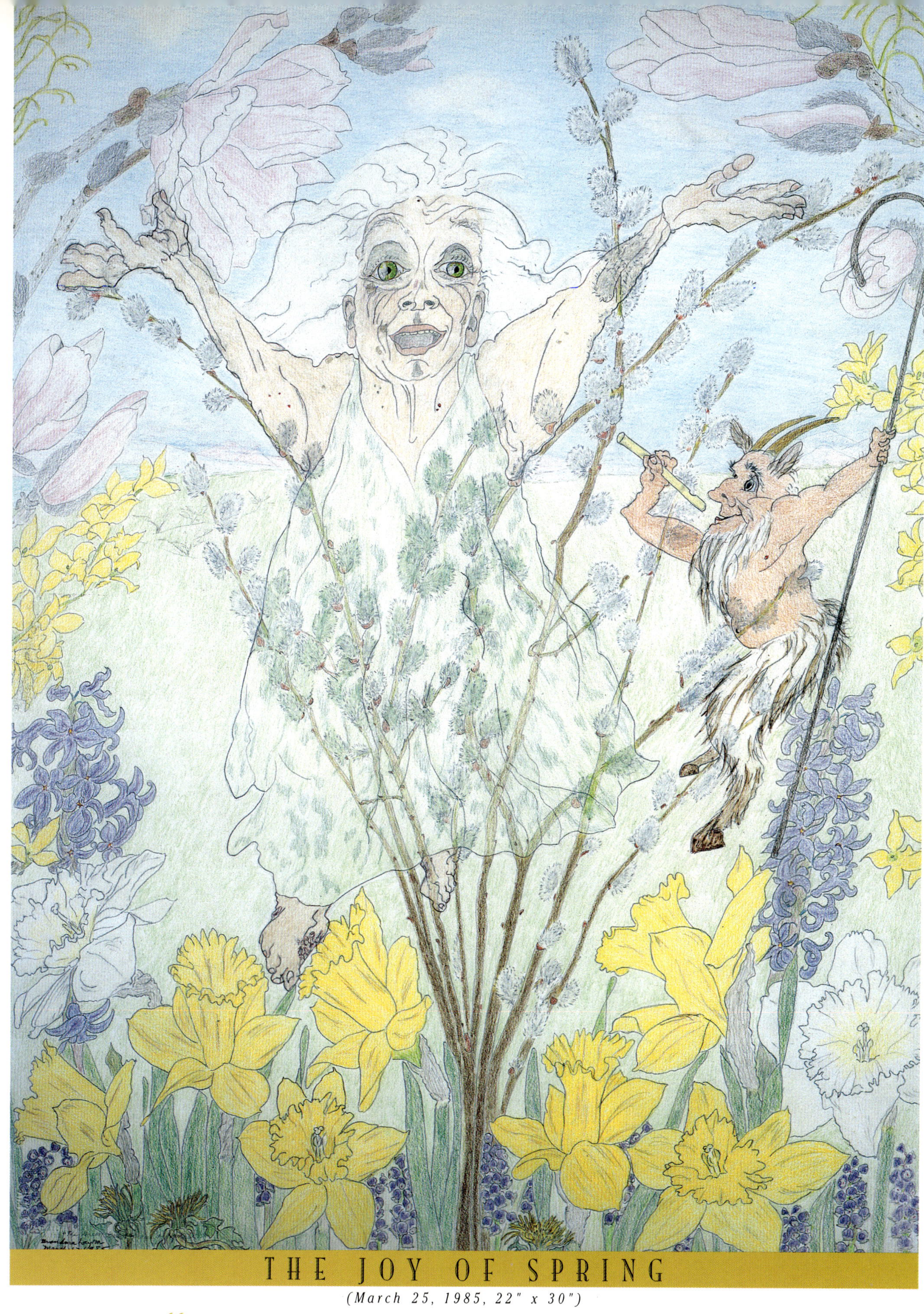

THE JOY OF SPRING

(March 25, 1985, 22" x 30")

" *Spring arrives while Pan plays his pipes, adding a touch of homesickness.* **"**

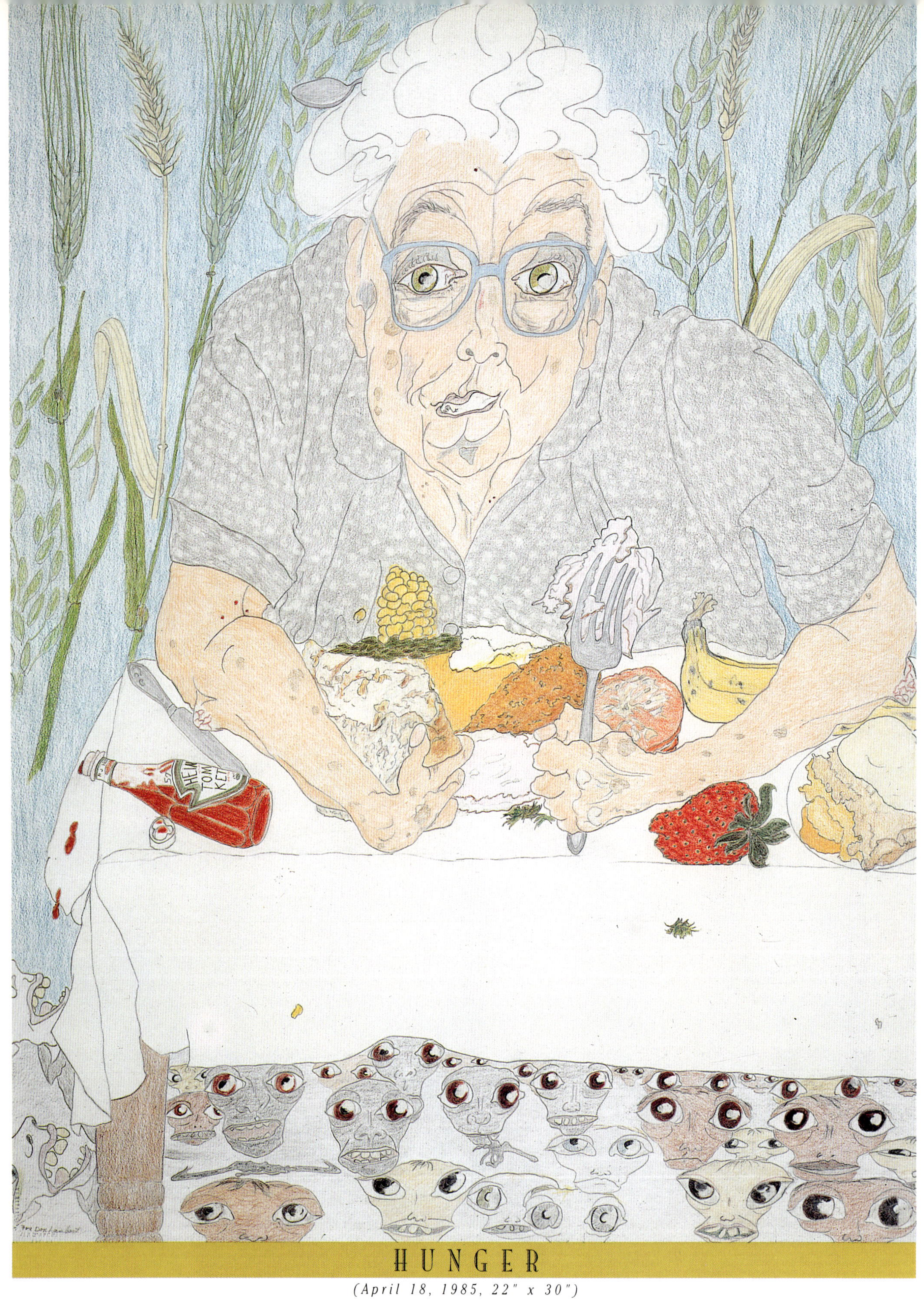

HUNGER

(April 18, 1985, 22" x 30")

"*She pigs out at her table, where a few crumbs fall and overturned catsup trickles down very slowly into hungry, open mouths.*"

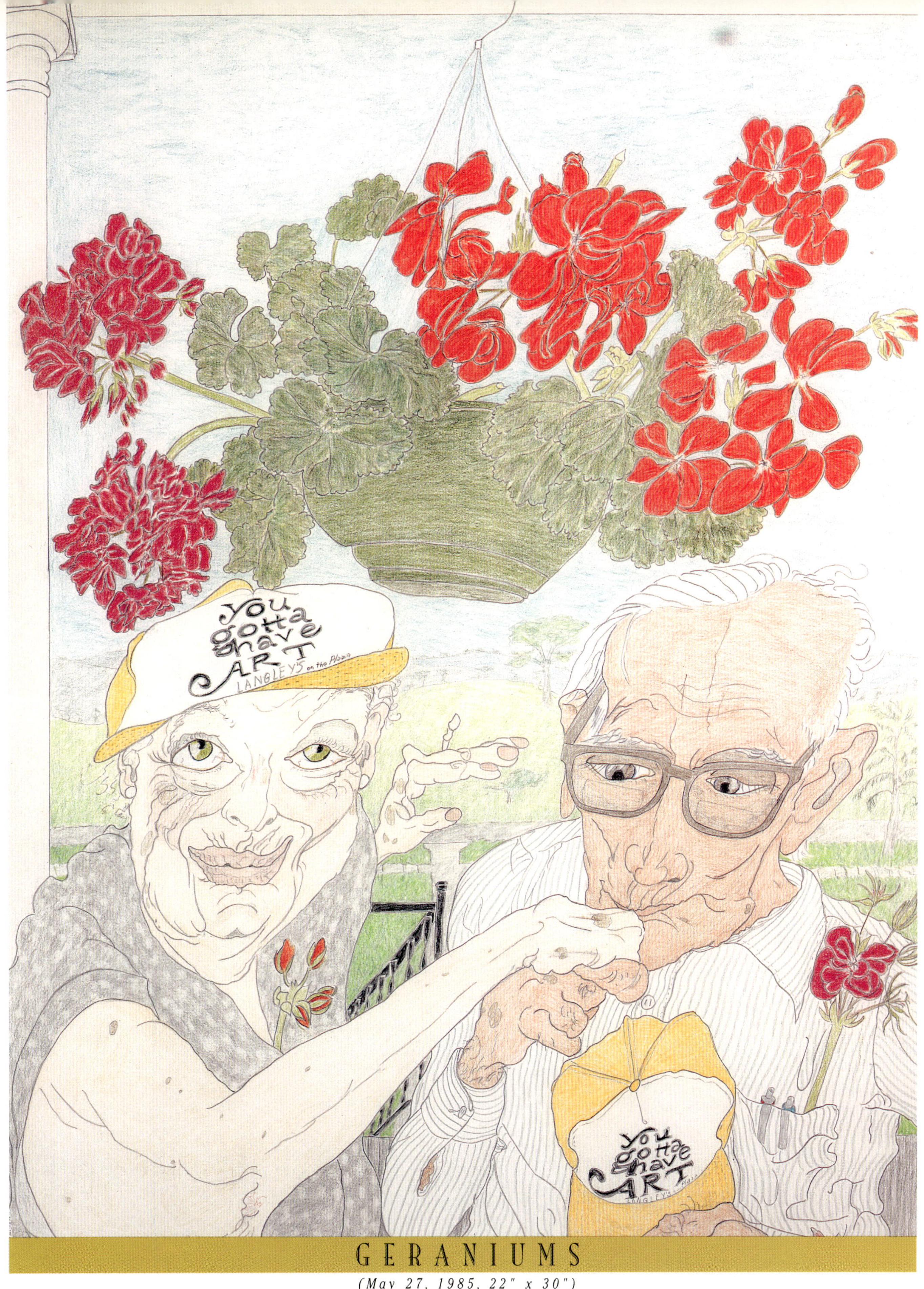

G E R A N I U M S

(May 27, 1985, 22" x 30")

From the collection of the Friends of Art, Kansas State University, Manhattan, Kansas

"A warm, summer afternoon, a stolen kiss under the basket hanging on the front porch."

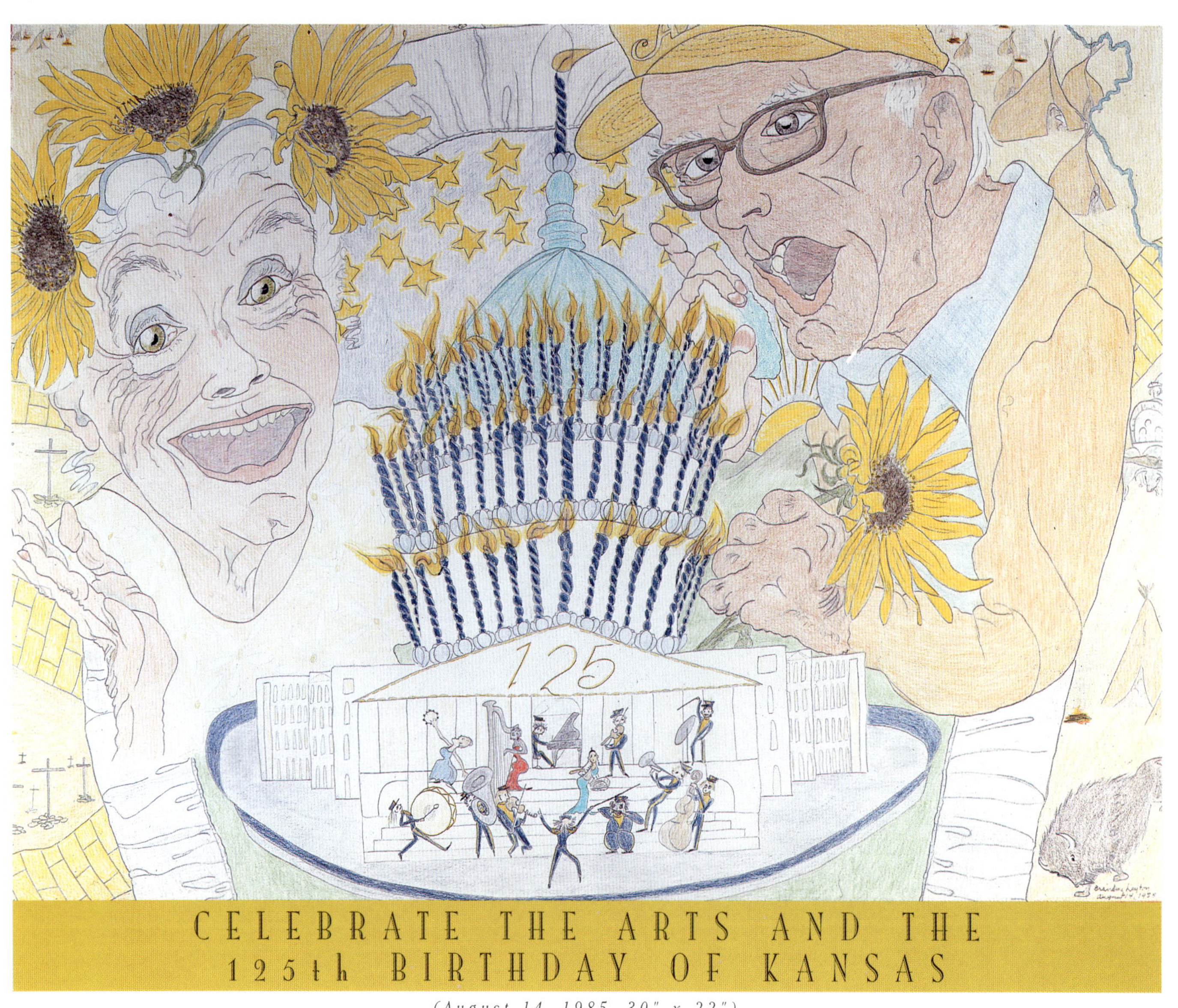

(August 14, 1985, 30" x 22")

Collection of the Kansas Museum of History, Topeka, Kansas.

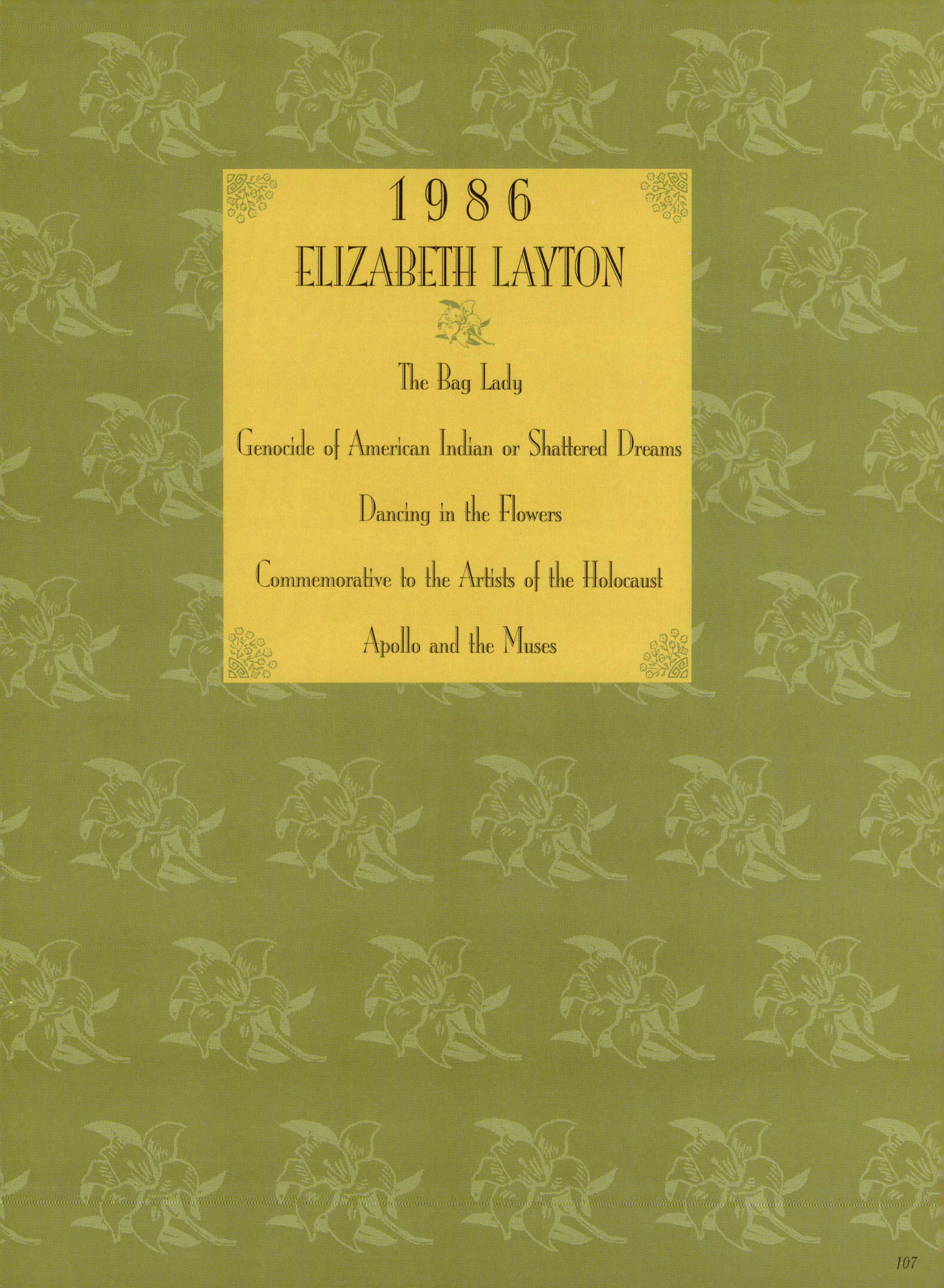

1 9 8 6
ELIZABETH LAYTON

The Bag Lady

Genocide of American Indian or Shattered Dreams

Dancing in the Flowers

Commemorative to the Artists of the Holocaust

Apollo and the Muses

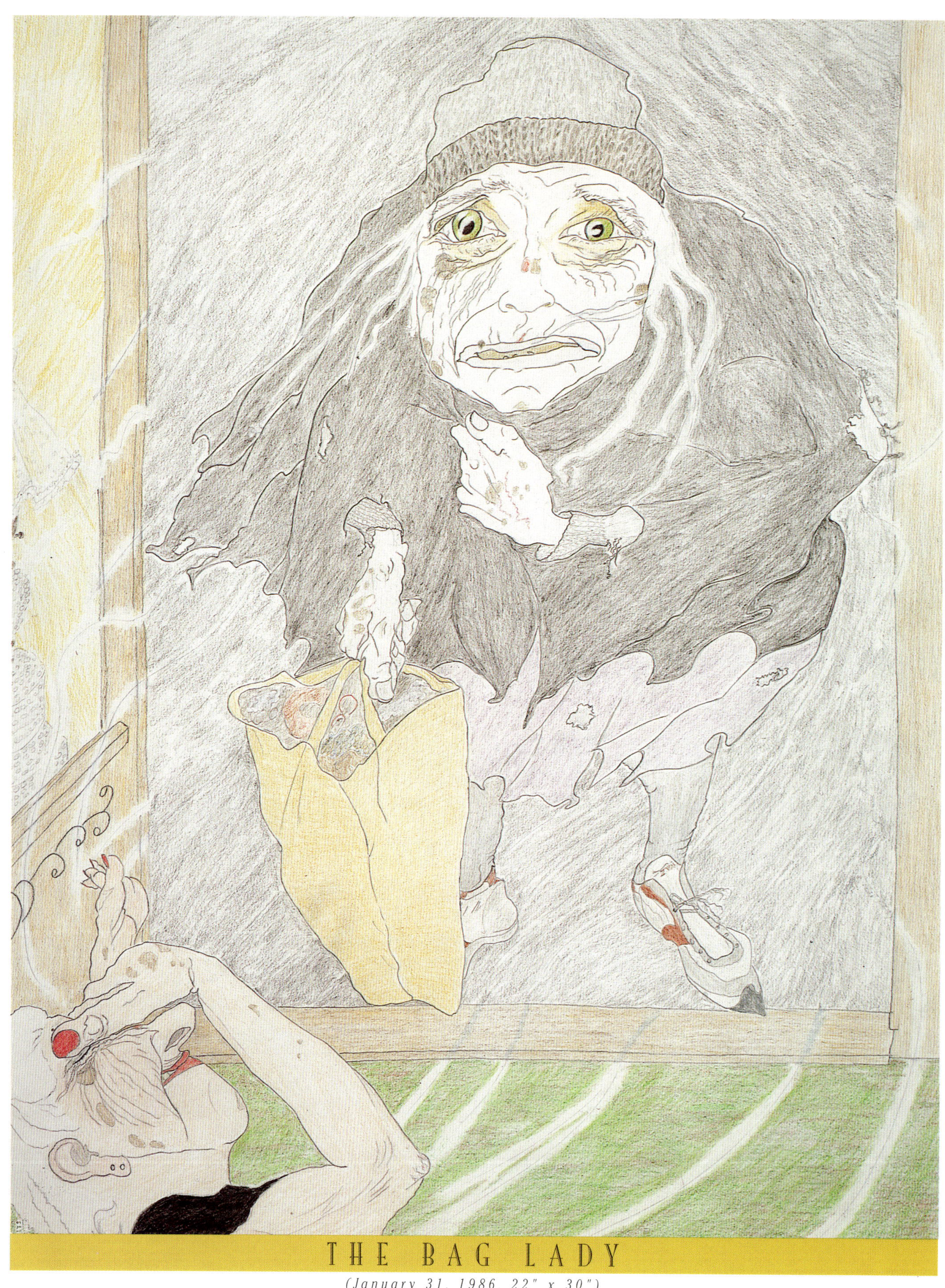

THE BAG LADY

(*January 31, 1986, 22" x 30"*)

"*This is my dormant bag lady — she disgusts me. I am afraid to look at her. I may become she at any minute.*"

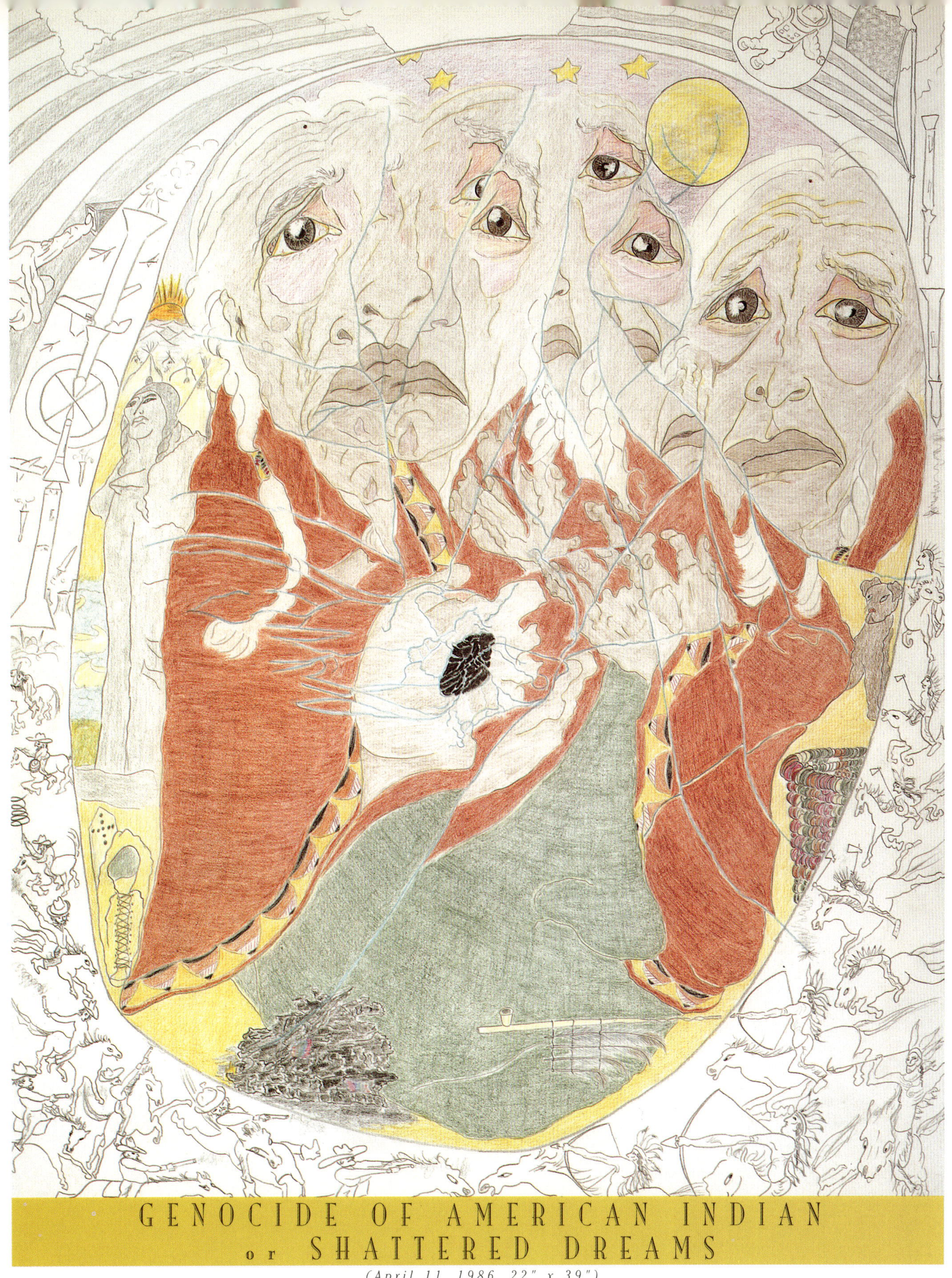

GENOCIDE OF AMERICAN INDIAN
or SHATTERED DREAMS

(April 11, 1986, 22" x 39")

"A culture within a culture. She is shattered by a mortal wound to the heart. Still she lives. As the Dakota Indian says, 'A nation is not conquered 'till the heart of its women are on the ground.' The bottom half of the border is from the black-and-white movies when the indian was always the bad man. The top half is the inhumanity of the present culture."

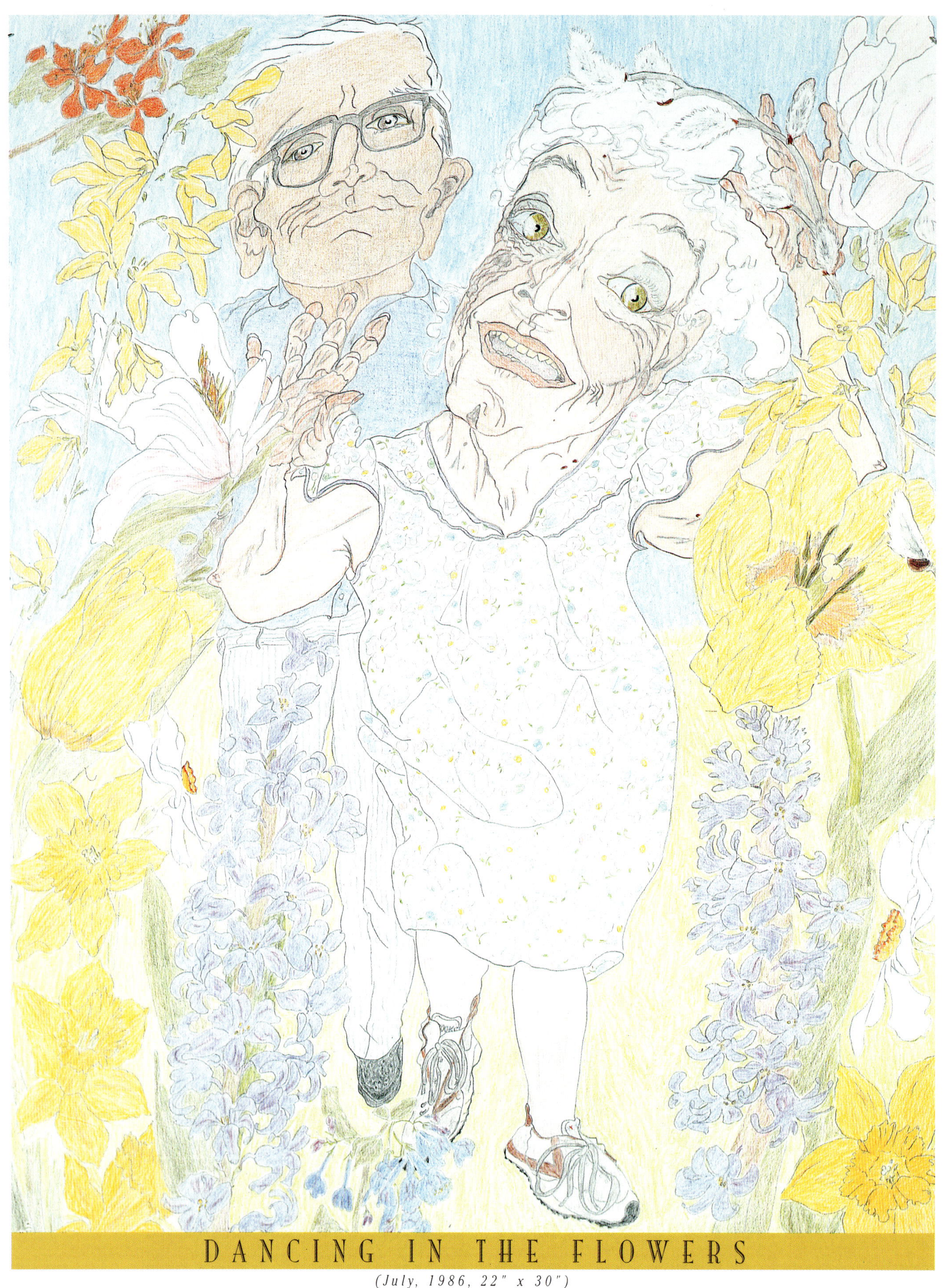

DANCING IN THE FLOWERS

(July, 1986, 22" x 30")

From the collection of the Honolulu Academy of Art, Honolulu, Hawaii

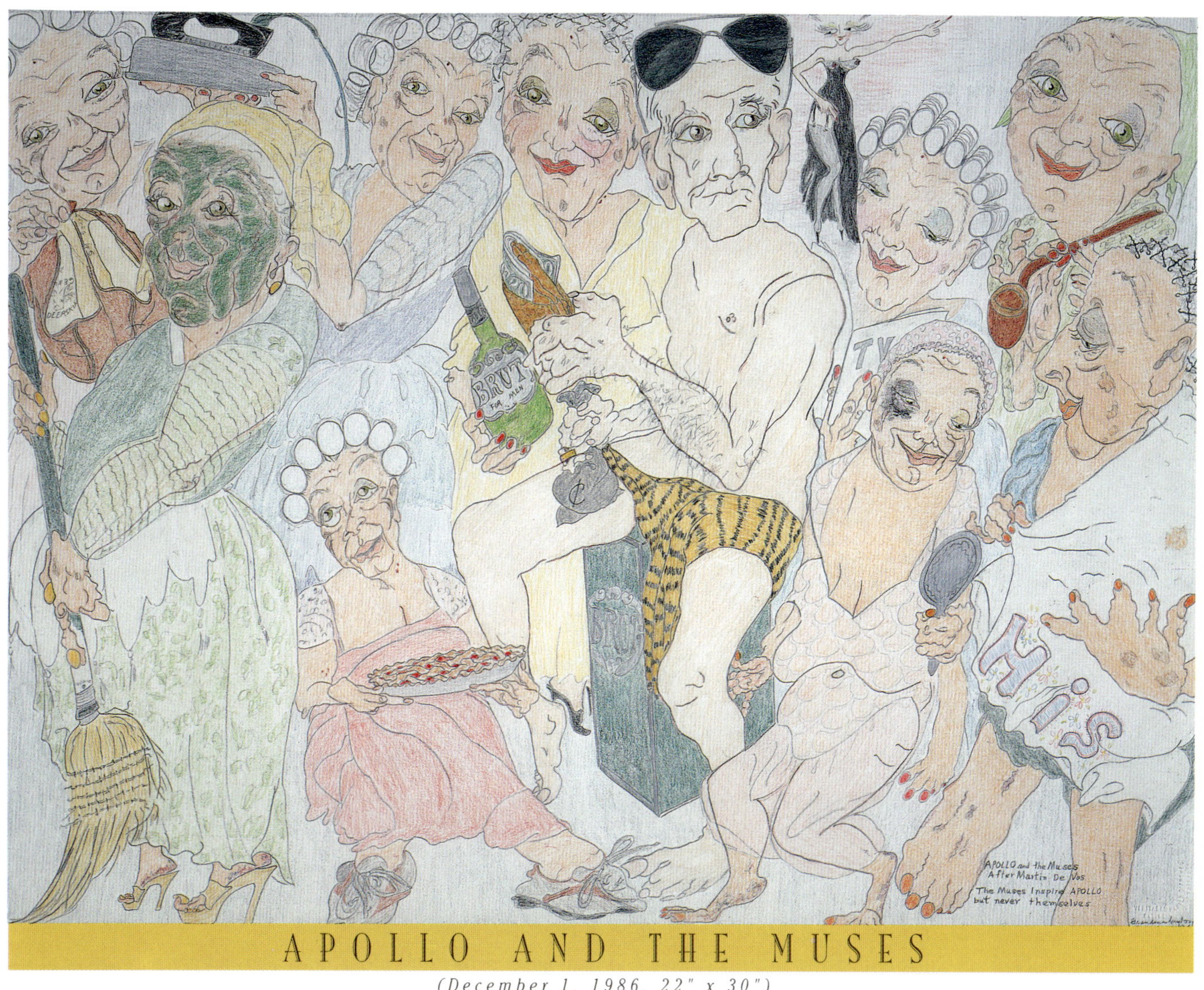

APOLLO AND THE MUSES

(December 1, 1986, 22" x 30")

"*This picture is about the battered women's syndrome. For the security that Apollo personifies with his tight hold on the wallet and money bag, the battered women muses may do several things, each muse bragging on what she does best. One uses a mirror to examine for shiner, a beaut; one hands him a bottle of Brut, asking for more; one tries her best to look like the stereotyped sex goddess as pictured on TV; one irons a neat shirt; one bakes a yummy pie; one sweeps things clean; one brings slippers; one brings his pipe; and one hugs the HIS pillow. All engage in various cosmetic absurdities. This could be what one man expects from one woman.*"

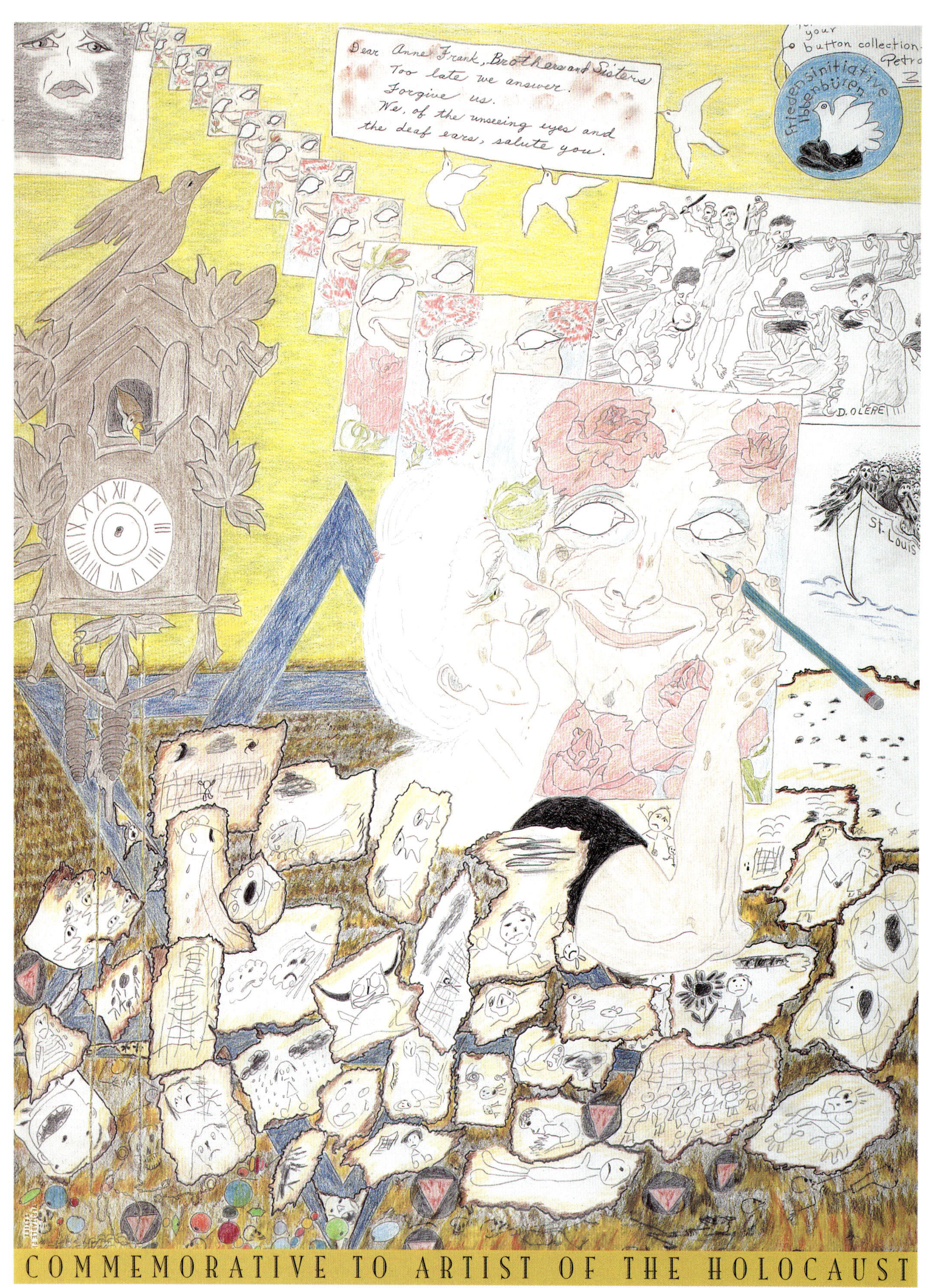

COMMEMORATIVE TO ARTIST OF THE HOLOCAUST

(December 15, 1986, 22" x 30")

66 *This is a picture of denial.*

When I was asked for a drawing about the Holocaust, I didn't have one.

Why not?

The answer had to be that I had always denied that it ever happened.
Here I sat, years on end, drawing flowers and smiling faces.

So I decided to draw a picture of denial. I drew these flowers and smiling faces ad infinitum.

Next day a young father was visiting us, just home from Amsterdam. He told of the high building where
Anne Frank hid from the Nazis with her family. He described the steep steps up to the bare attic room,
the one tiny window where they could look out on a dark night, down onto the flower garden in the back yard.

My steps and garden were already drawn, so I drew in a sad face in this little window.

It was crazy times, and Hitler was a madman, so the cuckoo clock.

This is a Commemorative for Artists of the Holocaust. The Children's Art. It must go on.
No two alike, all heart-breaking, all scorched and burned, along with vast acres of bodies, a Star of David,
gypsy beads, pink triangles of the homosexuals, old, debilitated children. The bones stand for the many
other group victims of the pogrom, and pogroms in other lands.

Artist David Olere, a concentration camp prisoner, drew "To Burn Their Sisters and Brother."

In the summer of 1985 two young women stopped to visit our home, one a young German girl who had been in our
country a year. When she reached her home she sent this Peace movement button from her hometown.

When my daughter saw the woman's black velvet dress, she exclaimed: "Oh, the black Nazi armband."

Last, my note.

Dear Anne Frank, Brothers and Sisters,

Too late we answer.

Forgive us.

We, of the unseeing eyes and deaf ears, salute you. **99**

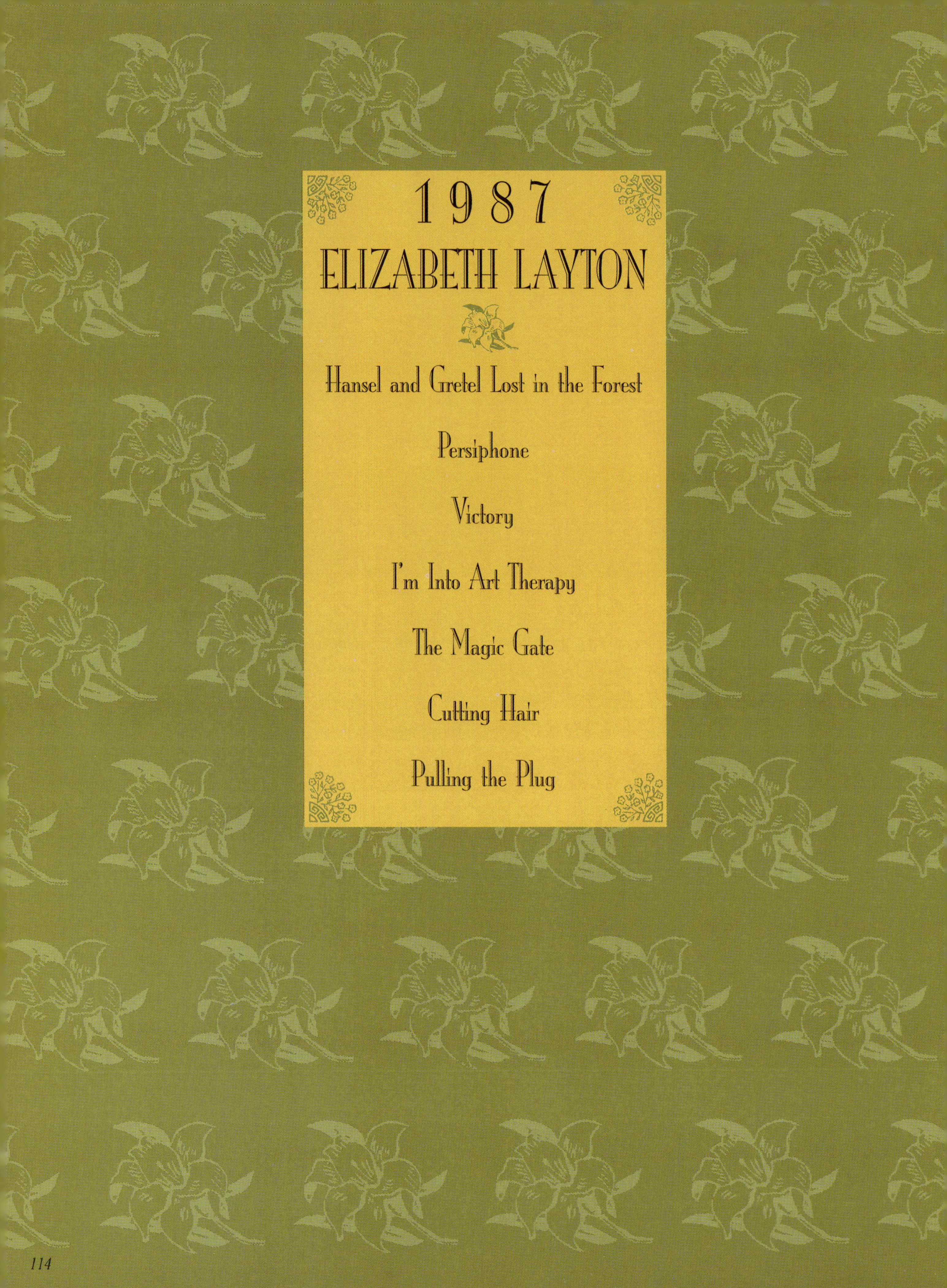

1987

ELIZABETH LAYTON

Hansel and Gretel Lost in the Forest

Persiphone

Victory

I'm Into Art Therapy

The Magic Gate

Cutting Hair

Pulling the Plug

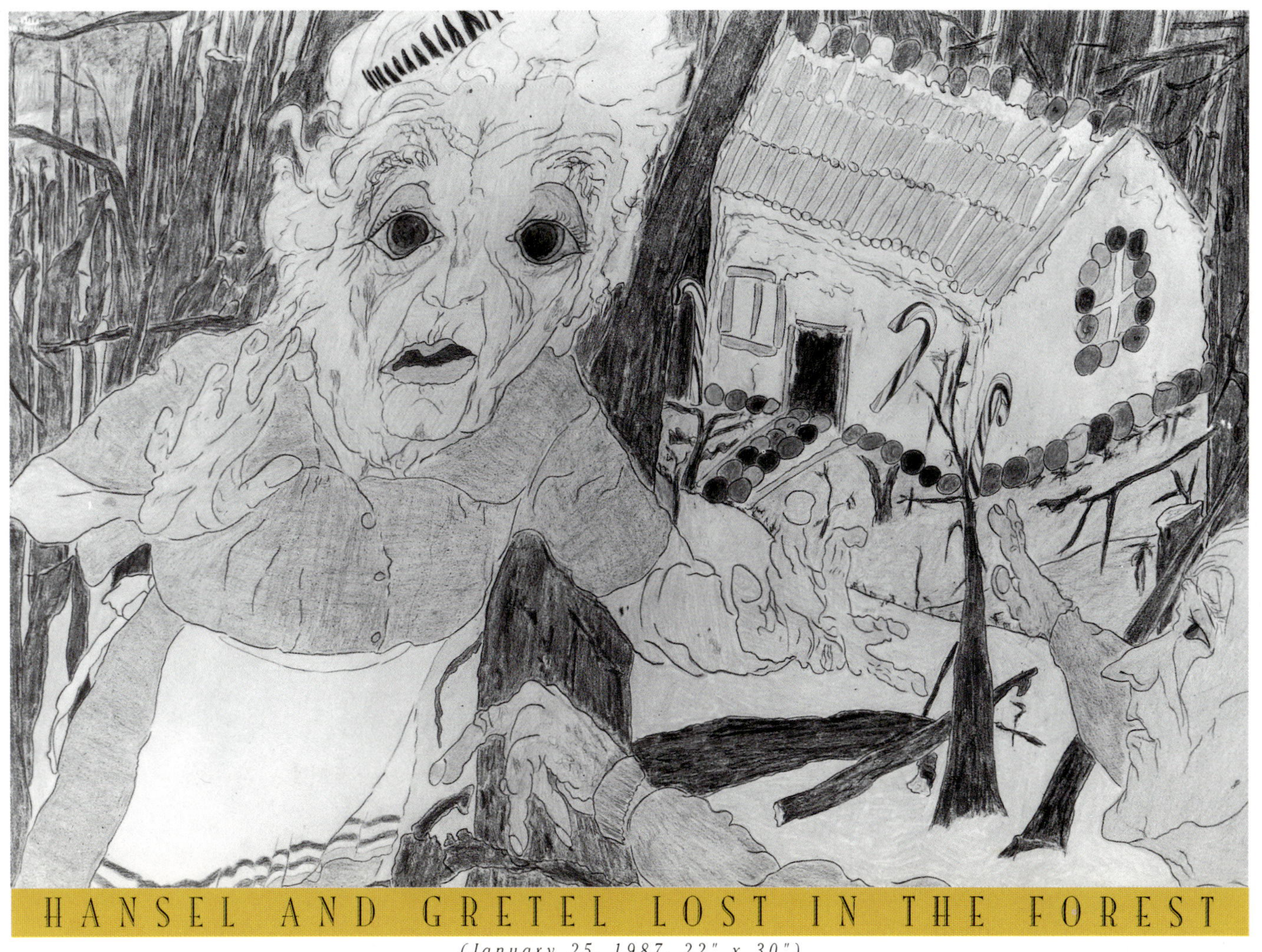

(January 25, 1987, 22" x 30")

Collection of the University of Kansas Medical Center, Kansas City

"*Hansel and Gretel are lost in the woods, at the candy house in the realm of the wicked witch. In the upper left corner is a patch of the 'beautiful woods' they came through.*"

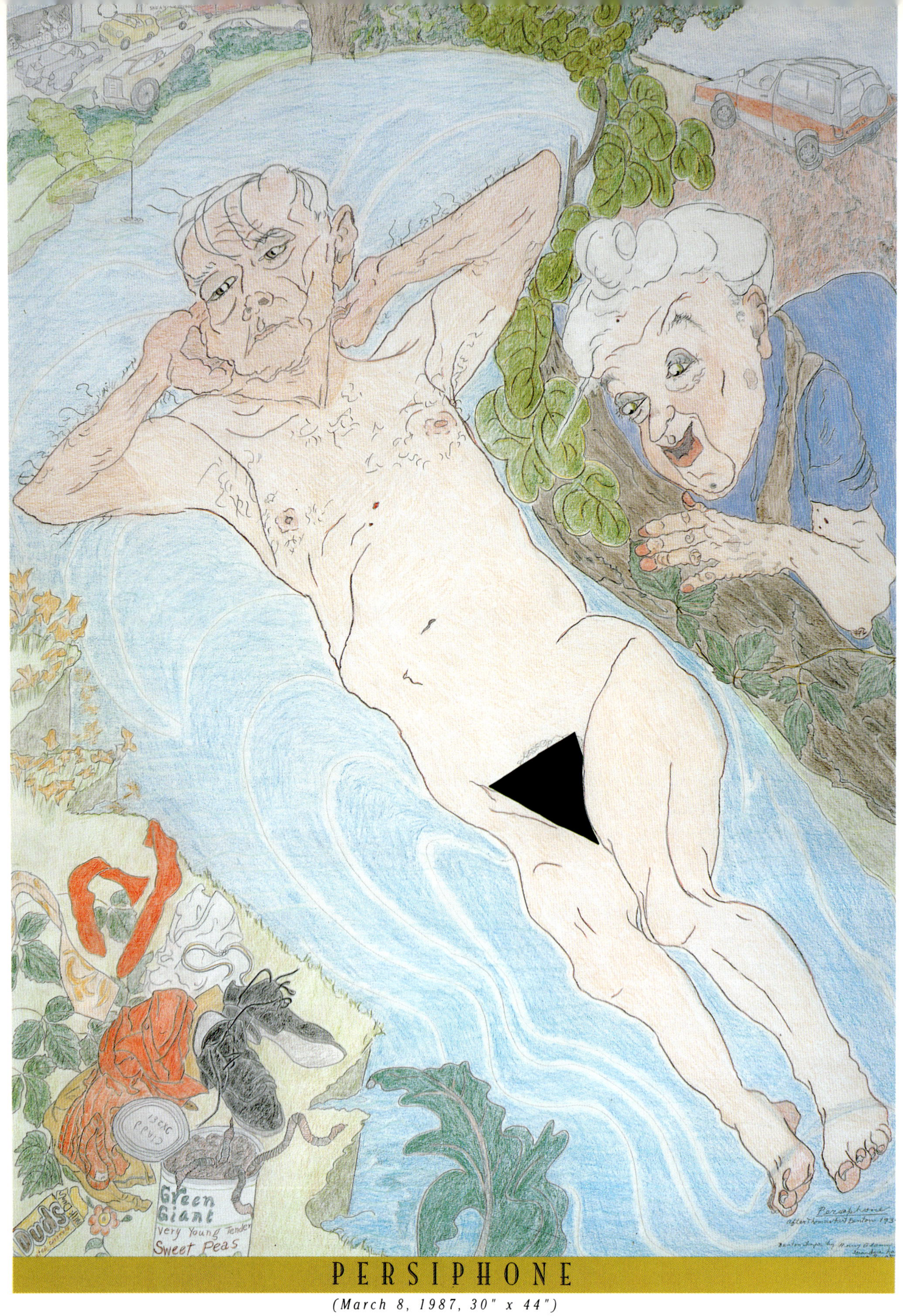

PERSIPHONE

(March 8, 1987, 30" x 44")

After Thomas Hart Benton

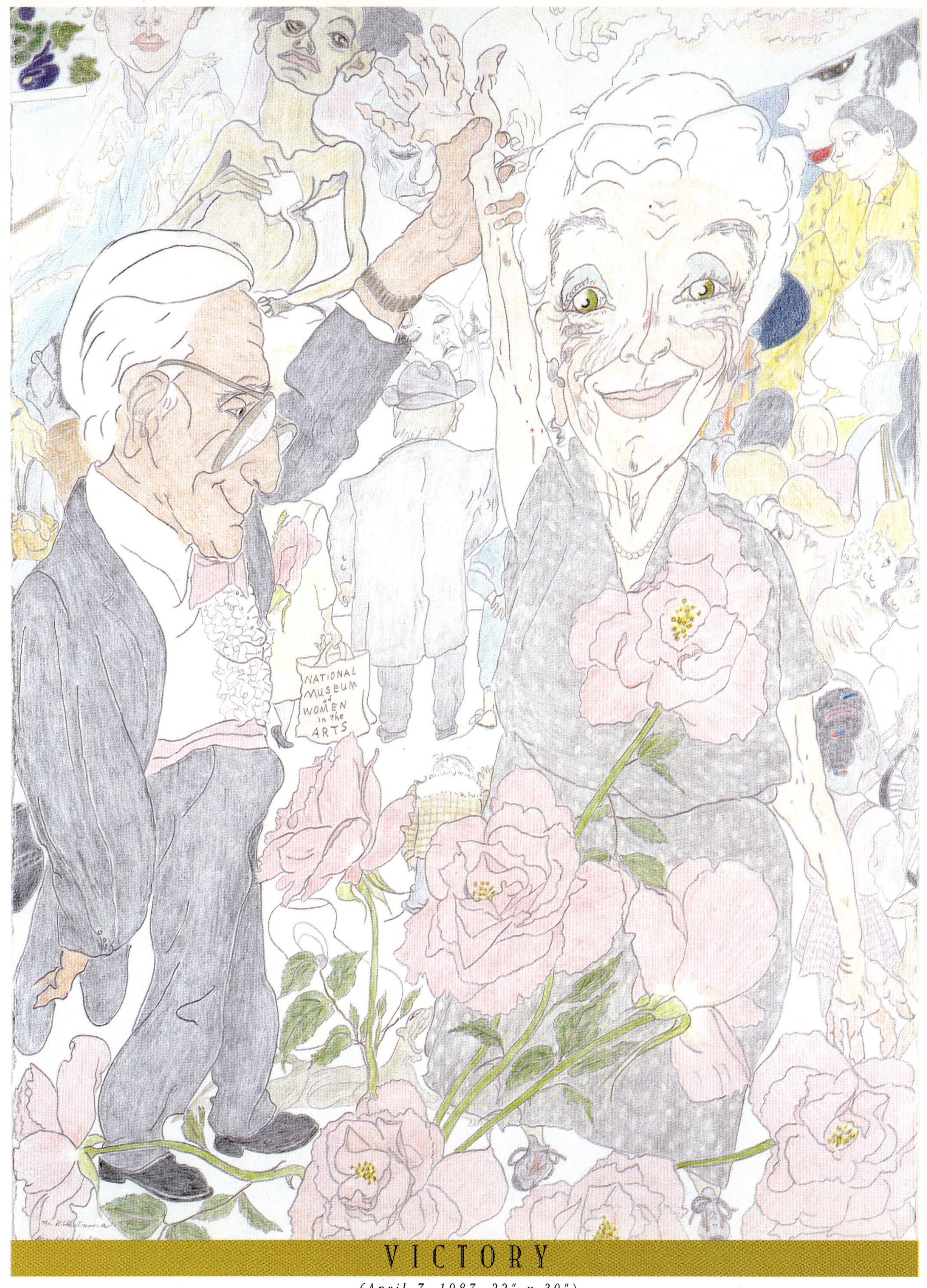

V I C T O R Y

(April 7, 1987, 22" x 30")

From the collection of the National Museum of Women in the Arts, Washington, D.C.

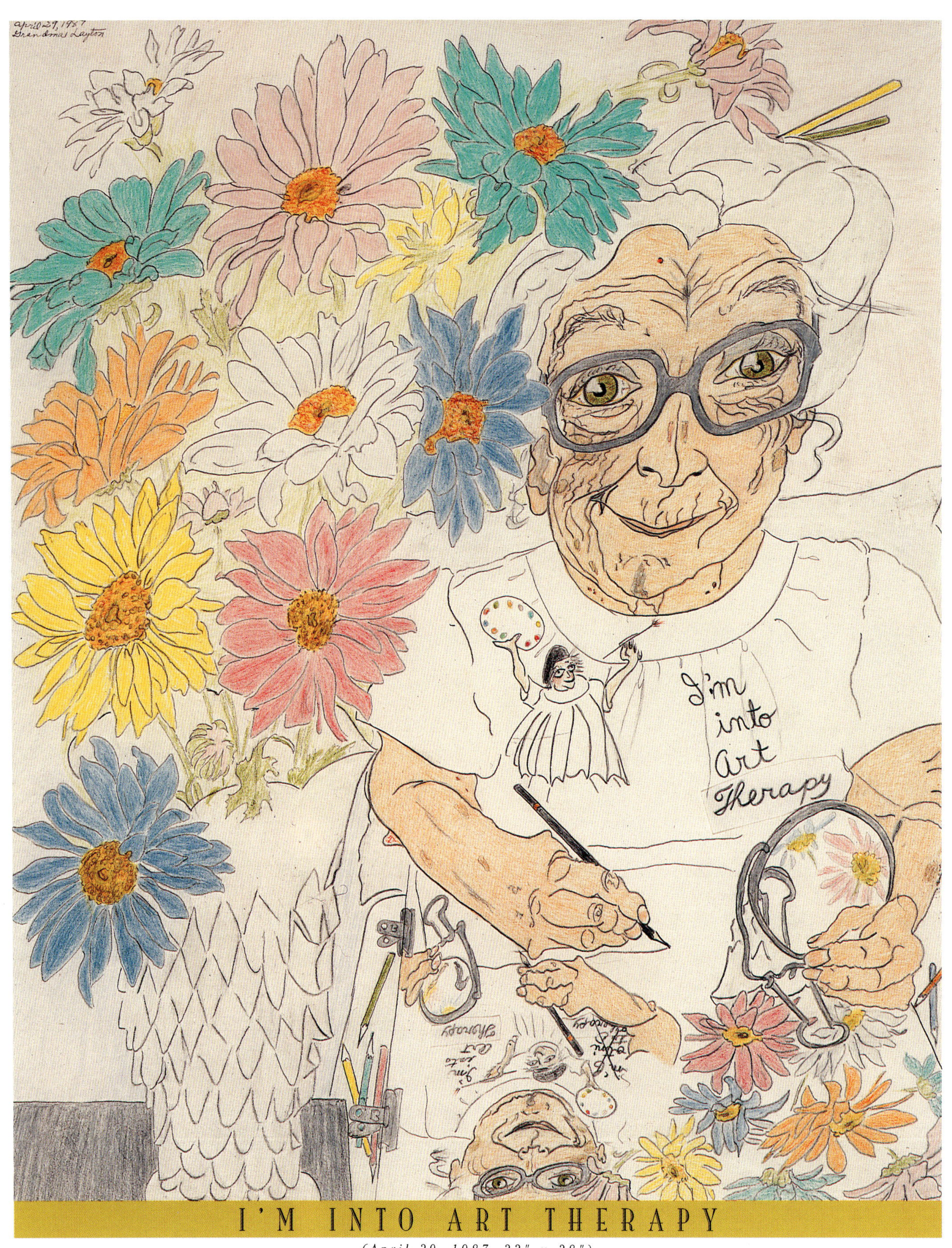

I'M INTO ART THERAPY

(April 29, 1987, 22" x 28")

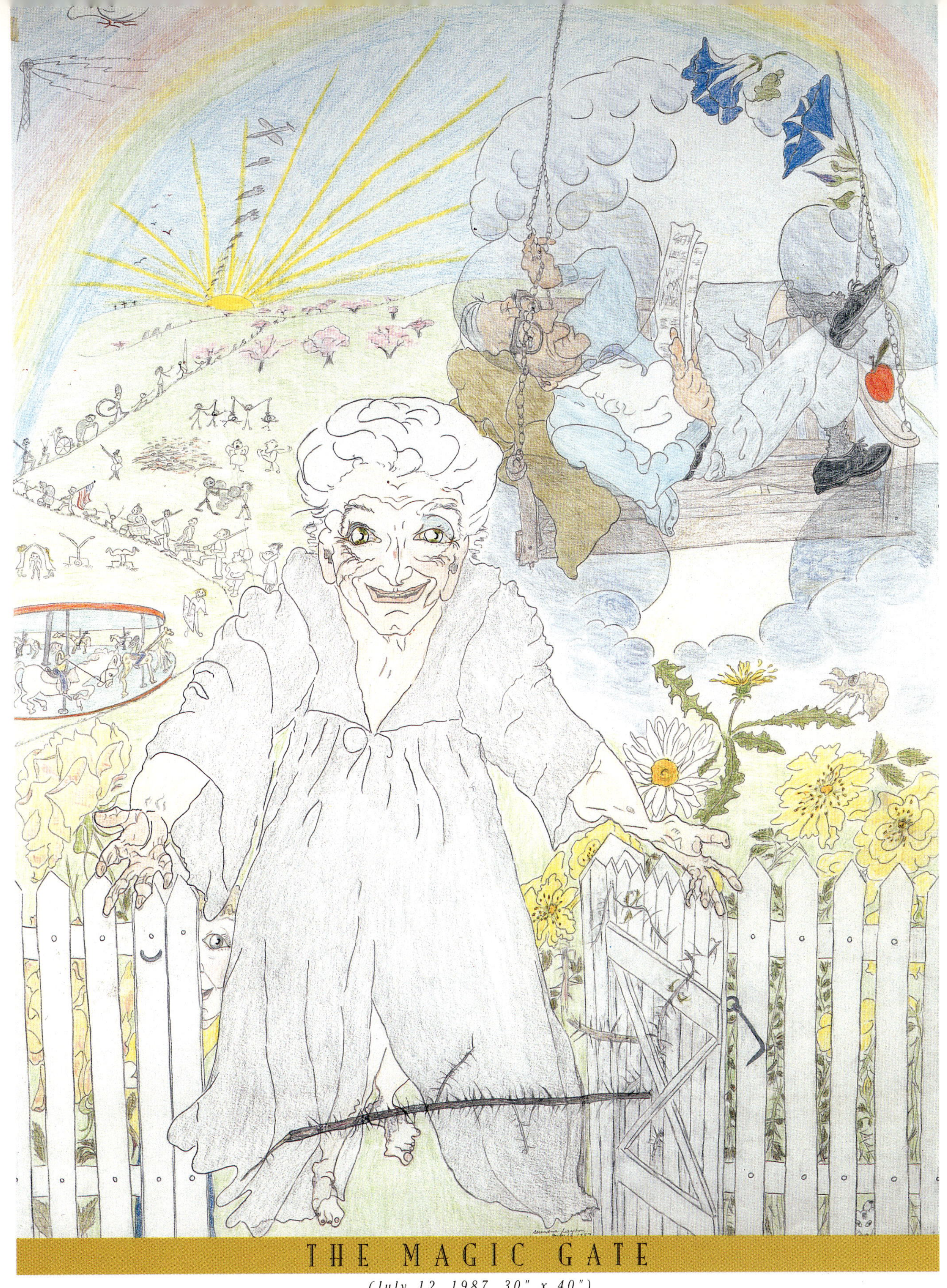

THE MAGIC GATE

(July 12, 1987, 30" x 40")

On extended loan from the University of Kansas Medical Center, Kansas City, Kansas

"She is almost through the magic gate to the cosmos. The gate opening up broke a thorny branch off the rosebush — the sting of dying. Behind her are ties to the earth — loved ones, wonderful worldly things, good and bad — her life. We can't see yet what she sees but the look on her face is joyous."

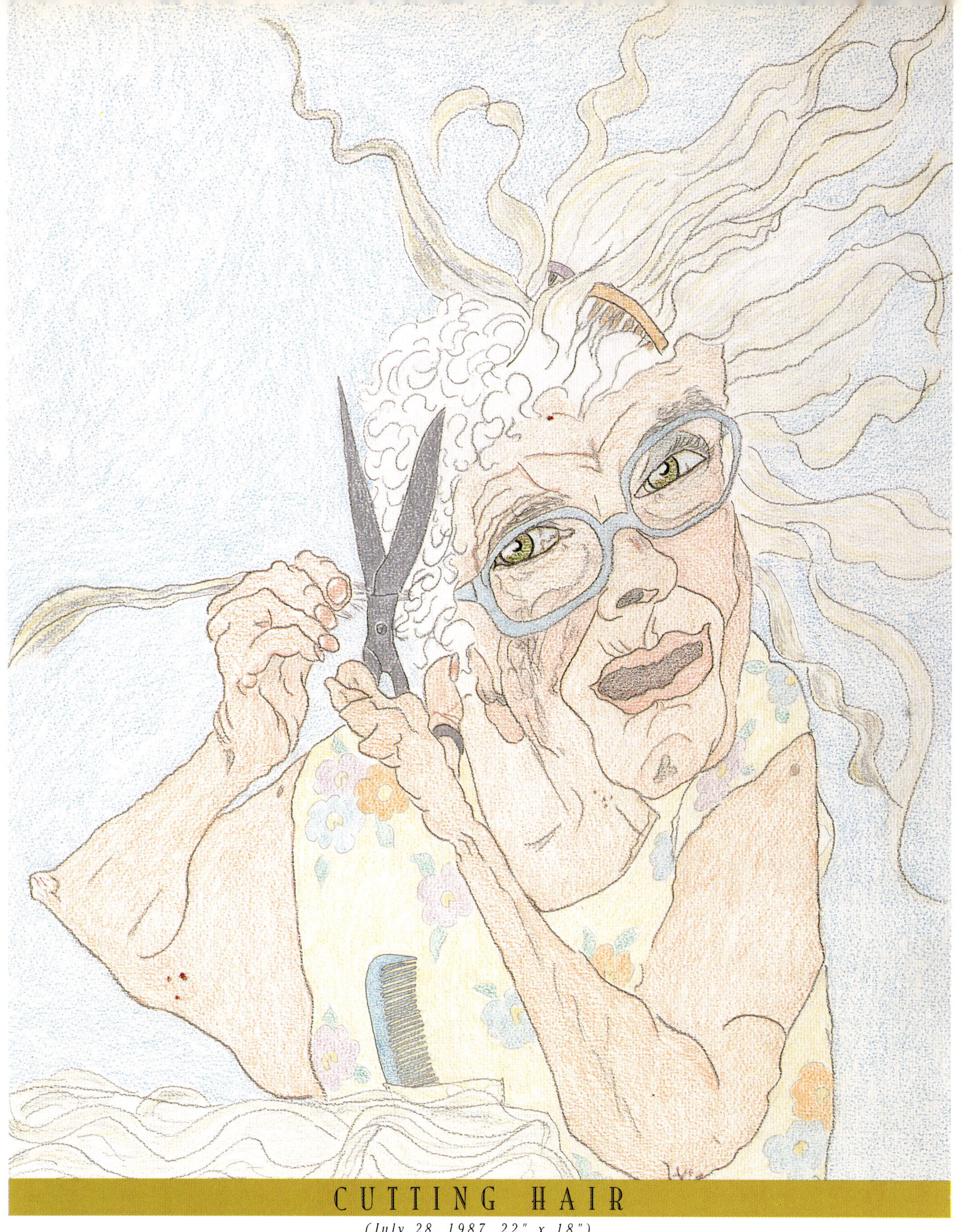

C U T T I N G   H A I R

(July 28, 1987, 22" x 18")

“*Last year after my sister had a massive stroke, the caretakers at the hospital cut her crowning glory, her long hair she'd always been so proud of. Later she realized what had happened, ran her fingers through the short locks, and shook the bedrails in her anger. 2,000 miles away I worried. What can I do to help her accept this? I'll cut my long hair and send her the word her little sister wants to look like her. I don't know that it helped her any, but I felt better for having done something. After I drew this picture I saw what I was doing — simplifying my life.*”

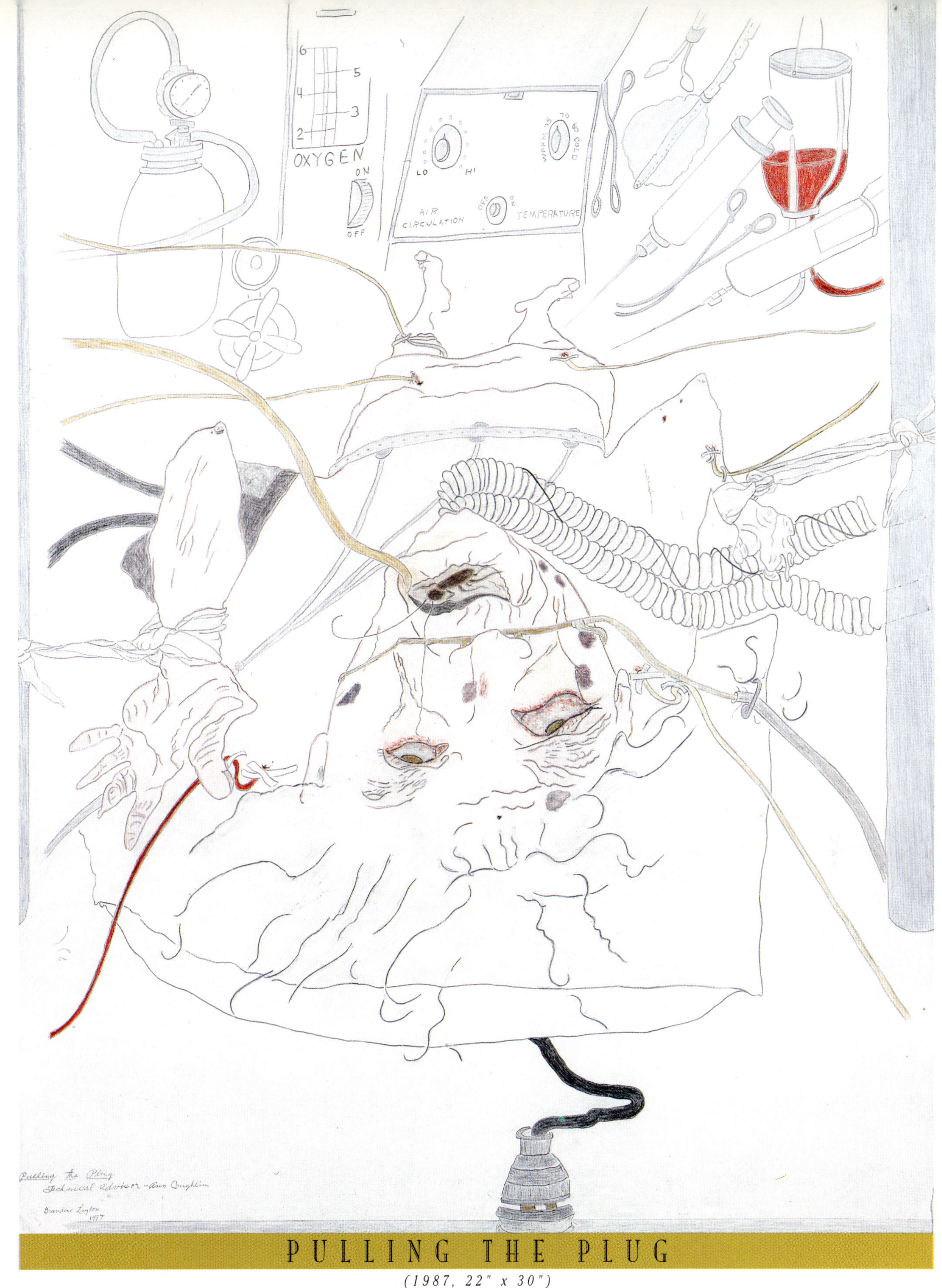

PULLING THE PLUG

(1987, 22" x 30")

" *Symbolic of the many means of keeping a body functioning. Restraint is a necessity.*
She has wasted minutes, hours, months. Would she want to add all that wasted time to this very end? **"**

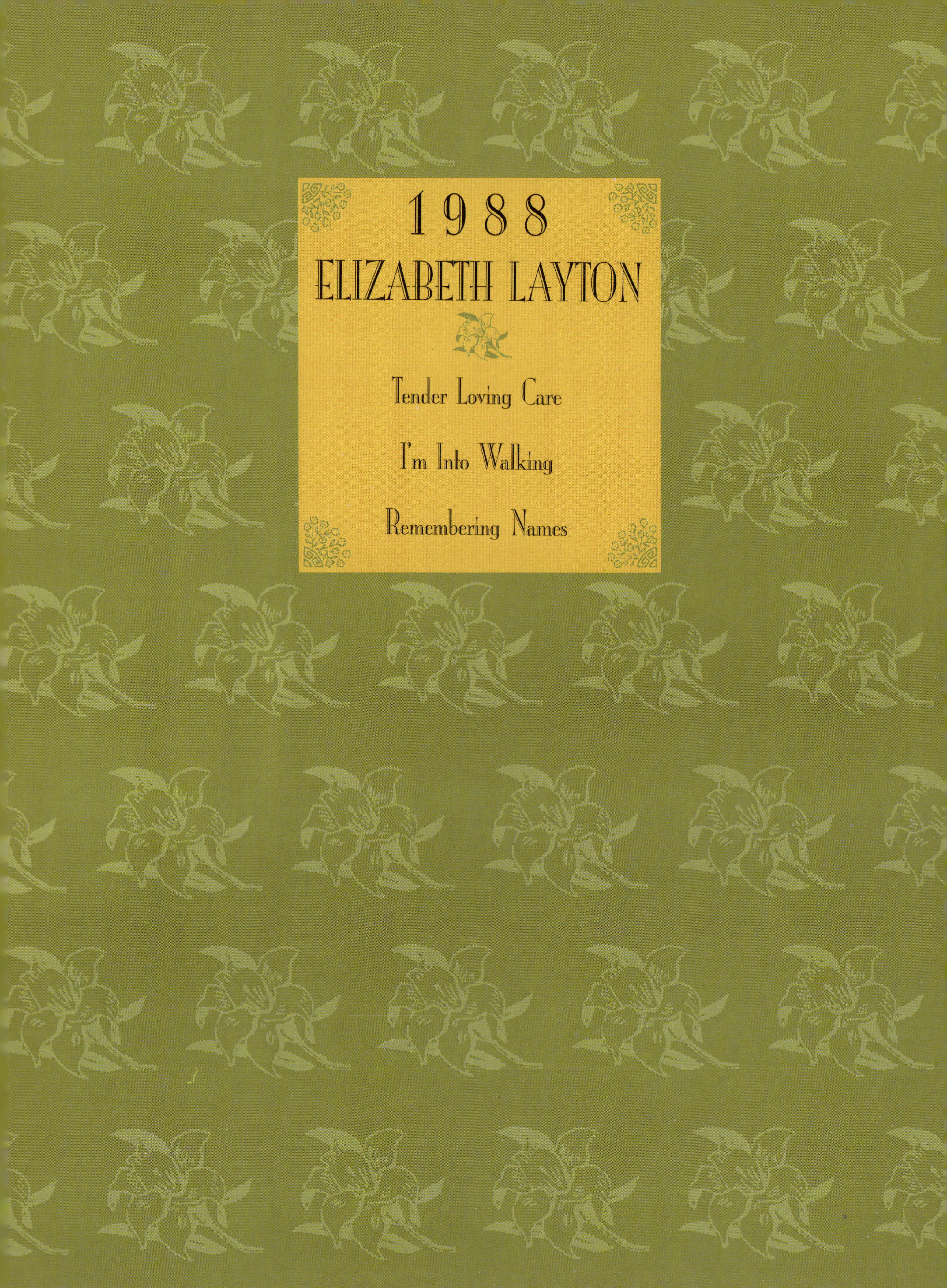

1988
ELIZABETH LAYTON

Tender Loving Care

I'm Into Walking

Remembering Names

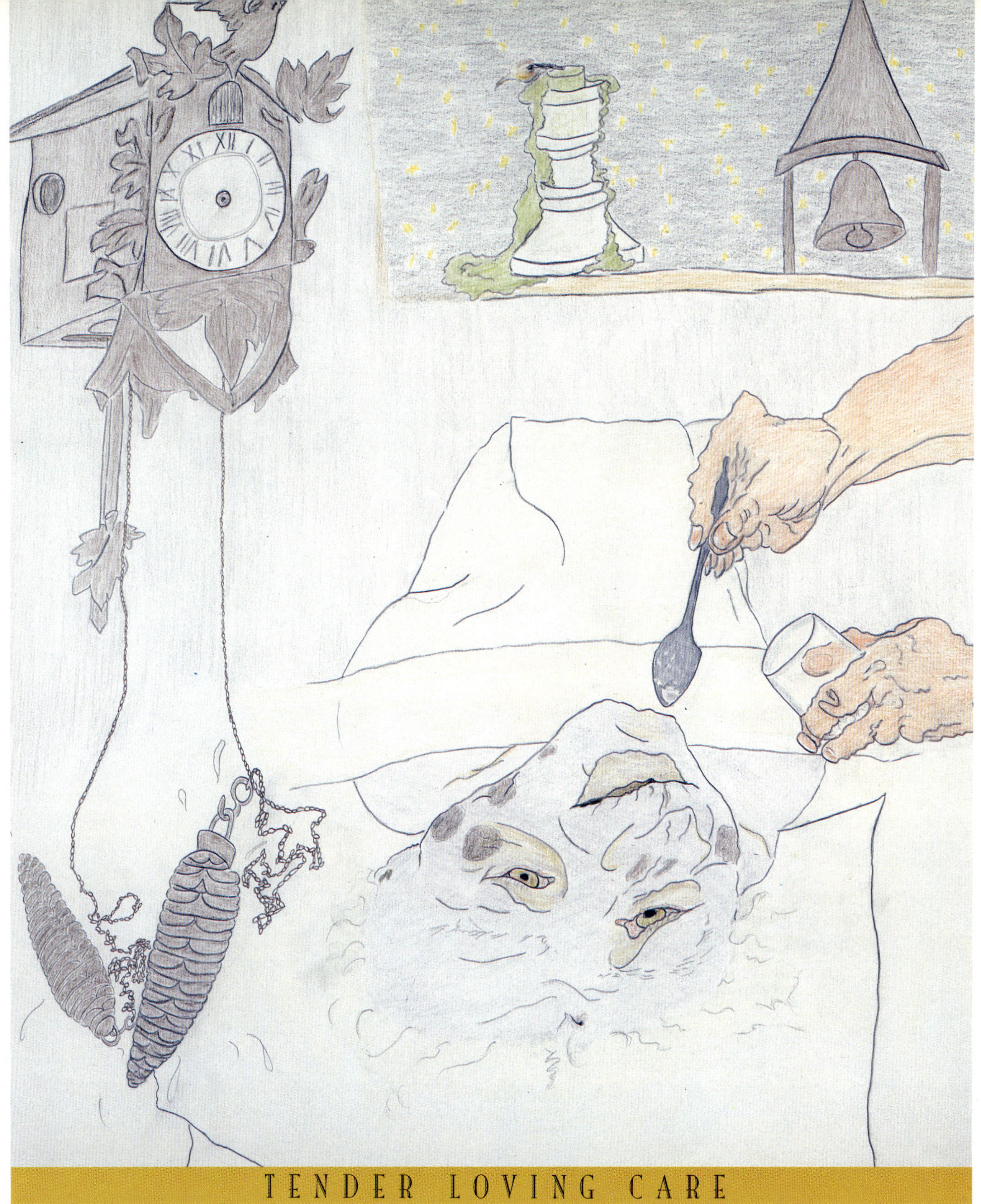

TENDER LOVING CARE

(January 21, 1988, 22" x 30")

"*Not every one is caught up in technology. Legal, financial, ethical puzzles engulf us. We have the answers — the procedures, the tubes, the machines, the know-how. When do we stop to open the envelopes and address the questions? What can we handle? How much technology can we live with? Is another Challenger exploding in our faces? Can we change so drastically in these few decades? For ages, man has struggled to accept death. In the traditional way of dying, we spoon-fed a little ice, not enough to sustain life but sufficient to comfort the body and nourish the soul. Sheets, clean and straightened, shelter a cherished privacy.*"

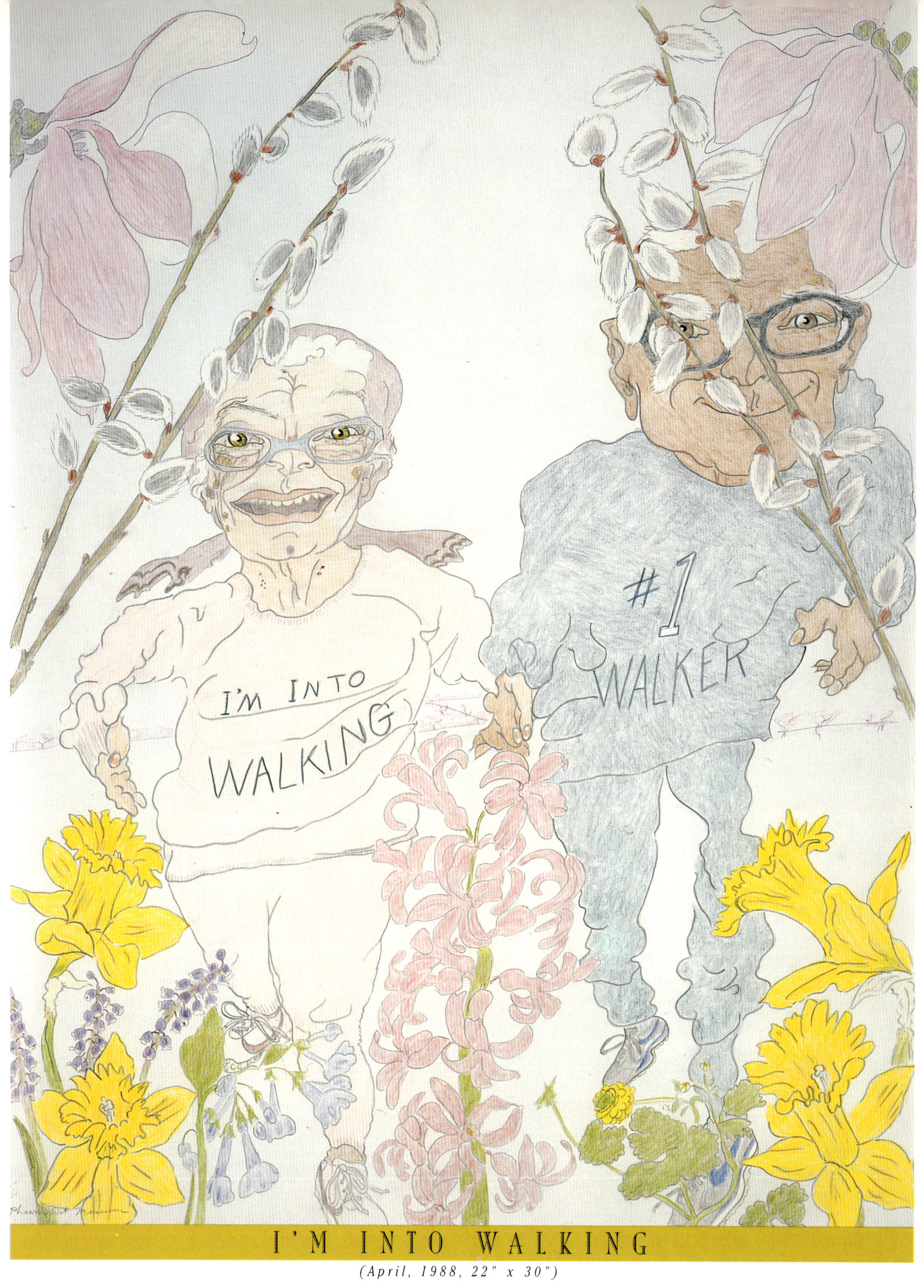

I'M INTO WALKING

(April, 1988, 22" x 30")

From the collection of the Phoenix Art Museum, Phoenix, Arizona

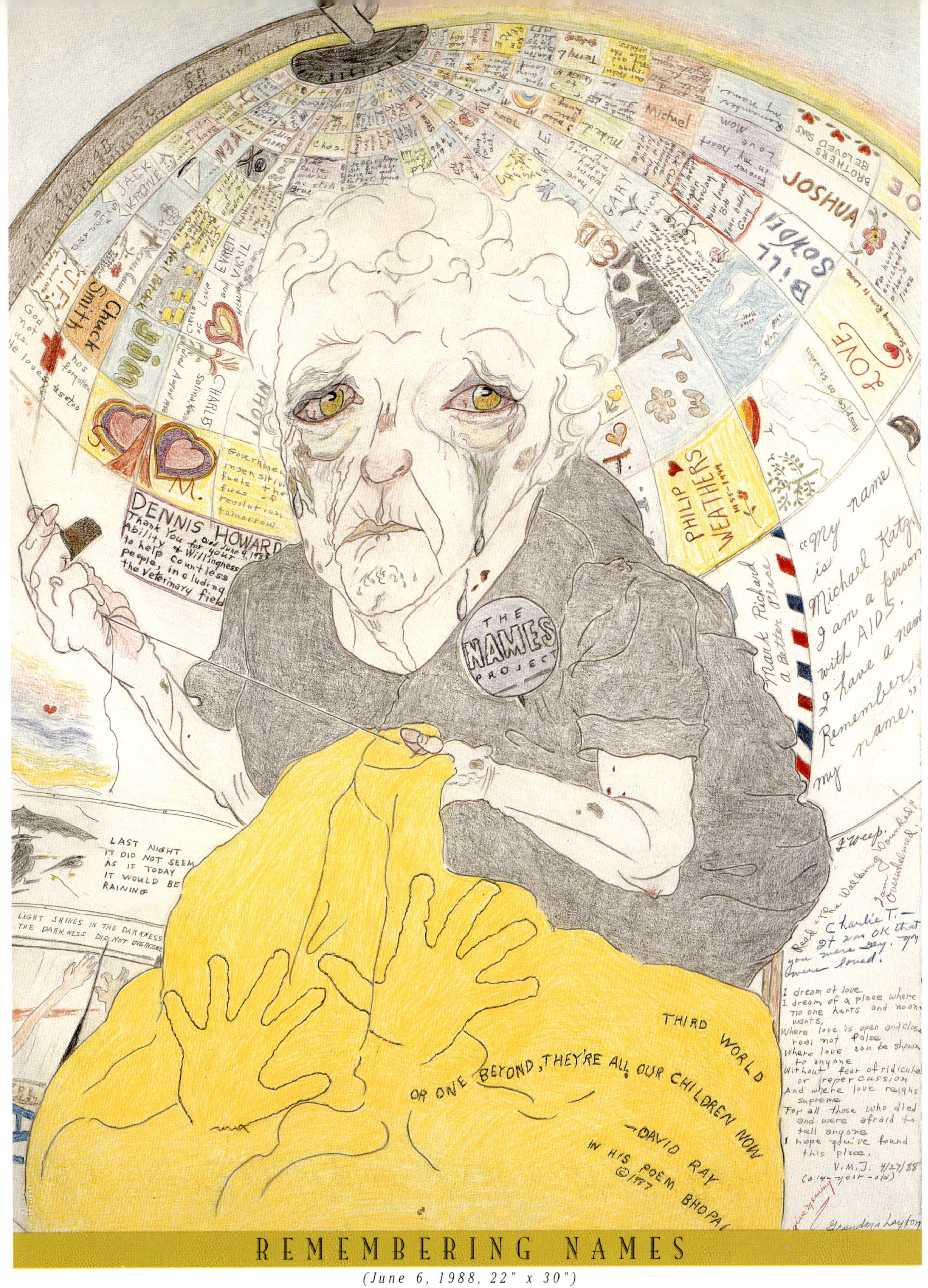

(June 6, 1988, 22" x 30")

"She embroiders her own block for the AIDS memorial quilt, with hand tracings by Benjamin and that beautiful line from the poem Bophal by David Ray. The other blocks are copies of actual panels from the quilt, shown here covering the globe."

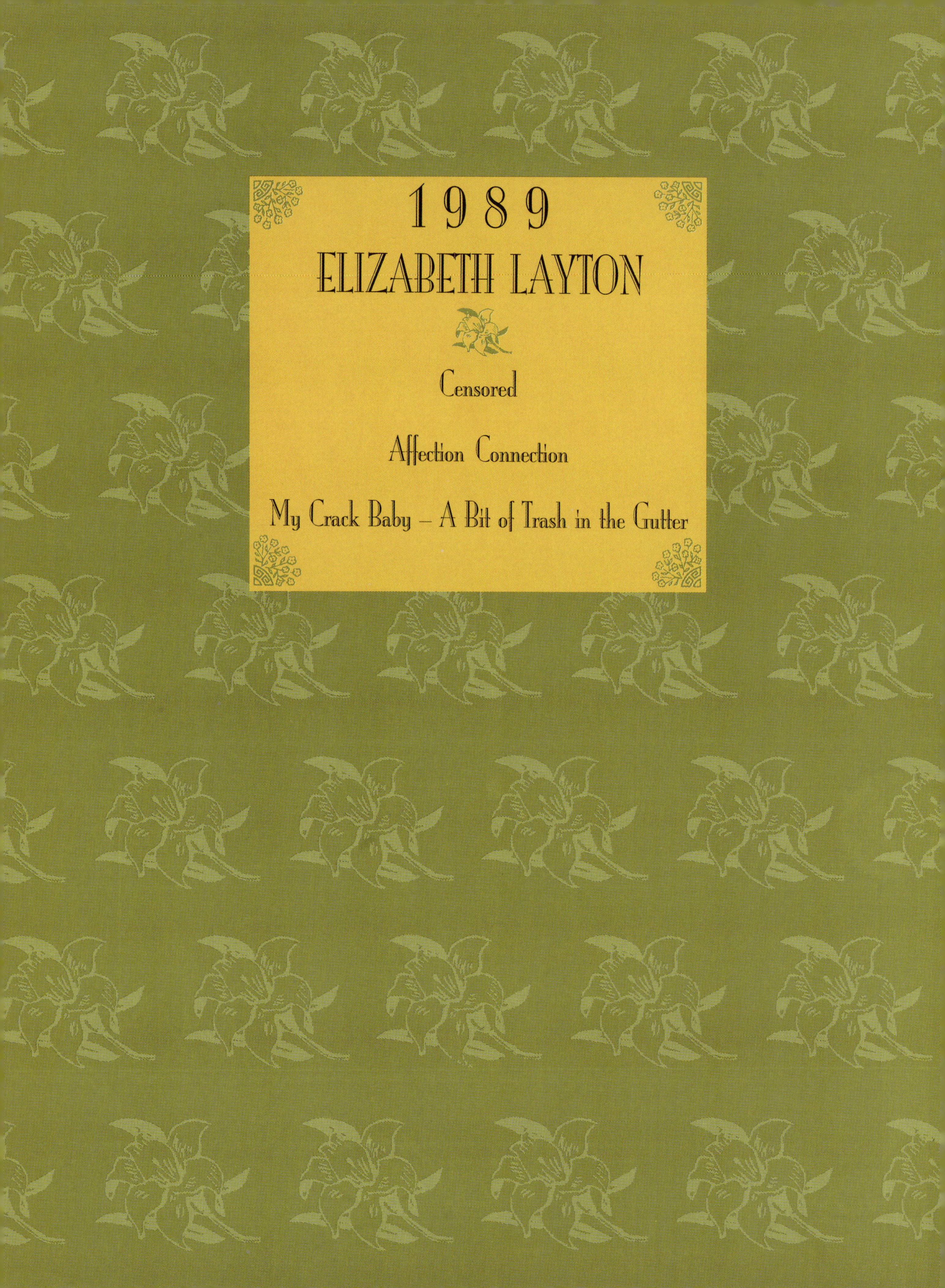
1989
ELIZABETH LAYTON

Censored

Affection Connection

My Crack Baby – A Bit of Trash in the Gutter

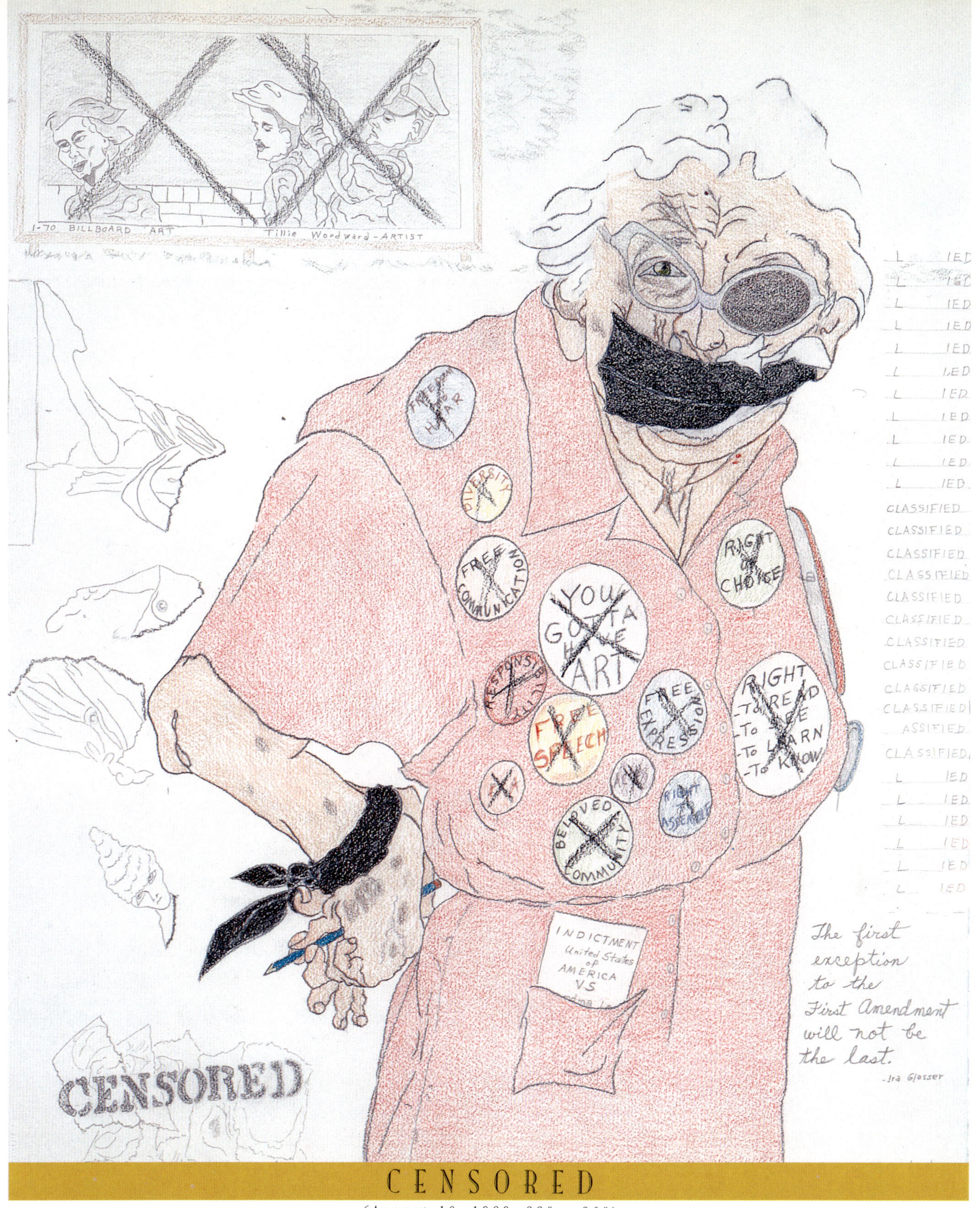

C E N S O R E D

(August 10, 1989, 22" x 30")

From the collection of the National Museum of American Art, the Smithsonian, Washington, D.C.

"This old woman is bound and gagged and can no longer draw. Her principles have been X-ed out. I guarantee you she feels like a zilch. In the background, from top left, counter-clockwise; Interstate 70 billboard art by Tillie Woodward, of a Nazi soldier hanging two Russian resistance fighters, which was censored and plastered over June 5, 1985; the Goddess of Liberty falling broken in China's Tianemen Square; a pile of the old woman's drawings torn up and censored; quotation, "The first exception (to the First Amendment) will not be the last" — Ira Glasser; sheaf of CLASSIFIED papers, beginning and ending with LIED."

127

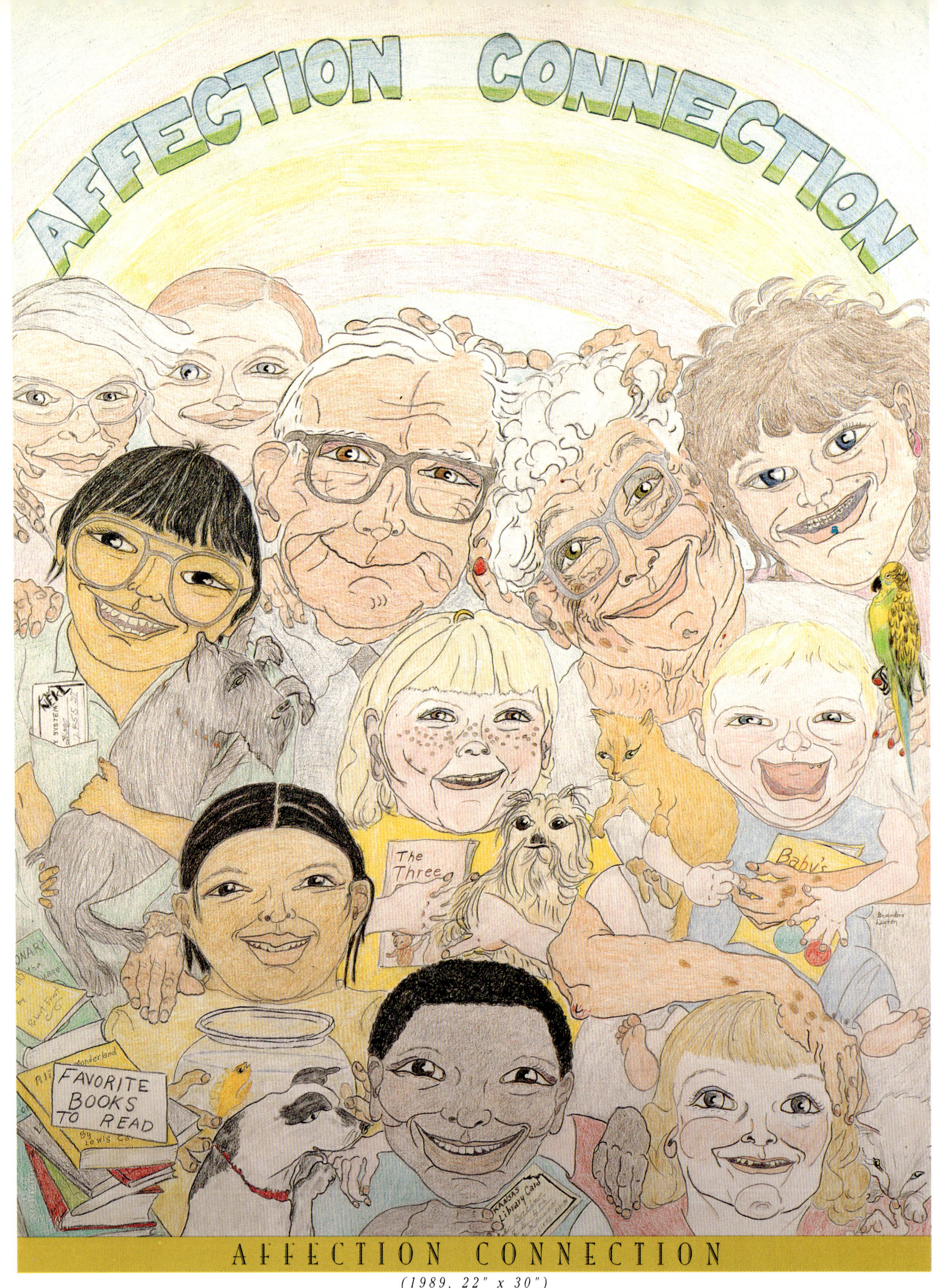

A F F E C T I O N   C O N N E C T I O N

(1989, 22" x 30")

From the collection of the Wellsville Public Library, Wellsville, Kansas

(Poster reproduction for summer youth reading program sponsored by Northeast Kansas Library System.)

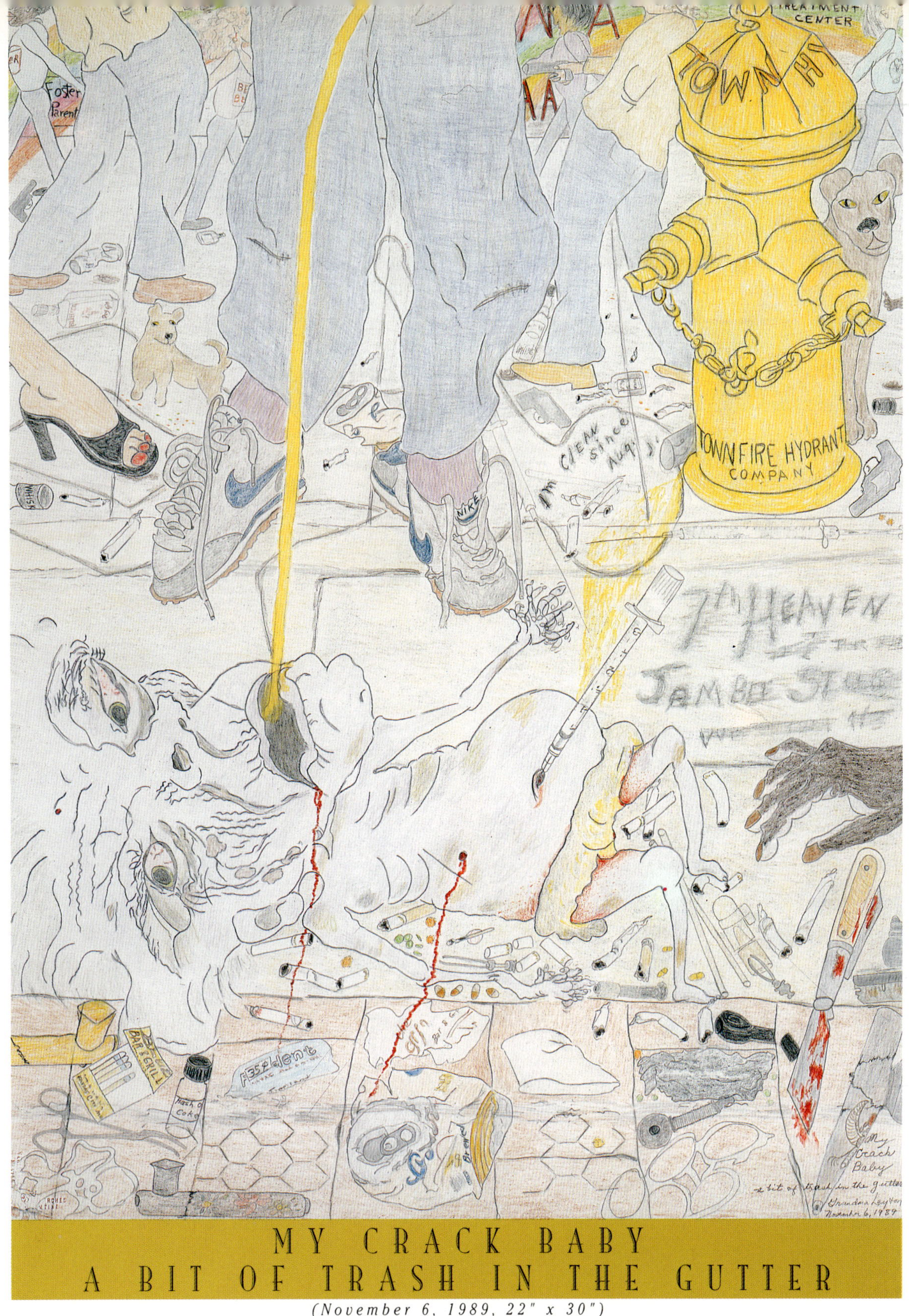

M Y   C R A C K   B A B Y
A   B I T   O F   T R A S H   I N   T H E   G U T T E R

(November 6, 1989, 22" x 30")

"A dog raises its leg against this street-corner fire hydrant. Part of his puddle trickles down on to the baby. A nerd on the curb relieves himself directly in to the baby's mouth. The baby lies in a gutter strewn with crack paraphernalia, beer cans, whiskey bottles, cigarette stubs, marijuana stubs, and a dead body whose hand has relinquished a blood-covered knife. Passersby on the sidewalk walk over the police's chalk outline of a dead body, and amidst more guns, liquor bottles and paraphernalia. Not many rainbows here, but on the storefronts are signs — People Who Care, Foster Grandparents, NA, AA, and Drug and Alcohol Treatment Centers."

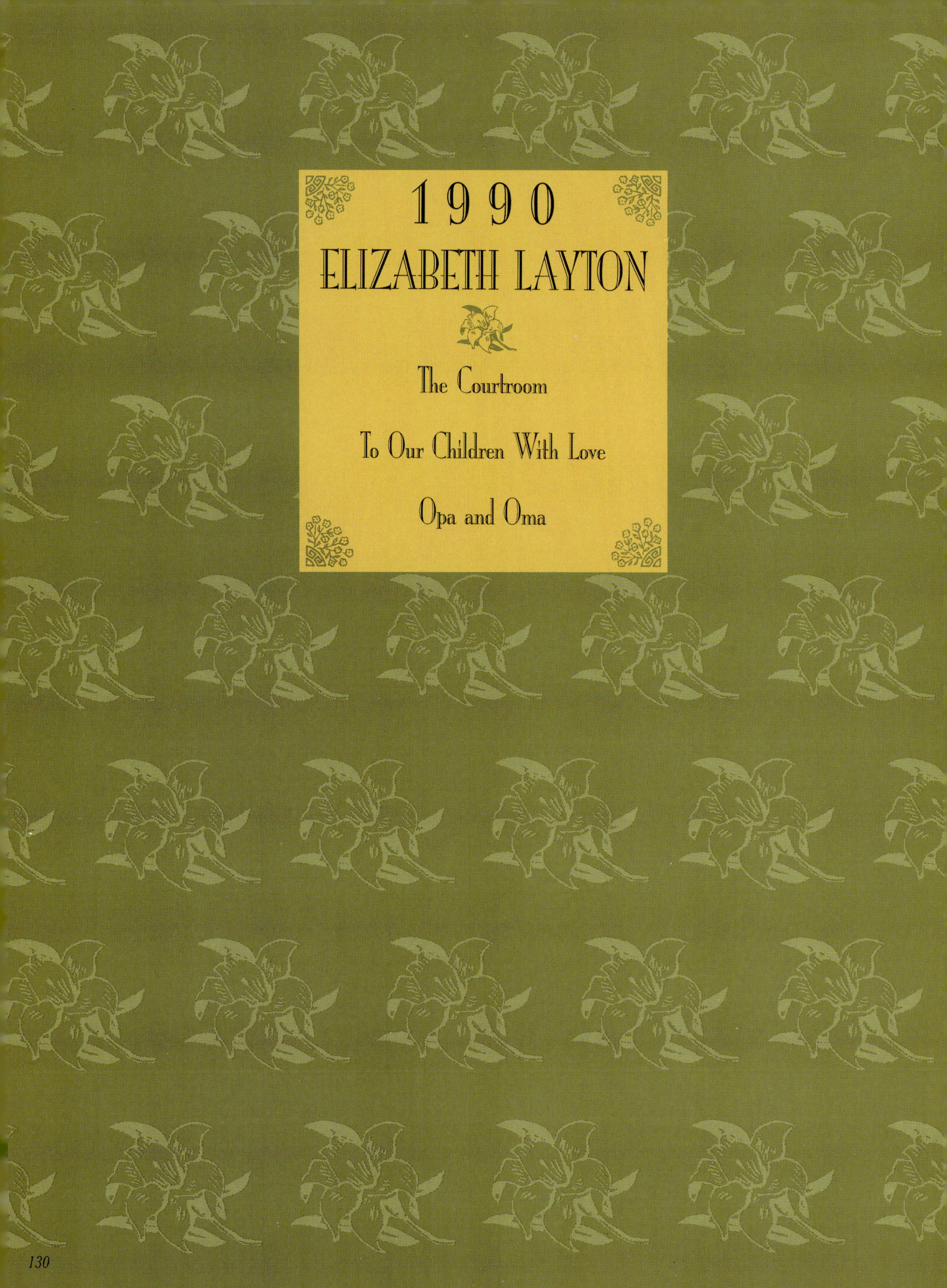

1990

ELIZABETH LAYTON

The Courtroom

To Our Children With Love

Opa and Oma

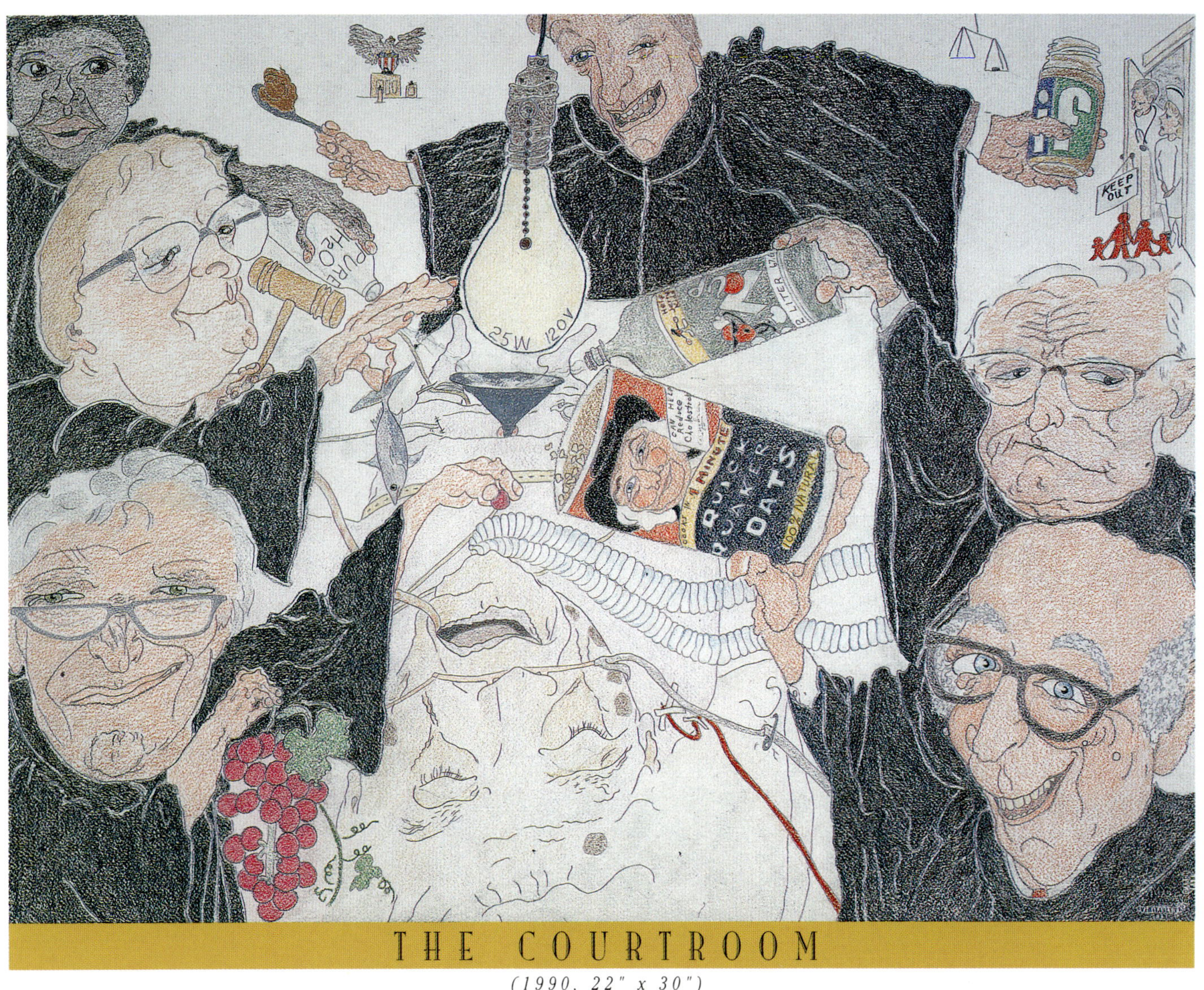

THE COURTROOM

(1990, 22" x 30")

66 *The sign on the door to the courtroom says, KEEP OUT. The doctors, nurses, and family are not allowed in. The comatose patient on the consultation table has a funnel leading directly into her stomach. Black-robed Justices pour in nutritious foods — artificial grapes, fish, oats, peanut butter, pure H_2O, 7-Up. The 25-watt light bulb symbolizes the dim illumination perfect strangers might have on the case.* **99**

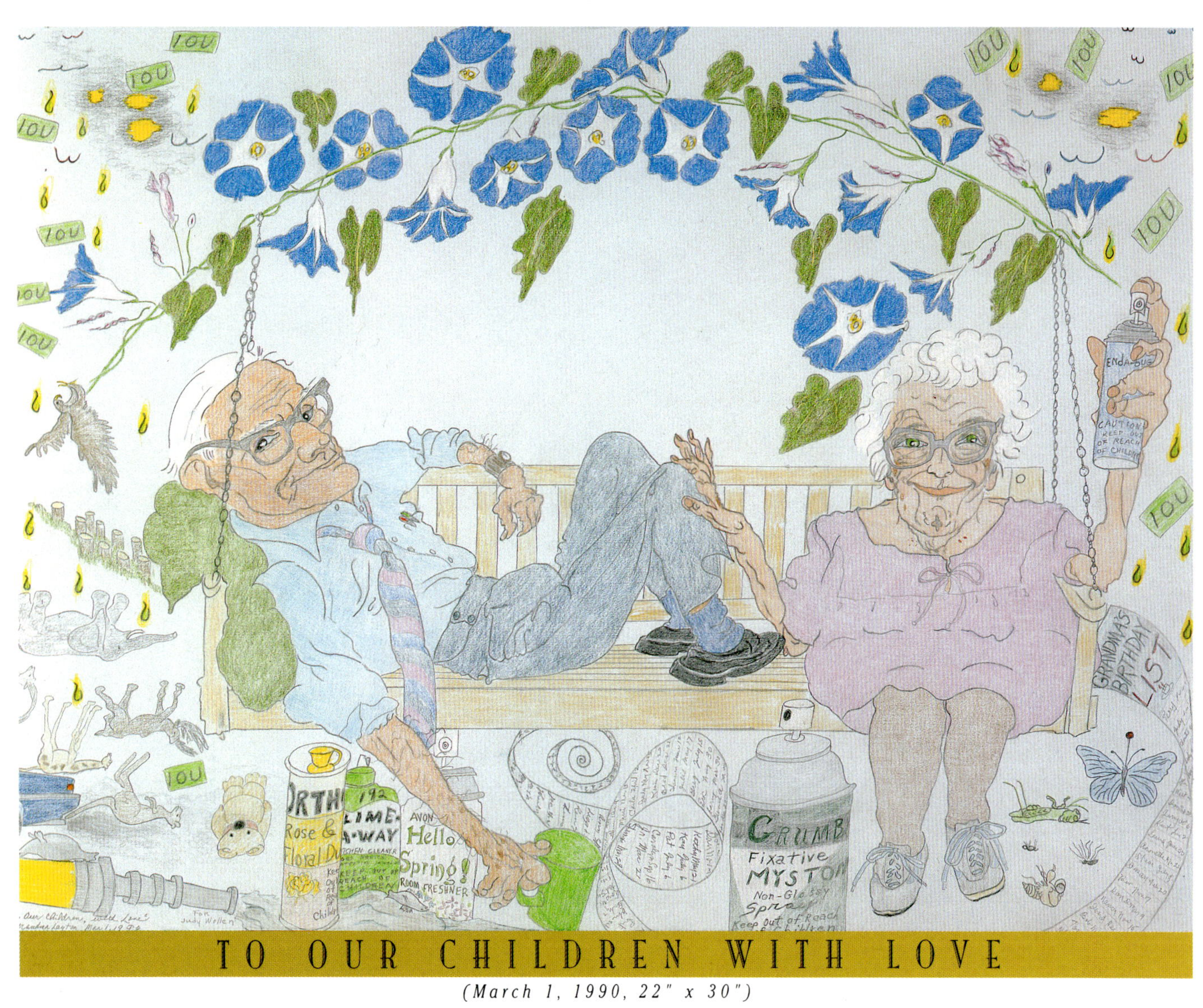

TO OUR CHILDREN WITH LOVE

(March 1, 1990, 22" x 30")

"*A benign old couple swings beneath the vines, innocently contemplating its birthday list which goes on ad infinitum. The couple sprays the air like mad, killing everything in the way. Water pours out from the hose, IOUs strew the place, acid rain falls. The sun shines brightly through the holes in the ozone.*"

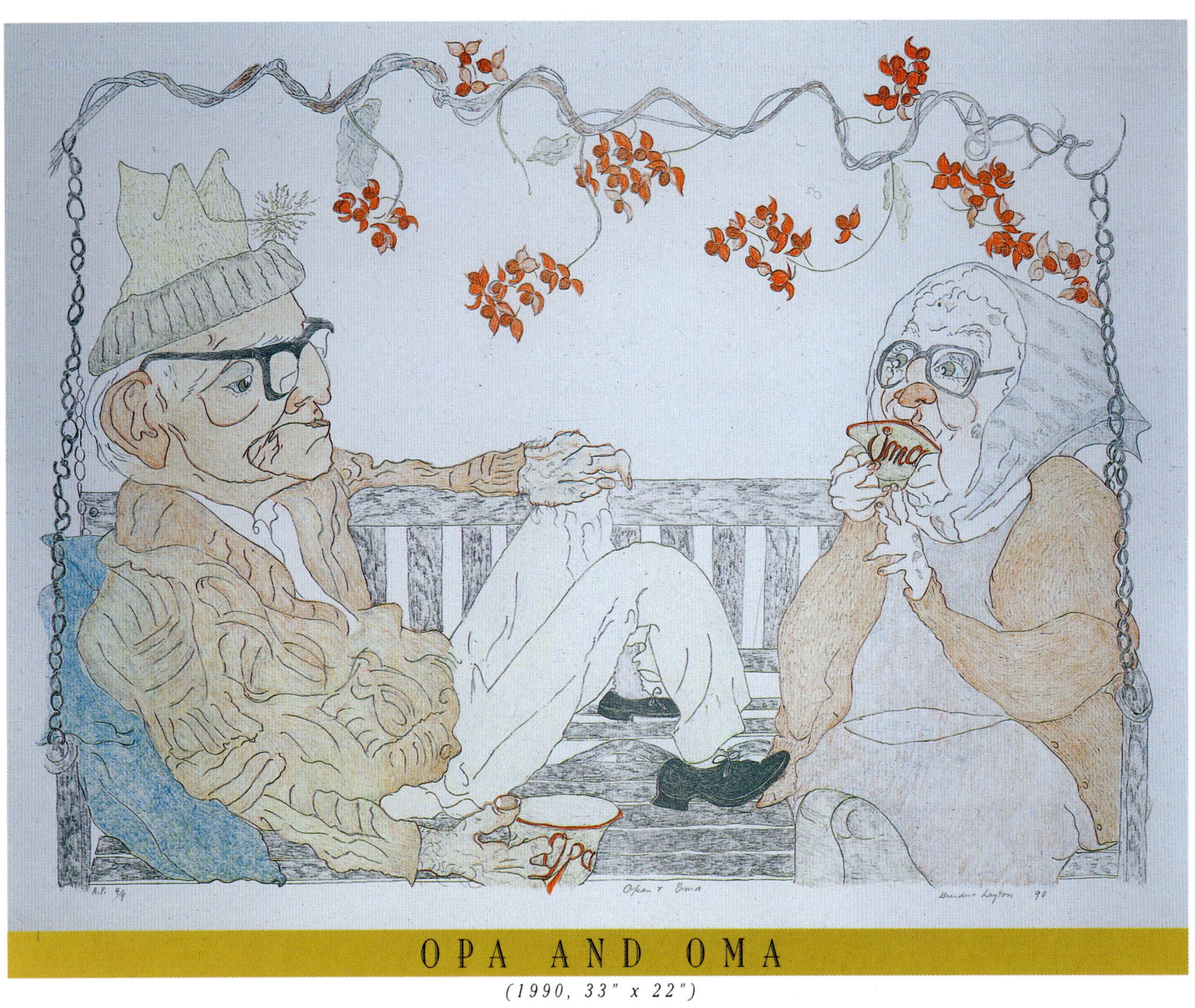

O P A   A N D   O M A

(1990, 33" x 22")

Five-color lithograph, produced in edition of 90, by Lawrence Lithography Workshop, Lawrence, Kansas

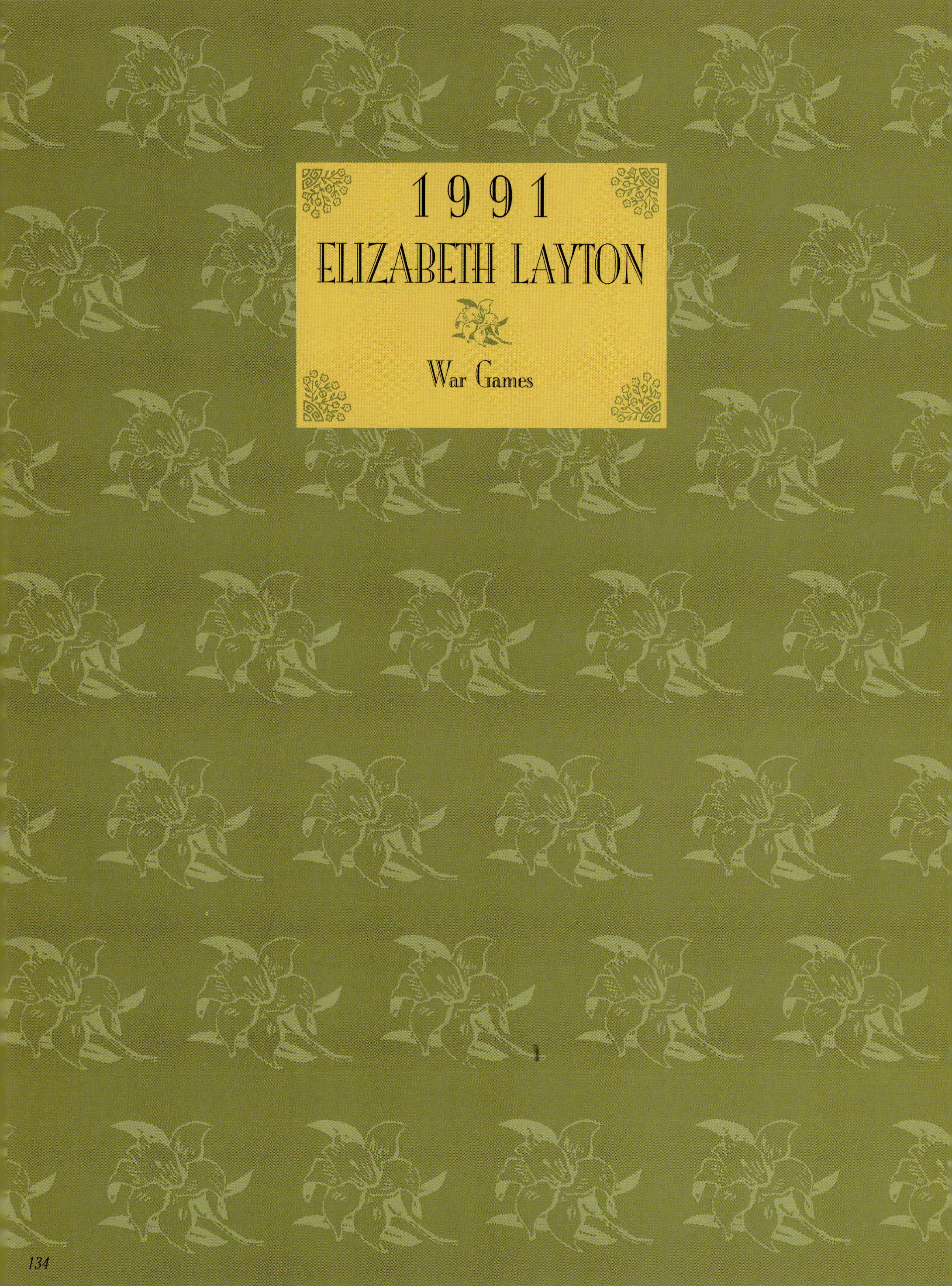

1991
ELIZABETH LAYTON
War Games

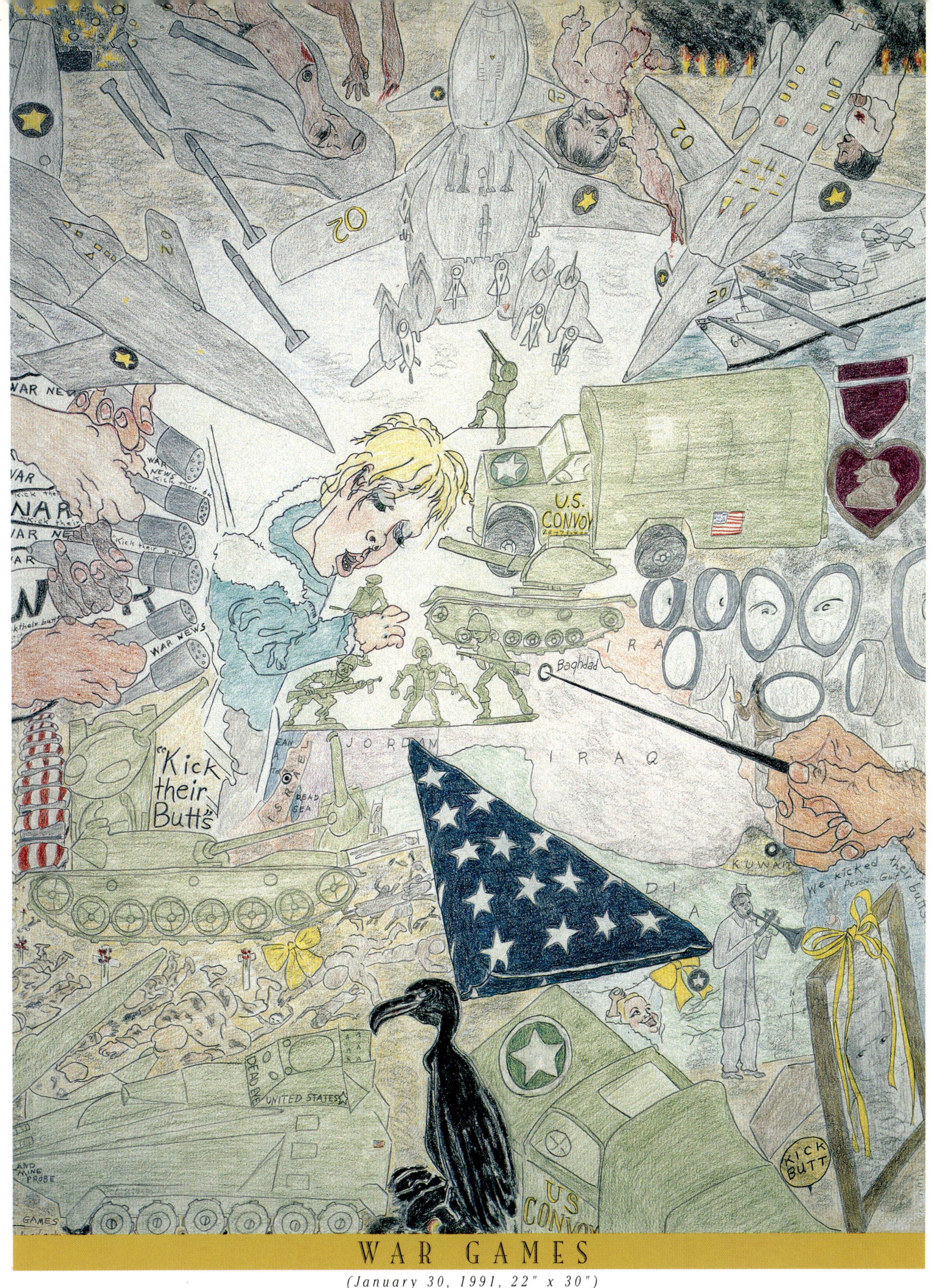

(January 30, 1991, 22" x 30")

❝*What was terribly frightening was the cheerleading aspect, 'We're No. 1.' I'm fearful of that attitude.***❞**

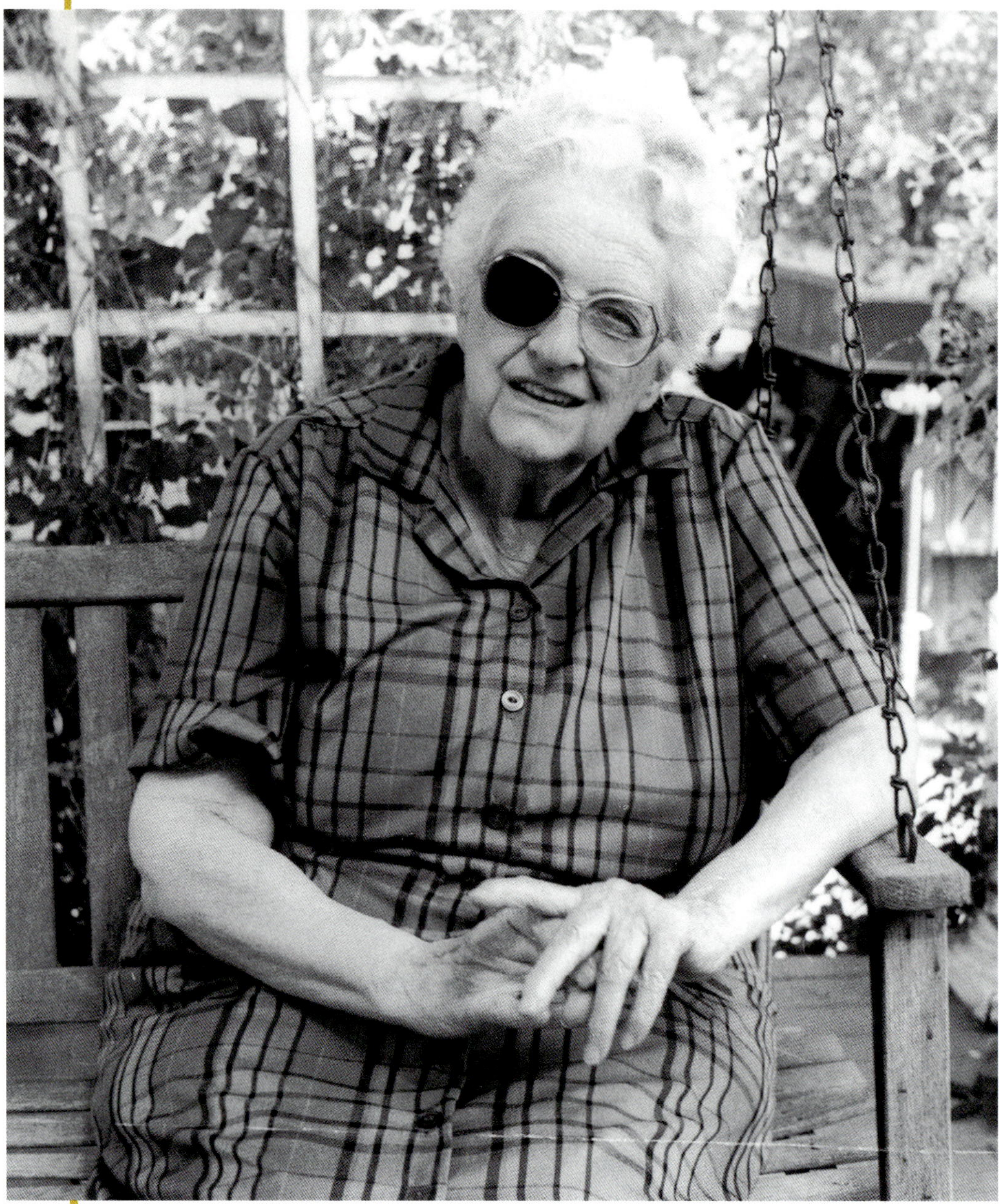

Elizabeth Layton at age 80.

A REMEMBRANCE

The teakettle is hissing. Water is hot enough for the instant coffee. It is supper time and I am invited. Elizabeth calls to Glenn, he's napping in the living room while watching a football game on television.

"Glenn, what do you want for supper?" He stirs from the reclino-rocker and smooths his white hair. He walks by the dining room buffet table crammed with photos of the kids, grandkids and greats. Some wear cowboy boots, some are in ballet tights. All are smiling.

He enters the kitchen and looks into the refrigerator which he knows is practically empty. "I don't know what I want, I'll have to think about it."

Elizabeth explains that Glenn's choices are limited, as are those of the guest. Glenn smiles and shakes his head knowingly. She gave up cooking years ago, although she was once a good cook. Her ham rolls are part of the family legend, now served only on holidays. These days, it is ham sandwiches, malt-o-meal, cottage cheese, store bought cookies and ice cream. Glenn orders oatmeal. She pours hot water into a small pan, pours in some "oats" and lets it simmer. I order and get a peanut butter and jelly sandwich. I know from experience it will have an extra thick portion of peanut butter. Elizabeth has a dish of fruit cocktail.

We discuss the goings on in Wellsville. Elizabeth announces proudly that "Glenn almost sold a house yesterday."

In his mid 80s, Glenn doesn't sell a house every day in Wellsville. Nor does he almost sell one every day. He would if he could find the buyers. The town's dream of becoming a bedroom community of Kansas City, 45 miles away, hasn't yet materialized.

Still in his coat and tie from his day of not selling real estate at his downtown office, he reports on other business. Since their grandson, Steve Layton, is president of the Chamber of Commerce, as well as a big wig in the local bank, Glenn keeps current.

"Thought you'd all want to know," he says with knowing mischief, "that KU won its game last night." He knows there will be only indifference from the other two at the table.

After supper, which concludes with the remainder of the package of chocolate chip cookies, Glenn returns to the football game. As always, Elizabeth rejects my offer to help with the dishes. No, she says, she'll do them later. We retire to the guest bedroom upstairs which doubles as her studio. The paneled walls are lined with clippings, postcards and other reminders of new friends. Christmas cards from the Jeters with Romalyn and Sally, a photo of Alberta and Marty, a drawing from Rita, one of Philomene by her husband, Lou. Across the windows are sheer, swagging curtains that one recognizes from many of her drawings. Hundreds of colored pencil stubs poke out of coffee cans on her makeshift drawing desk. It is an oak teacher's desk,. The top has been propped up to act as a drafting table. A mirror is nearby.

"Here's my new picture," she says about the almost finished drawing on top of the desk. It shows herself and Glenn, a vase of flowers is between them. "I want to give this to Norma who has been down here with Ann and Deb. She's been through some tough times, this might cheer her up."

I hand her the stack of booklets I'd brought with me, legal guides for senior citizens published by the Kansas Department on Aging. On the cover is one of her drawings — Glenn and Elizabeth on the front porch swing.

"How beautiful!" she exclaims. "The colors reproduced so nicely. And look at Glenn, he looks so handsome. Yihoo, Glenn, come up and see how handsome you look!"

He's asleep. He has appeared in many of his wife's drawings. She draws his outline quickly as he poses for her as Peter Pan, Christopher Columbus, Narcissus, or, more often, as a kind and smiling old man. "He's my favorite model," she explains. "He posed for me an hour this morning. He slept through most if it, that was fine with me because he held his pose."

His availability did nearly prove embarrassing a few weeks back, she explains. Glenn was posing for her modern version of Thomas Hart Benton's famous painting of Persephone which hangs at the Nelson-Atkins Museum of Art in Kansas City. She was doing a role reversal. Instead of having a beautiful young woman skinny-dipping with an old man peering through the bushes, Elizabeth would have Glenn skinny-dipping, and she'd be watching through the bushes. So, while Glenn was posing upstairs, some Sunday after-church company dropped by and rang the front doorbell. Glenn scrambled for his clothes, got to the front door just a bit late, and acted as if nothing out of the ordinary had happened.

Elizabeth shows me something else she is working on, a lithograph on literacy, being done with Mike Sims of the Lawrence Lithography Workshop. She enjoys the lithography process because of its closeness to the printing process which she grew up with.

Both voracious newspaper readers and non-television watchers, we discuss the news since our last visit. She was distressed to read that an area man was fired from his job when it was learned that he has AIDS. And that the courts have created additional barriers for the terminally ill who wish to die. I tell her about an editorial I found especially offensive, she hadn't liked it either.

We end with a bit more art business. Her exhibits are currently in Omaha and Dallas. Maybe we should give her drawing opposing censorship to the Smithsonian where, in Washington, it would more likely be seen by those she most wants to see it.

While we are talking, she puts a few more strokes of burnt sienna on the drawing and asks if I'll deliver it to Norma. She signs it, "Grandma Layton, for Norma."

In the drawing, so happy and vibrant, I barely see a trace of the woman who struggled with depression for 35 years and no trace of the fact that she has been blind in one eye since 1983 when two operations to reattach a retina were not successful. These new drawings seem unconcerned about her increasing imperfections while her earliest drawings exaggerated them.

It has been at these weekly suppers or lunches or drop-in visits since the winter of 1978 that I've come to know Elizabeth Layton. Throughout, I've been impressed by her warmth, her compassion, her fairness and her honesty. But what has impressed me most, in this world of self-absorption, has been her ability to transcend self to focus on "other." How she got to this point, I don't know.

Was it because of her years of depression, her recovery from it or her years of drawing herself — the years she came to know and accept herself? But in every conversation initiated to talk about "her," she managed to turn it around so she could talk about "you."

As I prepare to leave, Glenn comes to the door. Patting me on the back, he says, "Come back, Donnie." He knows I will.

I break off a sprig of honeysuckle from the front porch trellis, remembering that this is where I discovered this vine with its strong aroma some dozen years before. It is merely one of the discoveries I've made on that front porch — I can hardly imagine my life without these regular discoveries.

"Oh, say," Elizabeth says as I walk toward my car, "Did you remember to take those two drawings to the nursing home show in Kansas City?"

"Did it this morning."

"Thank you kindly," she says, waving as I drive off.

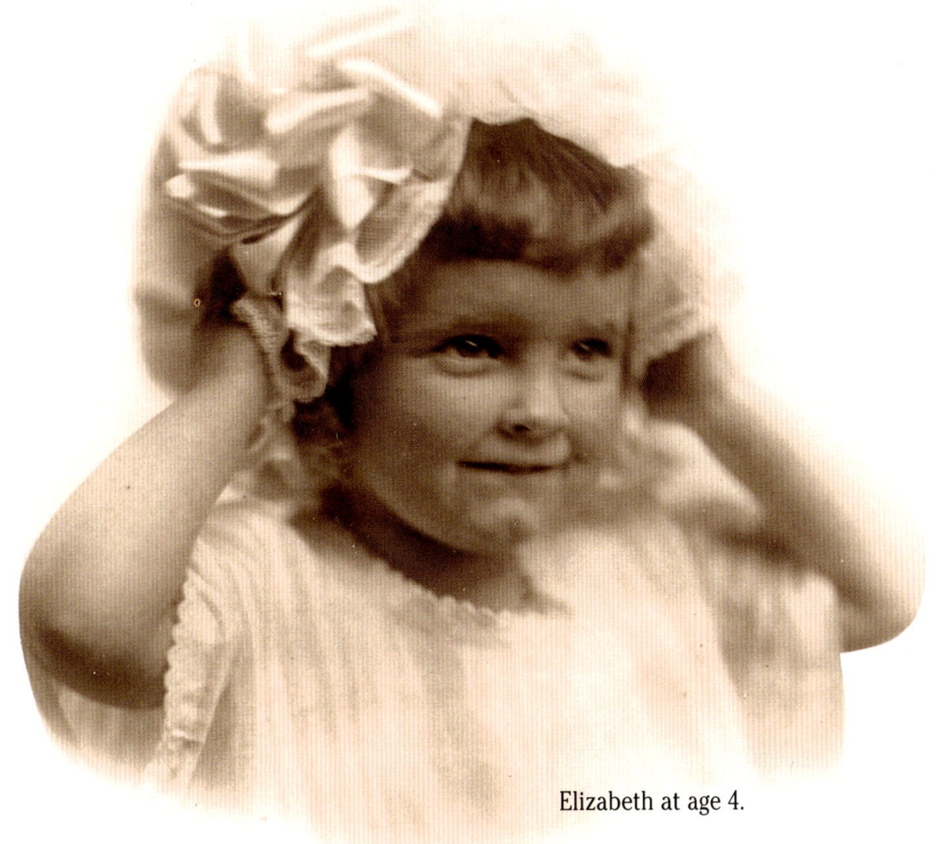

Elizabeth at age 4.

EPILOGUE

All these pictures and all these words seem not to answer the question. Why and how did Elizabeth Layton do it?

The answer remains unclear. It must have something to do with the enduring spirit, the power of creativity, the need to communicate, and aspects of being which we don't yet understand. We can be thankful that the talents of Elizabeth Layton were released, talents she maintained are in all of us.

Elizabeth Layton, age 83, died on March 15, 1993, at the Olathe Medical Center, in Olathe, Kansas, of complications from a stroke. Although her body had worn out, she said from her hospital bed that she was not ready to die; she had more work to do. Perhaps it was to write her story, something she often said she'd do after an anticipated blindness would have ended her ability to draw.

Elizabeth's survivors include her husband of 36 years, Glenn Layton; one son, Sherman Nichols, a retired physician; three daughters, Carolyn Layton, a housewife who helped with her mother's correspondence in her later years; Kay Russell, who in 1992 reestablished the *Wellsville Globe*, the newspaper that had been her grandfather's and then her mother's; and Julia Nichols, who is president of the Layton Foundation; a daughter-in-law, Alvera Nichols; three stepsons, Don, Robert and Glenn Layton; a stepdaughter, Beverly Dumler; 25 grandchildren and 26 great-grandchildren.

More than a half-million people have seen her drawings in more than 200 towns and cities. She drew nearly 1200 self-portraits during her 15 and-a-half year drawing career. She gave nearly all of them away to friends, museums, and charity auctions. Thus she raised more than a half million dollars for the arts, women's organizations, civil liberties, mental health, medical ethics issues, the visually impaired, and the Wellsville Library.

With her approval, nearly a hundred drawings were retained by the Layton Foundation. Sixty of those are on two national tours by Exhibits USA, Kansas City.

She received as many as 50 letters a day. Some were simple fan letters, others written in desperate struggle. Elizabeth always responded with wit and compassion. It is anticipated that these letters from her will be edited into a book.

Elizabeth Layton chose not to accept any money for her drawings and so, "didn't make a dime" from her art. Learning to draw had been such a wonderful gift to her, she explained many times, that she didn't feel right about profiting from that gift; "You don't sell a miracle."

Her rewards were many, however, such as the letter which follows.

"Thought you might like to know that I framed your drawing of you offering me the feather to fly with. I've hung it smack in the middle of the wall above my electric organ and I look up and say, OK, Elizabeth, I'm taking that feather. And I'm going to learn to play so well that I'll soar to heights unknown, to me, before.

I don't know a thing about art — just what I like or don't like and, frankly, the drawing that caught my eye in the magazine prompting me to read the article was the drawing of your husband in the windstorm. It disturbed me terribly. That, I said to myself, is weird. It looks like something from a nightmare. Who would draw such a thing? I got to thinking, golly, that's why they are calling her a genius. You wouldn't be afraid to tell an actress that she frightened you or made you mad or whatever. That only proves she played her role, how well she expressed herself and got her character across. That's what an artist does, too. And boy, can you do it.

I hope it gives you a nice, warm, satisfying feeling to know that you have been an inspiration to me. I thought I was too old and uncoordinated and slow and foolish to attempt to learn music. Well, I am all those things. But, you've proved to me that if its in there, it can come out. And I know that music is here in me.

Thought you'd like to know that I've been asked to play at my organ club's Christmas program."

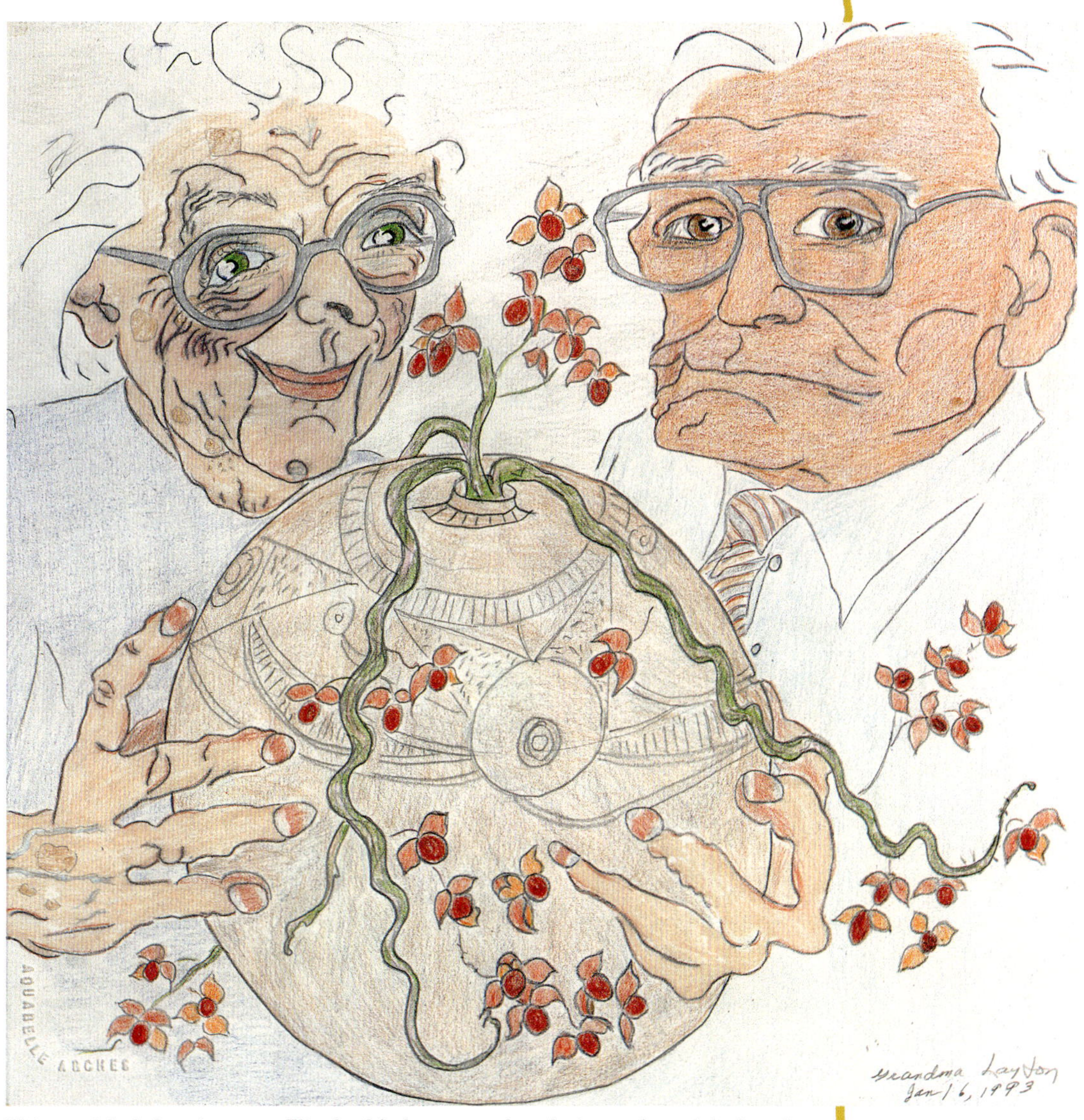

This untitled drawing was Elizabeth's last completed piece of work before her death. The ceramic pot was made by Pal Wright, her contour drawing teacher.

"You are more than the
'grandmother of us all.'
You are our conscience,
the voice from within our heart
that reminds us of what
is right and good and true."

— Unknown

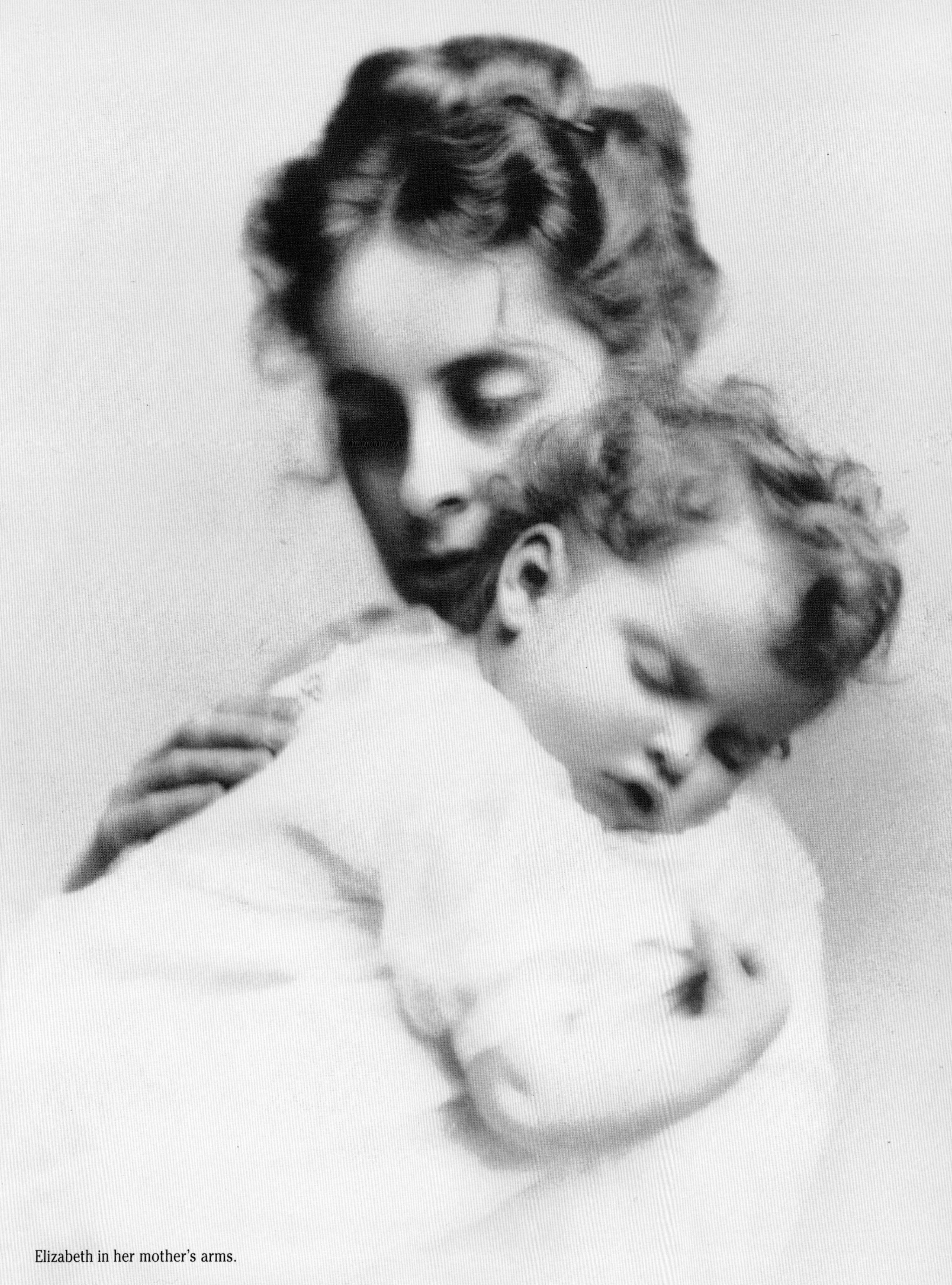

Elizabeth in her mother's arms.

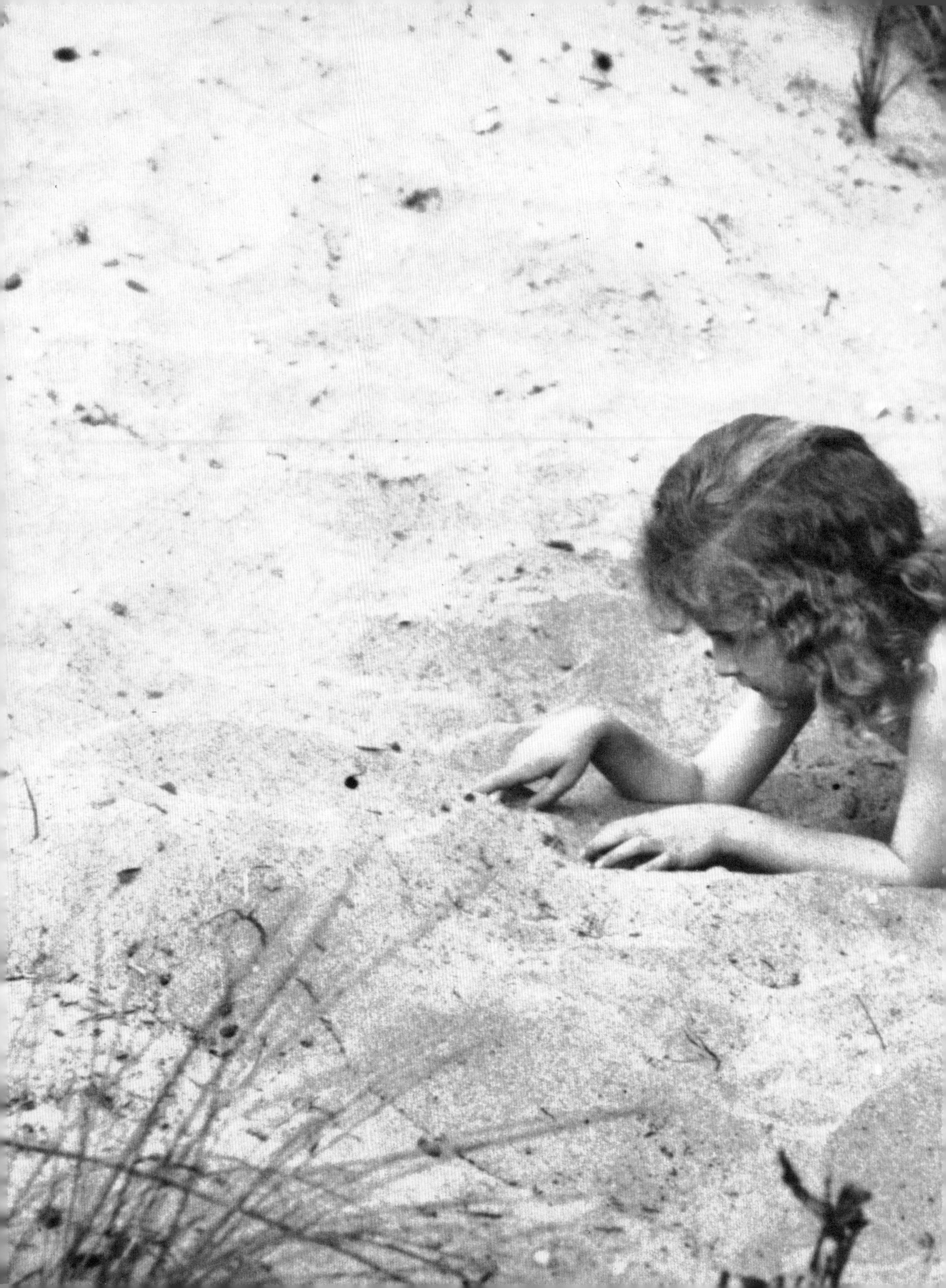